Advance Praise For

The Wisdom of the Buddha

This is a life-changing book! *The Wisdom of the Buddha* begins with the story of the Buddha's life and a detailed overview of his central teachings. These teachings are then applied to the realities of our daily life using clear analysis and step-by-step methods along with guided meditation practices. As a psychotherapist, I believe that Buddhist teachings and practices presented in this book have the clarity and power to produce genuine and positive change.

Joyce LeMieux Cameron, MS, MFCC

As someone deeply committed to mental and emotional health, I unreservedly recommend *The Wisdom of the Buddha...* It is written with clarity, and simplifies the learning and use of meditation and other mindfulness practices for the beginner without sacrificing depth of explanation. This book will be useful to a broad spectrum of people as well as any therapist wishing to learn these practices and to teach them to clients.

Nancy McCollum, M.S., Marriage and Family Therapist (retired), and Vipassana meditation practitioner

Dale Lugenbehl has written an accessible, personal, and eloquent introduction to Buddhism and mindfulness, useful not only for its scholarship but for language that translates Buddhist teachings into intelligible suggestions for practice. I would not hesitate to use this wonderful book in my classes, both academic and for interfaith adult education.

> Jonathan Seidel, Ph. D., Professor in Religious Studies and in Judaic Studies, has taught at the University of California at Berkeley, Stanford, and the University of Oregon, among other institutions. He is a rabbi and the Spiritual Leader of Or haGan in Eugene, Oregon.

Those in the West often view Buddhism as a foreign, esoteric religion with incomprehensible teachings. In *The Wisdom of the Buddha*, Dale Lugenbehl reveals the Buddha's teachings to be an intuitive, practical self-help philosophy which helps us live happier lives, be more compassionate and experience the world as it truly is. Chock full of concrete illustrations and examples, this book walks the reader through the core teachings of the Buddha, clears up common misconceptions in easy-to-understand terms, always with an eye toward personal application. Useful meditation exercises are offered throughout. Readers dealing with depression, anxiety, or addiction will find the chapters devoted to those problems especially helpful. In the last section of the book, the author demystifies some of the more profound teachings of Buddhism about "no self," death and the "oneness" of everything. This book is ideal both as a guide for personal growth and as a college textbook.

> Jeffrey Borrowdale, Professor of Philosophy and Philosophy Program Director, Lane Community College.

The Wisdom of the Buddha

Using Mindfulness to Change Your Life

Dale Lugenbehl

Contents

Introduction

The Wisdom of the Buddha is the book I wish had been available when I first became interested in Buddhism.

When I first encountered Buddhist teachings some 25 years ago I found them extremely intriguing but also frequently quite baffling. What could possibly be meant by "no self," or the idea that death is an illusion, or the teaching that suffering is created by the mind? My Western university education and previous years of college teaching in philosophy had not prepared me to comprehend something so radically different and alien. But still, there was something very appealing about the teachings and also about the manner of engaging life that I witnessed in people who actually did understand what was taught. They seemed to have a totally different way of engaging life and it had a magnetic appeal to me.

Over the years, through the help of many teachers, readings, dharma talks, and meditation retreats, I made progress in understanding what was being taught. The teachings, though a bit alien from the ideas we have absorbed from our society, turned out to be actually quite simple! Once understood and made use of with consistency, I discovered that these teachings had the power to totally transform my life.

The Buddha's teachings are really about suffering. The Buddha said that he only taught two things: the nature of suffering, and freedom from suffering. He said that each one of us has the ability to free ourselves from suffering, both the suffering that we cause ourselves and the suffering we cause out in the world around us.

Mindfulness—seeing what is really happening in each moment—is the central tool needed for this job.

The Wisdom of the Buddha is fundamentally intended as a practical guide to understanding the teachings of the Buddha and applying those teachings in our own lives to reduce suffering.

In making use of any such practical guide, it is essential to begin seeing the teachings as a system of methods, rather than as a collection of theories or doctrines. For a long time I did not fully understand this. Western philosophy has the intention of accurately *describing* reality. The Buddha, on the other hand, wanted to develop methods to enable us to *directly experience* reality. It is this clear seeing of our situation that makes it possible to change ourselves radically and thereby reduce our creation of suffering. The words that are used in Buddhist teachings only point to the experience—they direct our attention and help us know how and where to look. The Buddha's teachings are like ladders that, when we climb them, provide a new vantage point from which we can clearly and directly see for ourselves both the external world and our own internal world of thoughts and feelings. Wrapping ourselves up in studying the ladders is missing the point. The ladders—the teachings—are intended to be used as tools for reaching a better view of things. The Buddha's focus everywhere and always was on the practical.

Because Buddhism is a collection of methods to see reality more clearly and change ourselves, it is not at all necessary to become a Buddhist in order to benefit greatly from what the Buddha taught. In the history of the world, there have been many Buddhas—some of them were Buddhists and some were not. What is important is not our chosen path to enlightenment, but our becoming more enlightened. And there can be more than one useful path to the same destination.

My own teachers have been many: Thich Nhat Hanh, Charlotte Beck, Eckhart Tolle, Sharon Salzberg, Jack Kornfield, Joseph Goldstein, Pema Chodron, Alan Watts, Phap De, Lama Dorje, and many more.

2

Some of these teachers I have known personally, and many I have known only through their books and recorded dharma talks. And of course the greatest teacher of all has been my own moment-to-moment experience in applying the teachings to my own life, and in helping others to learn through sangha work and through the teaching of Buddhist meditation to others. The central intention in writing *The Wisdom of the Buddha* is to pass along what was given to me and help people transform their suffering into joy the way that my teachers helped me.

The *Wisdom of the Buddha* combines an in-depth introduction to Buddhism with the practicality of a spiritual self- help book. The first five chapters explain and give insight into the foundation teachings of the Four Noble Truths, the Eightfold Path, mindfulness meditation, and the nature of suffering and happiness.

The next ten chapters bring Buddhist teachings to bear on transforming our lives through learning how to: break the grip of habits, end arguments and power struggles, deal with difficult emotions and strong desires, see the essential nature of all addictions, deal with anxiety and depression, become more accepting, and cultivate compassion and reverence for all life.

The final two chapters provide much needed insight into the Buddha's most difficult and freeing teachings of all: the true nature of the self(the teachings on "no self"), relative and absolute truth, nirvana, impermanence, and our mistaken understandings of death.

In the beginning, some of what the Buddha taught can be mystifying, so I have tried to present the teachings using simple and accessible language, practical techniques, eight guided meditations, personal stories, and numerous quotations from master teachers to provide inspiration along the path toward deep personal transformation. Nonetheless, many Buddhist teachings will require prolonged study and practice to be fully understood. May this book serve as an aid to that process.

PART ONE

The Big Picture

CHAPTER ONE

The Life and Mission of the Buddha

To most people, the Buddha was a mysterious figure from long ago who talked about things like peace, and calm, and reincarnation and lived in some far off place. Who, in actuality, was the Buddha? And what was his mission during the time he was alive?

We can begin to answer these questions with the recognition that the Buddha never said he was anything other than a human being, essentially no different from you or me. He had achieved a remarkable insight into the nature of the world, and human beings, and believed he had found a path to eliminate suffering. An astounding central feature to what the Buddha taught is his claim that all the rest of us could achieve the same insight and freedom from suffering that he had. The story of this particular human being began about 2,500 years ago with the birth of a child named Siddhartha Gautama in what is now the country of Nepal. Siddhartha would later become known as the Buddha. The life of the Buddha unfolded in three basic stages, beginning with his birth into a royal family.

The Three Phases in the Buddha's Life

Siddhartha's father was king of a large province and Siddhartha was a prince who was in line to eventually become king. He was given the best education of the time by private tutors, had the best of food, clothing, accommodations, and entertainments available to him. He was also deliberately sheltered from the painful circumstances of the outside world: poverty, sickness, the deterioration of aging, death, and all forms of suffering in general. He married at a young age and had a son. His family was a happy and loving one.

As time went on, life in the palace and its endless round of pleasant activities came to seem more and more hollow to him: feasts, concerts, parties, plays, games, royal ceremony. Surely, there must be something more to life than just this. Siddhartha eventually came to gain a knowledge of the suffering, fear, and anxiety of the outside world. He became determined to find what he called "The Way," meaning by that a path that led to liberation from suffering, including the suffering that comes with death.

The second stage of Siddhartha's life began at the age of 29, when he decided he must leave the palace to find the path that leads to the end of suffering. When he left, his wife gave him her blessing for his quest, he put on the ordinary clothes of a servant, and began his determined search for "The Way." Siddhartha deliberately sought out spiritual masters and people of wisdom to see what they could teach him. During this time, he tried a multitude of spiritual disciplines: various forms of meditation, fasting, study, research, reflection, renunciation, and personal discipline.

Finally, after six years of intense spiritual practice, he had his ultimate awakening experience in which he saw through to the true nature of reality and the causes and cure for human suffering. This began the third stage in Siddhartha's life. He became a teacher.

Shortly after his final awakening, he encountered some of his friends and former spiritual seekers, and his appearance was so transformed that they asked him "What happened to you?" Siddhartha responded very simply, saying only "I have awakened."

At this point Siddhartha was about 35 years old. He intended to share what he had learned with others in order to alleviate the suffering they were causing themselves as well as others. It is at this time that he became known as the Buddha. The word "Buddha" literally means "one who is awake." Most people go through life as though half asleep, or not fully conscious. Most of us simply act based on following some "life script" prevalent in our culture, doing what we are "supposed to do," and not really *consciously choosing* how to respond to life. The Buddha woke up in the sense that he became fully conscious and saw things the way they truly are.

Awakening From the Trance

My own high school years were largely spent in this half-asleep state. At that time I was fortunate to have a few spontaneous small moments of becoming awake. One of these moments I remember vividly. I was dating someone who was the sort of person you were "supposed to" want to date—looked and dressed the right way, popular, involved in the right school activities, and so on. Yet one evening when I was driving home with this girl I had the very vivid and immediate realization that I was definitely bored, and furthermore, that I was *always* bored when I was with this person. This arose in my mind with stunning clarity. The question then arose, "If this is always boring, *why am I doing it?*" When I reflected on this question the next day, the only answer I could give myself was "This is what everyone else wants to do; this is what you are supposed to do. But at the same time, it just feels hollow to me." Looking back at it now, I can add words like "It all felt so artificial, false, scripted, and contrived, with everyone just acting out some role that they had been taught to play; there was no real sense of personal connection or aliveness in any of what I was doing."

But I didn't have enough clarity to have said any of this at the time. All I could say was that I knew with absolute clarity that I had absolutely no genuine interest in doing what I was doing—not now, nor any of the previous times I was with this person. For a few short moments, I became awake in one small area of my life. This was a tiny but still very powerful experience of momentarily awakening from the trance of unconsciousness and being in touch with what was real in that moment—one small moment of mindfulness, of paying attention to

7

what was happening right here right now, both outside of myself and also in my mind and emotions. This was potentially the beginning of freedom and authenticity. Unfortunately, at that time I had no idea what came next or what to do *instead of* following the path of my conditioning. But that small opening proved to be the start of something.

The Buddha's awakening was total, and extended to the deepest possible level. He now saw the world and human experience as it truly is. He saw the causes of all of our blindness and suffering, as well as the methods needed to remove this blindness. The next 45 years of his life, until his death at the age of about 80, he devoted himself to teaching and founding monasteries all over what is now Nepal and India. During his lifetime he ordained more than 1,000 monks and nuns.

The Buddha's Mission

The Buddha never said that he was a god, or was sent by god, or that he was fundamentally any different from other people. He was simply a human being who, through his own efforts, had awakened. He also said that each of us could do the same thing, and that we could do it in the life we are living right now. Buddhist teachings contain the idea that we all have something that has come to be called "buddha nature," which is the natural human capacity to wake up, see reality as it is, free ourselves of suffering, and to operate from a place of wisdom, compassion, and inner peace.

The teachings about waking up are intended to apply to everyone in all cultures and in all time periods. Whether a person wakes up or not is determined by their actions, and it makes no difference whether you are male or female, rich or poor, of some particular nationality or race, or old or young. According to Buddhism, there have actually been *many buddhas*, some of them members of other spiritual traditions such as Christianity, Taoism, or Judaism, and even secular philosophers. The central hope in what the Buddha taught was *not* mastery of *doctrines*, but fundamentally changing how we relate to life. The idea is not to become a *Buddhist* (someone with an impressive *verbal* knowledge of the teachings), but rather to become a *buddha* (someone who engages life from a place of clarity and wisdom). Buddhist teachings are intended as a powerful vehicle for creating deep personal change.

The Buddha wanted us to realize that it is not the *events* that life presents us with that cause us suffering, but rather it is *our response* to those events which causes suffering. Once we see what is going on more clearly, both outside us and in our own minds and emotions, we can begin to consciously choose more skillful responses to life and stop causing so much suffering.

Receiving Teachings from the Buddha

The Buddha would teach anyone who had a sincere interest in receiving the teachings. Typically, it was necessary to ask the Buddha for teachings, and sometimes to ask more than once so as to demonstrate an intention that was sincere. The monks and nuns in the monasteries that the Buddha founded helped with this teaching. The teachings were never to be sold; they were to be offered freely to anyone who asked for them. This was done because there was the recognition that if the teachings were offered in exchange for payment, there might have been a temptation to tell people what *pleased* them rather than the truths that they *needed to hear* in order to set themselves free.

The Buddha lived in an oral culture and the teachings were passed down orally from one generation to the next. The Buddha's wife, Yasodhara, and his son, Rahula, were eventually ordained into the Buddha's circle of teachers. Rahula apparently had a remarkable memory and was able to memorize, from a single hearing, entire discourses from the Buddha. These talks were then taught to the other monks who would chant them as a way of memorizing the teachings. It was not until several hundred years after the Buddha died that the teachings began to be kept in written form. It is only in the last 30 to 40 years that the teachings have become widely accessible to people living in western cultures. We owe a great debt to a relatively small number of people who have been instrumental in bringing the teachings of the Buddha to the West: Thich Nhat Hanh, Alan Watts, Joseph Goldstein, Jack Kornfield, Sharon Salzberg, and Charlotte Beck, just to name a few.

The Buddha was intensely concerned with the deepest questions in life: Who am I really? What is death and can it harm us? What is morally correct action? Can there be freedom from suffering? How can I change myself at the deepest level to become happy and at peace?

Personal Responsibility

The Buddha's approach to these life questions is unique in a number of ways. In the original teachings there is essentially no reliance on tradition. The Buddha taught that the mere fact that something has always been believed or done should not be seen as a good reason for continuing to do so. We must have real evidence to know that something is true, because the teachings of tradition have often been proven to be incorrect. At one time, for example, it was widely believed that draining blood from sick people was a useful and necessary medical therapy, but we now know that this traditional practice was not an effective treatment and in fact harmed the patient.

Similarly, the Buddha did not believe that any teaching should be accepted simply because it came from some authority, whether the authority was a person, a church, an institution, a school, or a book. Even the Buddha's own teachings were not to be accepted as true simply because the Buddha spoke them. The Buddha held that the real test of a teaching is found in each individual's personal experience—he asks us to try a teaching out in our own lives and find out for ourselves whether it has value or not. Only if it rings true in our own experience should it be accepted.

At the age of 80 and on his death bed, the Buddha gave the following final instruction to his monks and nuns.

> *Therefore... be lamps unto yourselves. Betake yourselves no external refuge. Hold fast as a refuge to the Truth. Work out your own salvation with diligence."* (1)

At the core, this means three things. The first is that each of us must illuminate the truth for ourselves, that each of us has the *capacity within us* to discover the truth. Secondly, we must not look for anything outside of us to tell us what is true: no teacher, book, or tradition-- everything must be tested in one's own life. And third, each of us must discover for ourselves what is necessary for our own personal transformation and commit ourselves to doing the work. By personal transformation, the Buddha meant changing ourselves at the deepest possible level to free ourselves of delusion, ignorance, hatred, ill-will, and suffering. According to these teachings, no one can do this work for us; we must each do it for ourselves. Others can inspire us or provide pointers along the path for us, but ultimately each of us must find what steps to take and then take them.

Two Kinds of Lives

The Buddha taught that there were two fundamental kinds of lives: one he called random and passive, and the other kind he called intentional and assertive. He explained the random and passive life by giving the metaphor of a leaf in the wind. Imagine it is the fall time of year, and a leaf has become detached from a tree and it is driven first north, than east, then up, then down. *Its motion is totally determined by the outside forces acting upon it*: the force of wind, gravity, and physical objects it runs into. The leaf does not *consciously decide* in what direction it will move. It simply *reacts* to external forces acting upon it.

11

Our lives are often like this—we find ourselves doing things only because that is what others are doing, or because it is how we were raised, or because of what we have absorbed from television, movies, advertising, or family. What is the likelihood that any of us would have the same political, religious, or social views that we have now if we had been born into a home in a different part of the world? Much of the time, we are simply driven by unconscious beliefs absorbed from our surroundings and rarely do we rise above that to differentiate what is real from what is simply the result of our having been deeply conditioned. Is our habit of pursuing more possessions and status coming from a place of seeing clearly or is it simply the result of acting out our social conditioning from a mind that is still half asleep?

The second kind of life, intentional and assertive, is directed by our own conscious choices. This kind of life can be understood quite well if we imagine a small row boat in the middle of a wide river. Imagine yourself lying in the bottom of the boat and drifting. The path of the boat is totally determined by outside forces: water currents, wind, and rocks and logs jutting out of the water. Now imagine yourself getting up and taking a seat in the boat, picking up the oars, and rowing the boat in *a direction consciously chosen by you*. This is the experience of an intentional and assertive life. Imagine what it *feels* like to be in the boat in this manner. Even if you never reach some specific destination, your entire experience of being in the boat has been totally transformed—it *feels* radically different from the experience of drifting. It is this consciously chosen, fully awake and aware life that the Buddha held out to each of us as a real possibility.

Focus on the Practical

The most central feature of the teachings offered by the Buddha is that they were intended to be very practical. On many occasions, people would attempt to get the Buddha to answer theoretical or abstract philosophical questions: Is the universe eternal or did it have a beginning in time? Does the universe extend infinitely in all directions or is it limited in size? The Buddha frequently responded to these questions with silence. However, on one occasion, a monk named Malunkyaputta asked such questions and the Buddha answered with a story that has come to be known as The Parable of the Arrow.

The Buddha asks Malunkyaputta to consider a man who has been shot with an arrow dipped in poison. His wound is life threatening. Other people present want to run for a doctor but the man refuses, saying that before he will accept medical treatment he must know: Who shot him? Of what tribe was the man a member? From what kind of wood was the arrow made? The Buddha points out the foolishness of all these questions—unless the man gets medical treatment, he will surely die before all his questions can be answered.

In a similar manner, the world we live in right now is full of great suffering: murder, war, prejudice, hatred, injustice, and disease are everywhere in the world. Seeing and doing something about all this suffering must be our top priority, not answering theoretical questions. No matter whether you decide that the universe has always been here or not, war, greed, hunger, and all the rest will still be taking place unchanged. The Buddha made this abundantly clear in his closing remarks to his monk's question.

> "Why, Malunkyaputta, have I not taught all
> this [the answers to theoretical questions]?
> Because all this is *useless*, ...it does not lead to
> peace, to supreme wisdom...
> And what have I taught, Malunkyaputta? I
> have taught that suffering exists, that suffering
> has an origin, that suffering can be ended, that
> there is a way to end suffering. ...This is useful."
> (2)

Putting our focus on attempting to answer theoretical questions typically just serves as a distraction from doing the real work of fundamentally changing ourselves and how we relate to life. The

13

Buddha stated that "Whether the world is finite or infinite, limited or unlimited, the problem of your liberation [from ignorance and suffering] remains the same." (3) Having answers to theoretical questions does not move us one inch further along the path of freedom. Changing our way of engaging life and healing our suffering must be our top priority, not answering theoretical questions.

The Buddha once said that he *only taught two things*: the nature of suffering and freedom from suffering. As we come to know more about what the Buddha taught, we realize that he actually *only taught one thing*. When we truly *understand how we create suffering*, *that understanding automatically frees us from it*. Once we see clearly which of our behaviors are causing our suffering, all desire to continue with those behaviors simply disappears. This teaching will be dealt with in depth in a later chapter.

Methods Rather Than Beliefs

Buddhism differs from Western religion and philosophy in that it is not primarily concerned with beliefs. A belief is an attempt to describe some aspect of reality in words. Beliefs can be thought of as word maps of reality. When my word map disagrees with yours, we often think we need to argue with each other and prove the other wrong. In many ways, the history of Western philosophy can be seen as the history of philosophical arguments over maps.

Rather than being focused on beliefs, Buddhism is better understood as a collection of *methods*, or "practices" as they are called in Eastern traditions. The English word "practice" comes from the Greek word "praxis," which means "doing" or "action." Meditation, for example, is a practice—it is something you *do*.

Buddhist practice has essentially two purposes. The first purpose is to help us to see reality as it actually is. The word "reality" here refers to both external and internal reality. It is important to be able to see more clearly what is going on right here and right now in our

14

immediate external environment, and also important to see clearly what is going right here and right now in our internal environment of thoughts, emotions, and bodily sensations. The second purpose of practice is to help us to achieve personal transformation—change ourselves to become wiser, kinder, more at peace, free of suffering, and more able to be of good service to those around us.

Practices are not attempts to "map" or describe reality. And, since a practice is something that you *do*, there really is not much about which to argue. Essentially, you try out a practice for yourself, and it either works or it does not. Much of the learning in tribal societies takes place along these lines. At some point one of the tribal elders takes a young person out in the forest and *shows them* how to find food or build a hut for shelter. Then the youth tries doing it for herself, with possible corrections from time to time from the teacher. There is no need to quibble about the definition of "food" or "proper hut," or convince others that only the one method works or is best. The youth tries out what has been shown and it either works or it does not. There may be a need to adjust one's technique, or perhaps the method that was taught never works for this particular person and a search is begun for something else.

The same attitude applies to Buddhist practices regarding meditation, speaking more mindfully, practicing reverence for life, or practicing generosity. We simply do the practices as best we can (perhaps with some correction or suggestions from a wiser person), and then notice whether they are effective in helping us to see things more clearly and to change the way that we respond to life's events.

The idea of spiritual or philosophical practice is a bit alien to Americans because we are so used to arguing about theories and beliefs. My Western training in philosophy certainly instilled this habit in me. As a philosophy student and later as an instructor, I might have been interested in the subject of compassion, but it would have revolved around trying to define compassion in words, or perhaps proving that compassion was a higher value than justice or some other thing. The emphasis was on words and arguments (reasoning) and convincing others regarding some *belief* about compassion.

The Need for Doing

The Buddhist Zen monk Thich Nhat Hanh once said that "ideas about understanding and compassion are not understanding and compassion." (4) When I first started learning about Buddhism, I found such statements to be self contradictory and incomprehensible. When I learned more, I saw these statements as quite simple and containing great truth. Thich Nhat Hanh was simply saying that *verbal discussion of* understanding and compassion is not actually *behaving with* understanding and compassion. We can discuss the meaning of compassion and how it relates to other values all day long and still not be one bit more compassionate in our lives. It is essentially the same as the rather obvious truth that "ideas about health and fitness are not the same as being healthy and fit." No amount of reading exercise books or watching exercise videos or talking about exercise with friends will make us one bit more fit—there must be *praxis*; there must be *doing*. There must be action of some sort—lifting weights, swimming, yoga, running, hiking, or some other form of activity.

In what the Buddha taught, there is the recognition that a very powerful way to *become* more compassionate is to *practice acts of compassion* during our day-to-day doings. Each time we engage in a compassionate act, our capacity for being compassionate becomes stronger. The reverse is also true. Each time we are presented with an opportunity to be compassionate and do not act on it, we strengthen our tendency toward lack of compassion. There is a powerful principle at work here: Everything we do, like it or not, strengthens some tendency in ourselves. Every time we steal, it weakens our inhibition against stealing and makes it a little easier to steal next time. Seeing this very clearly is the crucial first step toward change.

16

Some practices work well for some people but less well for others, which is why the Buddha said that there were "84,000 dharma doors." "Dharma" is a Sanskrit word which means something like "truth teachings" to help one along the path of self transformation. So what the Buddha was really saying here is that there are a lot of different practices that can be used to reach the same destination, much like there are many exercise programs that can produce an excellent level of physical fitness. In later chapters we shall take a very close look at many of these specific "dharma doors" or practices and learn how to make use of them to produce beneficial changes in our own lives. A piece of good news here is that one can make use of these practices without having to give up any of one's useful existing beliefs or dharma doors in their present religion or philosophy. One can benefit from Buddhist teachings without becoming a Buddhist, just as one can enjoy Italian food without needing to be an Italian.

Although not a Buddhist, the ancient Greek philosopher Epictetus spoke eloquently about a similar focus on practicality and the importance of action rather than theories.

> ...Do not speak much...about philosophical
> theories and precepts: but do that which
> follows from them. For example, at a banquet
> do not say how a person ought to eat, but eat
> as you ought to eat. ...For even as sheep do not
> cough up their grass to show how much and
> how well they have eaten; but when they have
> digested their pasture... [their health and
> energy is obvious for all to see]. Do you also
> not show your theories to people, but show the
> acts which come from their digestion." (5)

Notes for Chapter 1

1. Smith, Huston, *The World's Religions: Our Great Wisdom Traditions, Revised Edition*, San Francisco: HarperSanFrancisco, 1991, p.99.

2. *Easwaran, Eknath,* "Introduction to *The Dhammapada,*" *in The Dhammapada,* Tomales: Nilgiri Press, 1985, pp. 39-41. Translated by Eknath Easwaran)

3. Nhat Hanh, Thich, *Zen Keys*, New York: Doubleday, 1995 p. 42.

4. Nhat Hanh, Thich, *Interbeing: Fourteen Guidelines for Engaged Buddhism, Third Edition*, Berkeley: Parallax Press, 1998, p. 5.

5. Epictetus, *Enchiridion*, New York: Prometheus Books, 1991, translated by George Long, Sections 46.

CHAPTER 2

The Central Teachings: The Four Noble Truths

When people asked the Buddha for teachings, he always started with what has come to be known as The Four Noble Truths. Essentially all of the Buddha's teachings are contained in some way or other in the Four Noble Truths.

Overview of the Four Noble Truths

The first three of the Four Noble Truths, on first examination, appear simple and obvious—some might even say "boring." The fourth truth often seems totally unrealistic. However, when correctly understood in all their depth, these four ideas are profound and life changing. The Four Noble Truths say the following.

1. Suffering exists.

2. Suffering has causes.

3. The creation of suffering can be eliminated by eliminating its causes.

4. The causes of suffering can be eliminated by following the eight-fold path.

It is important to emphasize that the Four Noble Truths are more accurately viewed as practices rather than beliefs—they are all things that *involve doing something*. Let's take these truths one by one and examine their deeper meaning, and how they work, starting with the teaching that suffering exists.

First Noble Truth: "Suffering Exists"

On the surface this seems to be an obvious truth because anyone can see that the there is suffering in our own lives: we get sick or injured, we lose jobs, people we care about move away or die, we become frustrated or angry when people don't behave in ways we think they should. And not only is there suffering at the personal level, there is also a huge amount of suffering at the global level: murder, war, persecution, prejudice, injustice, brutal governmental regimes, and the list goes on and on. We all know this. How is pointing out that suffering exists the least bit helpful?

The First Noble Truth helps us by reminding us to *practice noticing* that we are often suffering greatly but are not consciously aware of it—perhaps we just have this background feeling of tension or nothing ever being right, but the feeling is barely on the edge of our conscious awareness. We may even be completely unaware of it. Think of someone who dreads the sound of their alarm clock telling them to get up and go to work, whose stomach starts to knot up every morning as they pull in to the parking lot at work, who has a sense of guilt and tension while at their workplace where their tedious job is to help in the manufacture of a product that harms people. They then leave work exhausted, only to fight rush hour traffic on their way home to a house where all the family members are constantly going in different directions. The dread, knotted stomach, guilt, tension, tedium, and sense of disconnection are all happening, but there is not a fully conscious awareness of them. And of course we are very good at distracting ourselves in various ways so that we don't have to feel much of what is actually going on inside us or around us. Maybe once in a while we have the sensation well up that our life is not working but we quickly distract ourselves with endless activities, food, or alcohol so that we lose touch with our inner discomfort.

20

The teaching that suffering exists asks us to actually get in touch with and really experience our suffering and what is going on in our life. Until we get consciously in touch with the suffering that exists inside ourselves and acknowledge its presence, *nothing in our life changes*. Nothing changes until we notice and acknowledge to ourselves: "When I pay attention to *how my life actually feels moment-to-moment*, I realize that there is a lot of pain in my life. My life is really not working well right now." This is the crucial first step that is absolutely necessary for deep personal change.

People who work as drug counselors can tell us something here. Suppose you are an old friend who has not seen me for a long time and suddenly discover me sleeping on the sidewalk one night. I have a piece of cardboard pulled over me and an empty gin bottle in my hand and smell strongly of alcohol. You say to me, "Dale, I think you have a real problem with alcohol. You need to get some help." And suppose I say back to you "I do drink a lot but I'm doing just fine. I like sleeping on the sidewalk. Leave me alone." This is what psychologists call "denial." I am basically denying that there is anything going on in my life that is not just fine. What any substance abuse counselor will tell us is that until someone gets out of denial and acknowledges the existence of a problem, they will simply stay stuck in their dysfunctional behavior. Getting in touch with suffering and acknowledging its reality is always the first necessary step toward change. Without acknowledging the existence of our suffering, no meaningful change is possible.

This applies at every level. Sometimes a person is so out of touch with their own body that they don't go to a doctor until they have a tumor the size of a grapefruit. Before any healing can take place that person first has to acknowledge what is going on and that they don't feel so well. We sometimes even deceive ourselves into believing we are fine because the thought that things might not be fine terrifies us. This often happens with health issues, and in fact can happen in any area of our lives.

So the First Noble Truth tells us to practice paying attention to our moment-to-moment experience and notice when there is suffering present and acknowledge to ourselves that it is real. At that point, healing becomes a possibility. The First Noble Truth also tells us to practice paying attention to and acknowledge the suffering that is going on outside ourselves: suffering in other people, other creatures that we share this planet with, and suffering in the natural world and the environment whose health is essential to keep us all alive.

As simple and profound as this truth is, it has often been greatly *misunderstood*. The First Noble Truth that "Suffering exists" has often been taken to mean "Life is *nothing but* suffering," or that "Suffering is *inevitable*," or that "Suffering is 24/7." This all sounds very dismal and bleak. If we are paying attention to our moment-to-moment *experience*, however, we can see for ourselves that this is not the case. Even in the midst of great hardship, there are often moments of humor, personal connection, beauty, and even joy.

We also can ask ourselves a question: "Why would the Buddha spend 45 years of his life walking all over what is now India and Nepal to teach people how to *free* themselves from suffering? Why would the Buddha do this if suffering is *inevitable*?" The whole point of the Buddhist program is to give us a *treatment* for suffering. What can be truthfully said here is that *life as typically lived contains a great deal of suffering*. The promise held out by the Buddha was that it was possible to *understand how suffering is generated*, and then to *free ourselves from it*. As we shall see, The Fourth Noble Truth is essentially a comprehensive and detailed program for deeply changing ourselves so that we can stop *creating* suffering.

Second Noble Truth: "Suffering Has Causes"

The Second Noble Truth says that "Suffering has causes." The First Noble Truth could be viewed as *acknowledgement of the problem*, and the Second Noble Truth could then be called *the diagnosis*. This is

22

definitely a piece of good news! If suffering just dropped on us at random intervals during our lives, that would indeed be extremely disheartening: " Yes, I am suffering but there is absolutely nothing to be done about it." But if suffering does have causes, then maybe something can be done about it. The Second Noble truth, like the First, is not a theory. It is the *practice* of carefully observing our lives to see *how* our suffering comes to exist. Often we need some help in seeing the causes of our suffering, and that is precisely what the teachings of the Buddha are intended to provide.

It's a little like going to a doctor. I've finally acknowledged that there is something wrong in my life (the First Noble Truth), so the next step is to go to a doctor to find out about it. The doctor says, "I know what is wrong with you; I've seen this affliction many times before and know what causes it." This is the good news of the Second Noble Truth: suffering has identifiable causes. As we shall see later, the causes of suffering are in the mind.

The Second Noble Truth has also often been misunderstood. Probably the most common misunderstanding is to represent the Second Noble Truth as saying "The cause of suffering is tanha." "Tanha" is a Sanskrit word that is usually translated into English as "desire" or "wanting," leaving us with an incorrect statement of the Second Noble Truth which asserts: "The cause of suffering is desire." Though a common interpretation, it is deeply mistaken for several reasons.

First of all, the Buddha said that suffering had *multiple* causes: unskillful desire, ignorance, greed, delusion, and so on. However, in oral cultures people have to rely on memory to retain information and they often use simplifying devices as an aid for both remembering and for communication with others. One such device was to use the first item in a list to stand for the entire list as a way of making communication more streamlined and efficient. So the list of causes of suffering was often referred to by the first item in the list, which in this case was unskillful desire. So over time, unskillful desire came to be seen as the primary or only cause of suffering. Over time, *unskillful desire*—one particular *kind* of desire—simply slipped into being understood as *desire in general*, which is quite different from what the Buddha actually taught.

What the Buddha actually taught in regard to this was that *certain kinds* of desire cause suffering. These desires were called unwholesome or unskillful. Craving would be one type of unskillful desire. Craving is like desire on steroids. Craving is desire taken to the point where I absolutely have to have the object of my desire—*not* having what I want is totally unacceptable; *getting* what I want is *completely nonnegotiable*. A good example of craving would be the state of mind of a heroin addict who has not had his regular heroin dose. Such a person feels they *must have* their drug, and will do virtually anything—rob their brother's life savings or commit armed robbery—to get what they want. When we are in this state of mind our view of things is extremely distorted and we make very bad decisions. If I *absolutely have to have* a particular new car I have just seen, I am very likely to make bad decisions about how much to spend, the environmental impact of the car, its mechanical reliability and many other things.

A less intense desire (short of craving) can still be unskillful if the object of the desire causes harm. Consequently, my desire to have everyone like me would be an unskillful desire because I do not control other people's perceptions of me so this desire will certainly lead to suffering. On the other hand, the desire to become wiser and more at peace would be seen as a skillful or wholesome desire. Obviously, the Buddha had the desire to become enlightened and to alleviate the suffering of others. This is also a skillful desire, and is clear evidence that the Buddha did not see any problem with desire in and of itself.

So desire in itself is not a cause of suffering, much less the only cause of suffering. Suffering has multiple causes and unskillful desire (including craving) is one of those causes.

24

Third Noble Truth: "The Creation of Suffering Can Be Eliminated by Eliminating Its Causes"

The Third Noble Truth says that "The creation of suffering can be eliminated by eliminating its causes." When the doctor tells me that he or she knows what disease I have and that the disease has causes this is good news, but I am not completely out of the woods yet. The doctor may know what causes my affliction, but if there is no effective treatment for the disease my situation is very grim indeed. So the Third Noble Truth is an additional piece of good news because it says that *this particular disease Is curable*. The disease of human suffering *can* be eliminated by eliminating its known causes. So the first three Noble Truths can be seen as 1) acknowledgement that there is a problem, 2) diagnosis of the problem, and 3) recognizing that there is a cure for what ails us.

However, just like the first two Noble Truths, the Third Truth has a history of being misunderstood. By far the most common misperception is the idea that "Suffering can be eliminated by eliminating desire." As a student once said to me in class, "If getting rid of desire is the cure, then the cure is worse than the disease." And we know just how this student felt—the idea of getting rid of all desire seems impossible—and would life even be worth living if we *could* rid ourselves of desire?

As we have seen from our examination of the Second Noble Truth, the idea that we need to eliminate desire to eliminate suffering is simply a misunderstanding of what the Buddha taught. We actually need desire in order to be able to function. If I had no desires in the matter of whether I ate bread or a dirt clod for lunch, I would not live very long. Unskillful desire, on the other hand, certainly is a problem.

Another way of misperceiving the Third Noble Truth occurs when *the word "creation" is left out* of the formulation resulting in the statement that "Suffering [of any origin or type] can be eliminated by eliminating desire." This is a crucial omission. What the Buddha taught was that the *creation of* suffering can be eliminated. By leaving out the words "creation of" this common distortion of the Third Noble Truth seems to imply that *all* suffering can be eliminated: that I will never get sick or injure myself again or have a loved one die once I have mastered Buddhist teachings. It is important that we grasp fully the idea that what the Buddha called "suffering" is not the same thing as *pain and difficulty*.

There will always be a certain amount of pain, difficulty, and sadness in life (though even that can be *reduced* by wiser and more skillful action on our part). What the Buddha called suffering is something that we *add on to* the events of our lives by how we *respond* to those events. There is a huge amount of suffering that is caused by our response to events. In fact, the suffering added to events by our unskillful responses is often vastly more than what is caused by the events themselves. Unfortunately, however, we are typically totally blind to this fact.

As an example, suppose I get fired from my job. I feel hurt and now I need to look for another job and it may not be easy to find one. There is definitely pain and difficulty present. However, if I fully accept the reality of my situation and then do the things that I actually can do to improve things, there need be no additional suffering from this event. On the other hand, suppose my mind starts saying things like "This always happens to me, I'm just a born loser who never does anything right. The universe is just unfair and that's all there is to it. You are born, bad things happen, and then you die." The mental story that my mind is creating causes a huge amount of suffering that is simply piled on to the pain and difficulty caused by the job loss itself.

Like the preceding Truths, the Third Noble Truth is not a theory. When we begin the *practice* of carefully observing how our human minds work, we will discover that a large amount of our suffering is created by our *mental responses* to events, not the events themselves.

So a certain amount (sometimes a large amount) of pain and difficulty will always exist. However, the creation of huge amounts of additional suffering brought about by our mental response to events is totally optional—*that* is the part which can actually be eliminated. When our minds are no longer causing unnecessary trouble, *there can be a sense of well being and peace even in the midst of pain and difficulty*.

Think about this: If events were the real cause of suffering then everyone experiencing a given event would suffer to the same degree, and we know from experience that this is simply not true. My experience with two elderly women that I knew very well was very instructive for me. Both Ernie and Doris had experienced declining mental abilities as they moved into their late 80's and early 90's. Both of them had problems with memory and with their ability to perform various mental tasks. The fact that Ernie forgot things and could no longer balance her checkbook made her angry and full of self-blame and shame: "I used to be able to do this, I *should* be able to do this, I'm just a stupid old lady—I'm just so disgusted with myself." My lasting memory of Doris, however, was the time she was unable to remember someone's name or what had happened earlier in the day and she simply turned to me with this beautiful smile and said peacefully "I don't remember those things at all. My mind is just a sieve that won't hold on to much of anything." Both women were dealing with very similar mental decline, but Ernie was suffering, and Doris was free from suffering and at peace. The only real difference between the two was that Doris had learned to fully accept the reality of the changes in her life and Ernie had not.

Some people emerge from many years in prison bitter, cynical, and full of resentment. Others do not. Nelson Mandela spent 27 years in prison and emerged at peace, with kindness and compassion in his heart, even for his guards in prison. All of us have doubtless seen examples of different people responding very differently to the very same difficult and painful events: some suffer greatly and others experience little or no suffering beyond the pain of the event itself. This brings us to the Fourth Noble Truth.

Fourth Noble Truth: "The Causes of Suffering Can Be Eliminated by Following the Eight-fold Program"

The Fourth Noble Truth says that "The causes of suffering can be eliminated by following the Eight-fold Program." Traditionally, the phrase "Eight-fold Path" has been used here. However, the word "path" suggests taking separate steps, each step coming *after* the preceding one. So there is accomplishing the first step, and then moving on to the second step, which is then followed by completing the third step, and so on until one reaches the end of the path and is "finished." This is like thinking that you need to master healthy eating and then once you have done that you can move on to work on appropriate exercise, after which you can start on working with developing good friendships. In the Eight-fold Program, there is no first step nor is there a sequence of steps. All eight elements are important, they all interact with each other, and they can and should be used in conjunction with each other. Thus it is more like a comprehensive and interconnected *program* rather than a path.

The Eight-fold Program is basically a course of treatment for what ails us, and the treatment is essentially *a system of training*. People recognize the need to train for a job, for an athletic event, to be able to give first aid, and to give birth to a child. But people rarely think that it might be necessary and critically important to *train for life itself*. The Buddha believed otherwise.

CHAPTER 3

The Central Teachings: The Eight-Fold Program

The Buddha wanted to use every available lever to help people heal themselves. The Eight-fold Program was intended to be very comprehensive and help us to work at personal transformation and healing in every area of our lives. Traditionally in Buddhism, the eight components of the Program have been called Right View, Right Intention, Right Mindfulness, Right Speech, Right Conduct, Right Livelihood, Right Diligence, and Right Concentration. The word "right" is somewhat off-putting to many Westerners who may hear it as judgmental or as implying there is only one right way. In what follows, I will utilize the terminology of Thich Nhat Hanh, who prefers to call the Program elements "Mindful Conduct," "Mindful Speech," and so on. This is closer to the Buddha's actual intention in that it correctly implies that these are eight areas of life where we would benefit greatly from *paying much closer attention* to what we are actually doing moment-to-moment. In a very real sense, each of the eight areas is a place where we can begin to make use of certain *practices* for paying attention and other specific *practices* for making beneficial changes in how we operate based on what we see once we have become more mindful.

Most of the elements of the Eight-fold Program will be dealt with in depth in later chapters, so for now we can begin with a brief overview. The following elements of the Eight-fold Program are presented in no particular order, although they are numbered for ease of reference.

1. Mindful View (traditionally given as Right View or Right Knowledge). Mindful View, or Right Knowledge, has a number of facets to it, and it is important to explore each of them in turn.

The first aspect of Mindful View begins with the recognition that a blueprint of accurate beliefs or perceptions is needed to move ahead in changing oneself. If I act on misperceptions I run the risk of making bad decisions and harming myself and others. There are two fundamental parts to this. First, I need to practice being aware of, and working, with the Four Noble Truths in each moment. I keep them always before me. Second, I need always to practice seeing the reality (the truth) of my present situation, behavior, and inner process. This could be called seeing the truth of the present moment.

A second aspect of Mindful View pertains to understanding how the truth is known. What the Buddha taught is not a collection of beliefs or theories. The Buddha's teachings were derived from his direct personal experience: from observation using his five senses and also from internal observation—introspection—of his own thoughts, emotions, and bodily sensations. According to the Buddha, the way that you and I can know that these teachings are true is the same way that the Buddha came to know their truth—the teachings are revealed to us in our own personal observation and experience.

The purpose of the teachings is not to describe or explain reality in words and concepts but rather to provide information that will help people know *what to do* (specific practices) so that they can *experience* what is real for themselves. The Buddha's teachings are basically *methods* to help people see the truth directly and in their own experience of life. The truth is *not contained in* the *words*, the words simply *point* us toward the truth and tell us where and how to look so we can experience the truth directly without the overlay of concepts and words. A sign pointing in the direction of the Grand Canyon is not the Grand Canyon and it is not even a description of the Grand Canyon.

But the sign can *direct our attention to a vantage point* from which we can *personally experience the reality* of the Grand Canyon.

A third aspect of Mindful View deals with the appropriate attitude to have toward the Buddha's teachings. Since these teachings are practices that *point* to the truth, they are truly like a sign with an arrow that says "Grand Canyon." The pointer or sign is not holy scripture, nor is it something we need to worship, or defend, or argue about—it is just a device that can help put us in a position to see a piece of reality clearly.

One of the Buddha's enduring metaphors was using the idea of a raft to cross a river as a way of explaining how his teachings should be understood. The purpose of the raft is to provide a method of transportation to get to the other side of the river. Once that has been accomplished, the raft is no longer important or needed. Once the Buddha's methods (practices) have achieved their purpose of producing enlightenment, their usefulness is over.

It is interesting to note that the Western philosopher Ludwig Wittgenstein expressed the very same idea when he said that his statements were like ladders that helped you scale a wall—once you reached the top of the wall, you no longer need the ladder to see the landscape. Similarly, the teachings are merely devices to put you at a *vantage point* so you can view the truth directly and for yourself. As Wittgenstein puts it, a person "… must surmount these propositions [and] then he *sees* the world rightly." (1) Once you have seen the landscape as it truly is, the ladder has achieved its purpose.

The fourth aspect of Right View teaches that most of our perceptions are mistaken, and that we need to practice asking ourselves again and again: Do I really know what I think I know? How much of what I think I see is real and how much is distortion added on by my mind? Thich Nhat Hanh offers the following:

> If ten people look at a cloud, there will be ten
> different perceptions of it. Whether it is
> perceived as a dog, a hammer, or a coat
> depends on our mind—our sadness, our
> memories, our anger. Our perceptions carry
> with them all the errors of subjectivity. (2)

What the Buddha taught was a set of methods, or practices, for *eliminating mistaken views*. Some views are more accurate than others, and we want our views to be as accurate as possible.

This brings us to the fifth aspect of Right View. Although the Buddha taught that some views are more accurate and useful than others, he also taught that *no view is absolutely correct*. The Buddha put forward the radical proposition that from the standpoint of ultimate reality, *all views are wrong views*. This is because any perception of reality is just a perception, *it is not reality itself*. Thinking about how we use maps can help us to understand this. Ultimately, no map is the absolute truth about the terrain, because it is only a map and not the terrain itself. However, it is also true that some maps are more accurate than others and the more accurate our maps, the better off we are for finding our way around.

The metaphor of looking at the sky through a drinking straw can help us to understand the limitation of all beliefs and perceptions, even our most accurate ones. If your straw is very straight and free of obstructions, *at best* you can see a very tiny part of the sky. But the sky, of course, is much bigger and richer than any such glimpse of the sky. Beliefs are much like straws. At best we can only obtain a partial clear view of reality, and we should not cling fiercely to any one belief or "straw," though some straws undoubtedly provide a clearer glimpse of things than others. Adopting the practice of seeing beliefs in this way can help keep us open to other viewpoints and eliminate the impulse to argue over differing perceptions.

2. Mindful Intention (traditionally given as Right Intent or Right Thinking). This teaching is primarily about priorities. If I am serious about transforming my life, that transformation needs to be a top priority. In all of our efforts at various kinds of personal change we often miss this. Suppose I am trying to save money. If my procedure is to shop and buy first, and then put whatever money happens to be left over into savings, I will never save much because my priorities are backward—savings is only getting the "leftovers;" what is presently coming first in my life is buying and spending. What I need to do is reverse this and make a conscious decision about how much I want to save each month, and then as soon as I receive my paycheck I need to put this amount of money into a savings account *before* I spend money on anything. Whatever is left after savings happens can be used for buying things and shopping. This is giving savings my top priority.

If I want to become healthy and fit, I need to make sure that exercising gets done as the first order of business before my life fills up with other activities and my energy and time have slipped away. If something is important, it should not receive the left over scraps of my time, energy, financial, or other resources.

Mindful Intention tells us to do the same thing with our desire to become more peaceful, grounded, present, and freer from suffering. People often *say* they want spiritual enlightenment but also say that they don't have time for meditation, retreats, reading and so on. But why don't they have time? Because much of their time is going to watching television, playing video games, taking drugs, gossiping with friends, getting chores done and a hundred other things. The fact here is that there is a clear choice. I don't have time for meditation because I am choosing to watch television three hours a day. I can't afford to go on a meditation retreat because I am choosing to buy an RV which comes with huge monthly payments. What is my top priority: choosing to do my usual activities or choosing to fundamentally change my manner of being in the world? When I see it this way I can make a conscious choice to fundamentally shift my intention and then my life begins to change profoundly.

3. Mindful Speech (traditionally given as Right Speech). I can begin to pay attention to my own speech: words I speak, words I write, and the words that are continually passing silently through my head. When I do this, I will find that it reveals a great deal of information to me about myself: my desires, priorities, beliefs, emotions, and mental processes. This practice of observing my speech as it occurs also needs to include some reflection on my motivation for saying what I said. For example, perhaps I pass a colleague in the hallway at work and she asks me "How are you?" I say "I'm fine," even though I feel terrible and this is the worst week of my life. So, first of all, I can simply *notice* my untruthful speech, and then I can ask myself what *motivated* me to not speak truthfully? Perhaps it was because I want people to see me as happy and successful and in total command of my life. If this is what I am doing, how is this affecting my relationships with other people? Is it preventing people from ever actually getting to know me? Observing my speech in this way is like holding up a mirror—it reveals important information about hidden parts of myself.

Secondly, I can use the process of *consciously changing* my speech as a tool for *changing myself*. Over time, speaking differently will change me on the inside. For example, if I change my deeply ingrained habit of constantly finding fault with myself I will, over time, start to do less of this and find myself feeling lighter and more optimistic. The topic of mindful speech and the specific practices for working with it will be looked at in some depth in a later chapter.

4. Mindful Action (traditionally given as Right Action or Right Conduct). This one is huge. A central principle here is that everything I do, like it or not, reinforces some tendency in myself. If the fear I am feeling prevents me from attempting to speak up about something wrong that is happening, that action strengthens my tendency to cave in to fear and makes it more likely I will do the same thing in similar circumstances in the future. However, if I take action even though I am frightened, then I have strengthened the opposite tendency of not giving in to fear and stepping forward to help the situation. Over time, my actions shape my basic mental and behavior patterns. To a large extent, my way of responding to the world is the result of all my past choices and actions. Just as with mindful speech, noticing and then reflecting on my motives for acting play a central role here.

The Buddha provided five guidelines to help us become more mindful of our actions and their consequences for ourselves and for the external world. These five guidelines have been traditionally referred to as The Five Buddhist Precepts, and have often been *incorrectly* seen as the Buddhist equivalent of the Ten Commandments. (3) The Five Precepts have typically been misunderstood as follows.

1. Do not kill.

2. Do not steal.

3. Do not lie.

4. Do not indulge in sex.

5. Do not use intoxicants.

Although this is a common understanding of "Buddhist ethics," it is incorrect because these teachings were not intended as rigid and narrow rules or commandments. Additionally, they were not intended as negative prescriptions having the form "Do not do such-and-such." Thich Nhat Hanh has more accurately reframed these teachings as The Five Mindfulness Trainings. (4)

1. Practice, and cultivate reverence for life.

2. Practice, and cultivate generosity.

3. Practice, and cultivate mindful speaking.

4. Practice, and cultivate sexual responsibility.

5. Practice, and cultivate mindful consumption and ingestion.

To *practice* something means to put it into action and make it part of your life moment-to-moment. To *cultivate* something means to nurture it and cause it to grow in yourself. The Five Mindfulness Trainings are a way of focusing our intention. Thich Nhat Hanh adds the following .

> Mindfulness trainings are practices, not prohibitions. They do not restrict freedom... When we fail, we lift ourselves up and try again to do our best. In fact, we can never succeed one hundred percent. The mindfulness trainings are like the North Star. If we want to travel north, we can use the North Star to guide us, but we never expect to arrive at the North Star. (5)

So as part of cultivating reverence for life we can work faithfully to minimize harm and killing, but also know that in walking across the lawn we cannot avoid stepping on and killing microorganisms. But our inability to do something perfectly need not stop us from reducing harm in all the places where we actually can do this in our lives. The idea that we cannot act with perfection applies in exactly the same way for all the other Trainings as well—we can still greatly improve how we behave in regard to generosity, speech, sexual responsibility, and personal consumption.

Reverence for life, and **Mindful Speaking**, are so large in scope that each has a separate chapter devoted to it later on. The Trainings on Generosity, Sexual Responsibility, and Mindful Consumption can be briefly summarized here.

The Training on Cultivating Generosity includes not stealing but is also much broader than that. Yes, it is important to refrain from taking what does not rightfully belong to us. But there is more involved here. We steal from future generations when we take more than our share of natural resources and leave others with an impoverished planet and diminished life prospects. So part of practicing generosity involves choosing to live a more modest lifestyle that is centered on what we truly need and not caught up in always striving for more and more. We must, as Gandhi put it, "Live simply so that others may simply live."

Also part of practicing generosity is the sharing of our time, energy, knowledge, talents, and wealth with people in real need. Generosity goes beyond only material wealth.

We also need to do our best to prevent others from stealing from and exploiting other individuals. We can practice withdrawing our support from corporations that steal from people in other countries, push people off their native lands, and plunder the resources that they rely on to live. We can refuse to buy the products of companies that behave in this way and tell them why we are doing so. Clearly, there is overlap here with practicing reverence for life.

In regard to the **Mindfulness Training on Practicing Sexual Responsibility** we might ask: How did this ever come to be understood as the much narrower prescription of "Do not indulge in sex?" The reason is that not indulging in sex was, and still is, part of vows required of a person wanting to join certain Buddhist monastic orders. So if you wanted to become a monk or a nun at certain Buddhist centers, it was necessary to take a celibacy vow. However, this is not required at all Buddhist monasteries and it is certainly not required of people who have no interest in becoming a monk or a nun.

For people who are not monks or nuns, practicing sexual responsibility means not engaging in sexual relations unless there is love and a long term commitment. It also means respecting your own commitment to another person and respecting the commitments of others. It includes doing your best to protect others from sexual abuse and misconduct.

Lastly, there is the **Mindfulness Training on Cultivating Mindful Consumption or Ingestion**. To *consume* is to acquire something or to use up something. To *ingest* something means to take it into yourself. So drinking and eating are forms of "taking in" and so is the consumption of alcohol or other drugs. We also take in visual images, words and ideas, products, and social interactions.

Much of what we put into our bodies, minds, and lives can be seen as poisons. This includes obvious things like alcohol, drugs, and unhealthy food. But there are other kinds of toxins as well: toxic conversations that are full of negativity, as well as toxic relationships, movies, television programs, music, recreational activities and many other things that poison us in various ways. All of these things take a serious toll on our physical and emotional well being. The practice here is to first *notice* that these things have become part of our life, and then to *notice* the very real suffering they cause. We can then begin the practice of actively removing more and more of these toxic influences from our lives and finding health enhancing things to replace them.

The Mindfulness Training on Mindful Consumption and Ingestion tells us not to accumulate wealth when others do not have enough and are suffering.

The culture we live in tells us that we live in a consumer society and that our personal consumption of more and more products is a good thing. But if we investigate a little, we may learn that residents of the United States comprise about 5% of the Earth's human population, but use 25% of all the Earth's resources that are used globally each year by humans. (6) If everyone lived the way Americans do, we would need three more planets just like the Earth to provide the necessary resources to support such an extravagant and wasteful life style. (7) Our excessive use of resources is depleting and devastating our planet home and making it difficult or even impossible for people in developing countries to have decent life prospects. Our excessive consumption will have a similar impact on the generations that come after us in the future—what kind of a depleted world will we bequeath to them to try to live in?

Our high level of consumption is also creating great suffering in our own lives right now. The more products we feel we have to have, the more hours we have to spend at paid employment to earn money to pay for those purchases. If we were to choose to consume fewer goods, our need for income would be reduced, and this in turn could allow us to spend less time earning money working at our jobs. When that happens, we could then have more time and energy and a less hectic pace to our lives. As a result, we might find that we are more patient and kind, we can take better care of our health, spend more time with friends and family, and do worthwhile volunteer work in our local community. Additionally, the less income we need from a job, the greater is the number of jobs that exist to choose from that will take care of us financially. It becomes much more possible for us to find a job that is truly fulfilling. All of this begins with paying attention to our level of consumption and to the many toxins we are unconsciously taking into our bodies and minds on a daily basis.

5. Mindful Livelihood (traditionally given as Right Livelihood). We spend a large percentage of our waking hours engaged in earning a living. Our jobs can literally make us sick, or they can bring us great joy and peace. The kind of work we do to support ourselves profoundly impacts us and impacts the world around us as well. Mindful livelihood begins with consciously *paying attention* to what is happening in our work environment and how we feel while we are immersed in it. Am I involved in making a product which harms other people, living beings, or the environment? How is my being at work impacting my emotional outlook on life—is it causing me to feel more and more "dead" inside?" Is it encouraging me to be more insensitive, greedy, or cynical? Other things that need to be considered regarding a job might be: How are employees treated? Is the speech used at work abusive or kind and compassionate? Are large amounts of resources wasted? Does production create a large amount of toxic by-products or severely deplete the supply of nonrenewable resources such as petroleum, coal, and natural gas? Does the business make a quality product at a fair price?

Our jobs impact us profoundly, even if we are not yet mindful enough to be consciously aware of it. Each time I help to sell a life-harming package of cigarettes or lie to sell a defective used car, it leaves an impression on my consciousness, creates internal stress and inner conflict, and can often create the habit of numbing myself emotionally which then carries over to the rest of my life.

Essentially, the teachings on mindful livelihood ask us to find work that provides us with the necessities of life in a way that is as consistent as possible with The Five Mindfulness Trainings: cultivating reverence for life, generosity, mindful speaking, sexual responsibility, and mindful consumption and ingestion.

In attempting to understand this element of the Eightfold Program we should not be thinking in terms of one list of "good" jobs and another list of "bad" jobs. It is incorrect to assume that being a doctor and a member of the healing professions is "good," but that being someone who serves alcohol is "bad." Whether a job is mindful livelihood or not depends in part on *how that job is actually performed by a particular person*. Clearly there are some doctors who maximize personal income at the expense of their patients' optimal health. Similarly, there may be some people who serve alcohol who do their best to encourage nondrinking or reduced-drinking options for their clientele, help to find rides for those who are intoxicated, or practice being a good listener to their customers who might be suffering.

If we are paying attention, we will notice that every job contains both elements of mindful livelihood and also elements that are definitely not mindful employment. There is always a mix of wholesome and harmful elements and the idea is to move toward having as many wholesome elements of employment as possible.

The teachings on Mindful Livelihood also include the idea that we should try our best to create worthwhile employment for others as well as ourselves. We can do this through being conscious about the businesses that we choose to support with our dollars as a result of what we buy or don't buy. If I choose to buy a fast-food burger, that helps to create low paying part time jobs with high turnover rate, and which also puts employees in the position of serving unhealthy food to people. On the other hand, if I buy organic potatoes at a local farmers' market, I am supporting a different kind of work place. In this case, I have a personal relationship with the person from whom I am buying, I have the opportunity to know how the business is run and that the employees are treated well and paid fairly. I know that the potatoes they grow are healthy to eat and do not cause poisons to be released into the air, water, or soil.

Additionally, we can begin to look deeply at what we might be doing to make it less likely that someone will actually choose a life-enhancing job when the opportunity is in front of them. If we grant a high level of approval and status to people who have great wealth and impressive possessions, we are creating powerful incentives for people to do whatever is necessary to arrive at that level of wealth—and this encourages people to accept jobs that harm themselves and harm the environment but produce an extremely high income. So there are many layers to mindful employment.

6. Mindful Effort (traditionally given as Right Diligence or Right Effort). In order to progress in our intention to see reality clearly and to change ourselves, effort is needed. But this is not the effort of gritting one's teeth, giving oneself a tongue lashing, and trying to force something to happen. The kind of effort that the Buddha talked about is gentle and compassionate toward ourselves, but it also needs to be a very *consistent* effort. It has sometimes been likened to filling a large bucket by adding one drop of water at a time. It looks as though not much is happening, but we know that each drop adds to the total and that in the long run the bucket will be full. The kind of effort that is needed here is that of a marathon runner, not of a sprinter. If we try to do things for which we have not laid the foundation we will fail and become discouraged. Pace, and laying a good foundation of doing basic practices first, are key factors here.

The Buddha once used what has come to be known as The Parable of the Lute to explain mindful effort to a monk named Sona. Sona used to be a musician, so the Buddha asked Sona what would happen if the strings on his lute were tuned too loosely, and Sona answered that the strings would make no sound. If, on the other hand, the strings were stretched too tight, what would happen then? Sona answered that the strings would break. The Buddha then said that doing spiritual practice "... is the same. Maintain your health. Be joyful. Do not try to force yourself to do things you cannot do." (8) Progress will come without forcing if we practice consistently, and work at not allowing fear to prevent us from looking at how our own responses to life are causing our suffering.

If we are practicing consistently and with appropriate effort, laying the foundation of the more basic practices first, our practice will not seem like drudgery and something we must force ourselves to do. Practice will sometimes be hard but it can also bring us joy. If we have a strong interest in something we always have energy to work on it— there is a certain fascination and "magnetic pull" to do the work. Most of us have had the experience of putting in many hours of work on something that we cared deeply about, and found it easy to generate the energy to stay with it. If we have *experienced the benefits* of something, such as meditation, we will have the motivation and energy to *continue* the practice. When we experience the benefits of an activity, we *want* to do it and doing it comes easily. If following a more mindful life-path *greatly reduced our suffering*, why wouldn't we have great enthusiasm for doing the work?

42

If we continue practicing and benefitting in this way, the beneficial changes we have made in our lives become well established and the new "default" setting for us. At that point the new behavior feels easy and natural.

7. Mindfulness (traditionally given as Right Mindfulness). This is cultivating our awareness of what is happening in the present moment, both in our immediate external environment and also cultivating an awareness of what is happening inside of ourselves: bodily sensations, emotions, and thoughts. The next chapter is devoted entirely to the practice of mindfulness, which is absolutely central in all of what the Buddha taught. The first step in any process of change is always seeing clearly *what is happening in this moment*, both externally and internally. As we shall soon see, there are many specific techniques—practices— that we can use to cultivate greater mindfulness in ourselves.

8. Mindful Concentration (traditionally given as Right Concentration or Right Absorption). This element of the Eightfold Program involves learning the skill of putting yourself in a condition where you can absorb, or perceive, reality as it actually is. In this state we are relaxed, alert, not lost in thought, fully conscious, and simply allowing everything we are aware of to be just as it is.

An incorrect form of concentration, we can call it unmindful concentration, occurs when we deliberately concentrate on something in order to avoid an awareness of something else. Suppose I am driving down the road in my car and the engine starts making a strange noise. My response to this is to turn up the sound on my radio so that I only hear the radio. This is using concentration on the sounds of the radio to distract myself from being aware of something I need to know about my car. It is basically a *dysfunctional strategy of avoidance*. Often, people also do this when they take drugs, watch a movie, or go shopping so that they do not have to feel their emotions. As a result, we may never deal with some important issues in our lives. With more mindfulness, we can begin to consciously *notice* when we are doing this and choose a more effective response for ourselves.

Essentially, this incorrect form of concentration is a way of avoiding knowledge of reality and thereby maintaining our ignorance. Clearly, this is likely to cause harm. We are quite good at doing this whenever something comes up that feels uncomfortable: anxiety, fear, or tension for example. As a result, we usually just operate within our comfort zone and no real progress in changing ourselves takes place. We simply stay "stuck" forever. With more mindfulness, our discomfort can *actually be seen as a sign* that we are about to get in touch with something significant, some part of ourselves that is keeping us stuck or obstructed. When we learn to work at the level of our obstruction, real change can occur.

In order to concentrate fully, it is necessary to drop all external and internal distractions so that the world—both external and internal—can be seen as it really is. This requires dropping all desires, judgments, attempts to control or manipulate things, and agendas, because these things act as distorting elements and filters that block accurate perception. In talking about dropping them, this does not mean dropping them out of our lives forever, but rather being able to let go of them in this moment. I then can see the tree in front of me, or my present emotion, just as it really is—rather than seeing it the way I think it should be, how I hope it is, how I have been told it is, or how it relates to helping or not helping my getting the things I want for myself.

Mindful Association

Although not part of the Four Noble Truths or the Eightfold Program, there is one other central teaching to know about as part of our starting point on the journey to seeing things more clearly and deeply changing ourselves. This has to do with the Buddha's recognition that the people we choose to associate with in life will have a profound impact on our ability to successfully change ourselves. This collection of teachings has traditionally gone under the name of Right

Association, but can perhaps more appropriately be labeled as Mindful Association for our purposes here.

Our choices of who to associate with can either make it much easier to succeed at changing ourselves or much harder. Let's look at how this works. Many people who smoke cigarettes would like to quit. If that's what we want to do, if we spend a good amount of our time around people who continue to smoke and who don't have any interest in quitting, it is going to make it much harder for us to quit. We can make it more likely we will be successful in quitting if we spend most or all of our time associating with people who have already successfully quit or never smoked in the first place, or people who are making a good faith effort to quit.

Similarly, if I am a college student and trying to get an education and my roommate has no interest in school and even thinks it's a waste of time, it will be much harder for me to benefit from being in school. Finding a roommate who is really committed to school and regularly attends classes, studies, and puts care and attention into schoolwork will make it easier for me to succeed in school.

The Buddha pointed out that nothing teaches or inspires the will to learn like a real-life example (or role model). Mindful Association is a powerful tool to facilitate change for at least three reasons.

First, a living example of what I want to become shows me that living this way is *possible*. If someone else has already done it, or is doing it, then clearly it is possible.   I have a living example of what I want for myself right in front of me. Having someone *show* me that it is possible is very different from reading or hearing about it in *words*.

Second, a living example provides me with a constant illustration of *how to live this way*. If I want to get off junk food and eat a healthy diet, spending time with people who are presently living that way shows me how to shop for good food, how to prepare it, how to store it properly, and so on.

45

Third, a real-life example shows me *the benefits* to be derived from living this way. My new friends who are eating healthy foods rarely get sick, are strong, have lots of energy, they're calm, their skin looks good, and they enjoy their food and their lives. This is very inspiring and motivating.

In making use of the principle of Mindful Association, it will probably also help me to minimize time spent with people who are "harmful association" and who will make it more difficult to maintain my commitment to changing myself. This is especially true when first getting started with a program of personal change. This doesn't mean that it is necessary to rudely tell old associates to go away—I can simply tell them that I am trying to make some specific changes in my life and that, for a while at least, I want to be spending most of my time with people who have already successfully made these changes. If they are really my friends, they will support me in my efforts to change. Later, when my new habits are strongly established, I may be able to spend more time with people who are still choosing to participate in harmful habits—I might even be able to be a Mindful Association influence for them and ultimately help them to be successful at change also.

Mindful Association works in exactly the same way in regard to following the Eight-Fold Program. If I have the intention of being more mindful, seeing my life more clearly, and moving toward greater wisdom and compassion it will help greatly to spend time with people who have already made these changes or who are making a good faith effort to move in that direction. People who exude negativity and are mired in behaviors I want to leave behind will be people I will want to consciously choose to spend much less time with—or perhaps even no time at all.

Notes for Chapter 3

1. Wittgenstein, Ludwig, *Tractatus Logico-Philosophicus*, London and New York: Routledge & Kegan Paul LTD, 1961, Section 6.54.

2. Thich Nhat Hanh, *The Heart of the Buddha's Teaching*, New York: Broadway Books, 1999, p. 53.

3. Smith, Huston, *The World's Religions: Our Great Wisdom Traditions, Revised Edition,* San Francisco: HarperSanFrancisco, 1991, p. 107.

4. Nhat Hanh, Thich, *The Heart of the Buddha's Teaching*, p. 94.

5. Nhat Hanh, Thich, *Interbeing: Fourteen Guidelines for Engaged Buddhism, Third Edition*, Berkeley: Parallax Press, 1998, p.7.

6. (Note (6): Worldwatch Institute, "The State of Consumption Today," January 8, 2019, http://www.worldwatch.org/node/810.

7. McDonald, Charlotte, "How Many Earths Do We Need?", *BBC News Magazine*, June 26, 2015, https://www.bbc.com/news/magazine-33133712.

8. Renata, "The Parable of the Lute," posted May 9, 2013, https://bychancebuddhism.blogspot.com/2013/05/the-parable-of-lute.html. The Parable is originally from the Buddhist scripture *Anguttara Nikaya*.

CHAPTER 4

Mindfulness and Meditation Teachings

Before we can do anything about changing our lives we must first see clearly what is going on.

Imagine a room containing 20 people and every one of them is wearing a blindfold that leaves them in total darkness. In addition, these people have had their blindfolds on for so long they do not even know that they are wearing them any longer. What would things be like in that room? People would be walking around, bumping into furniture and bumping into others and hurting themselves, probably getting angry, and lashing out at other people. There would be great deal of unhappiness. Now imagine that at some point you realize that you are wearing a blindfold and that you remove it. *Everything* is now different for you—you can see what is happening, see your own behavior and the consequences of that behavior, get your bearings, and stop hurting yourself and others. This is mindfulness—actually awakening from the darkness of our half-conscious state and seeing what is going on in our lives. And the good news is that we can actually train ourselves to be much more mindful.

Mindfulness is simply being aware of what is present right here and right now. It is a state of relaxed and alert attention to the present moment. When we are being mindful, we are not lost in thought, not worrying about the future and not chewing over the past. We are in direct contact with what is real in this moment: sounds and sights arising around us, bodily sensations, and the thoughts and emotions that are present.

Of course, we cannot be mindful of everything that is arising in any particular moment—to attempt this would leave us frantically trying to notice everything and feeling stressed out and overwhelmed. Frequently, we will find it necessary to choose to narrow our attention down to some specific slice of what is present in the moment: perhaps physical sensations, perhaps the emotions we are feeling, or maybe what is being said to us by the person we are with at the time. At other times, our mindful awareness can simply be receptive to whatever elements of personal experience present themselves to us: first a sound arising near us, then the wind on our face, then the color, pattern, and texture of a cloud arising in our field of vision, and then an emotion welling up inside us. This kind of mindfulness is often called "choiceless awareness." But whether it is choiceless awareness or a more concentrated and focused state, we are in direct touch with reality and not lost in thought.

Thoughts may arise, but when we are being mindful they can be observed like objects floating by in a river while we are seated on the bank. We can learn to simply observe what is present—whatever it might be—without being swept away by it. Being swept away by thought is what happens when we hike a trail in the woods and "awake" at some point to realize that we have not noticed a single thing along the trail because we have been lost in thought the whole time.

Mindfulness is not an intellectual operation. When we are in a mindful state we notice many things that we would otherwise miss. When we are absorbed in thinking, we miss many things that we would otherwise notice. If while you are speaking to me I am thinking about what I want to say next, I will miss much of the meaning of what you have just said. Listening mindfully means giving my full attention to your speech, just being receptive and taking in what is being said without trying to pass judgment on it or manipulate it in any way.

Not being judgmental is an important part of mindfulness. Perhaps part of what is real in this moment is that I am feeling anger.

The anger is real and it is here now. It does not matter whether it is justified or not, nor does it matter what caused it. Mindfulness is simply knowing that I am angry and feeling it fully without creating "mental stories" about it: "I shouldn't be feeling this way, I'm a bad person for feeling this way, I'm just an angry person." The simple reality is that *anger is here now*. The mental stories are just the mind's attempt to comment on what is here now, interpret it, figure it out, or distract me from just feeling it.

If we try, most of us can be mindful for a short period of time—it's actually not particularly hard to be mindful. If you ask someone to pay attention to the actual sounds arising around them without labeling or interpreting them, they usually can do it. But it won't last long—maybe only a few seconds—before they are distracted, almost always as a result of getting lost in their own thought stream: "Was that a car or a bus I just heard? I remember when I was on the bus yesterday a really unpleasant person sat next to me and..." So while it may not be hard to be mindful, it is hard to *remember* to be mindful; we have a tendency to continually slip back into being oblivious. As we continue to practice, we will find that we become better and better at *catching ourselves* not being present and then bringing ourselves back to the present moment.

Becoming More Mindful Day to Day

A simple example can help us here. There are two ways to sit in the park. One way is sitting in the park in order to wait for a friend to pick us up and give us a ride. Typically, this way of sitting in the park has us lost in daydreams or problem solving or with the mind jumping about from one idea to another, or perhaps glancing over to the street every few minutes to see if our friend's car is here yet—where can she be? Typically we are not noticing much of anything in our immediate external and internal environments.

50

The second way of sitting in the park is sitting in the park in order to be sitting in the park. In this case we are in direct contact with our experience: we are feeling the sun's warmth on our face, the tiny sensations of our hair moving slightly in the breeze, the hard pressure of the ground under our hip bones which we are sitting on, the pleasant warm vibration in our chest, the physical sensations of air moving into and out of our body, the sounds of birds in the trees. There is no need to try to frantically be aware of everything; we are simply in a relaxed and receptive state in which we are paying attention to whatever elements of "right-here-and-right-now" present themselves to us. We allow our attention to move from one thing to another without trying to "figure anything out" or advance some agenda. In this state of mindfulness, we are simply noticing what is present in this moment. Through practice, we can learn to be fully present in the park and, in addition, also be there to meet a friend. This applies equally well to any other activity: folding the laundry, vacuuming the floor, or chopping vegetables for dinner. We can actually experience each moment of each situation we are engaged in. The present moment is always where our lives take place. To not be present as we move through our day is to miss out on huge segments of our lives.

I had a very revealing experience along these lines when I first started college. I was an architecture student, so in addition to engineering and design classes, I was required to take drawing and painting. Art was a subject in which I had no background whatsoever. But, I thought to myself, how hard could it be? We were assigned to paint a building on campus, so I simply used my blue tube of paint for the sky, my green one for grass, and my red one for the brick building. My rendering, of course, did not look at all convincing. What I was doing was painting *from concepts* in my head rather than really looking at and *experiencing what was actually present. My mind was telling me that grass was green* but when I actually paid attention and got in touch with what was real and right in front of me in that moment, I saw clearly that grass was not simply green, it was many shades of green as well as shades of brown, yellow, black, and even blue. There were even some highlights from the sun that were bright white. Our thinking and our concepts often act as obstacles preventing us from seeing what is actually there.

Sometimes our tendency to not be mindful comes from our habit of pulling away from experiences that are unpleasant or difficult. Rather than "lean into it" and open ourselves to truly experiencing the fear that is present in us, our tendency is to "hit the eject button" and "bail out" of what we are feeling—very much the way a pilot might bail out when the plane is not flying well. When we don't like what we are experiencing we find some way of distracting ourselves or "changing the subject" to avoid experiencing what is happening. The practice of meditation is to learn to stay with more and more of what arises in our experience. Pema Chodron calls this learning to "maintain our seat on the [meditation] cushion." In meditation we learn to stay with our experience, to maintain our awareness of what is present rather than get up and leave because it is unpleasant or difficult or not what we were hoping for. An essential purpose of Buddhist meditation is to learn to stay connected to our actual experience, both during meditation when it is easier to do so, and in our day-to-day life when it can be much more challenging. It is this "staying connected" with our actual experience that is crucial to seeing clearly what is going on in our lives and therefore being able to make wiser and more conscious choices about how to respond to events.

Our tendency is to be unmindful almost 100% of the time—it is simply habitual and automatic, our "default setting" so to speak. But we can change things. Eckhart Tolle observes that we have a strong tendency to live in the past and in the future, and to only pay occasional visits to the present. We need to reverse this and have our "...*dwelling place* in the Now and pay brief visits to past and future when required to deal with the practical aspects of... [our] life situation." (1) With some consistency of effort, we can gradually change being in the present moment to our new default setting so that it becomes our home where we spend almost all of our time.

The Buddha taught that we can *train ourselves* to be more mindful by the practice of meditation. The word "meditation" is actually not a good English translation for what the Buddha had in mind. To meditate literally means to *think*. A premeditated murder, for example, means a murder that was *thought through* ahead of time. However, meditation is not concerned with *thinking about* anything, it is concerned with *experiencing* what is present in this moment. The word "meditation" is a translation of the Sanskrit word "bhavana," which literally means "to cause to be developed." Bhavana refers to Buddhist practices that are aimed at developing or strengthening certain mental and emotional qualities in ourselves.

How to Meditate to Increase Mindfulness and Concentration

The meditations that we will be learning about here are drawn basically from the vipassana tradition within Buddhism. Vipassana is also called "Insight Meditation" or "clear seeing." Buddhist meditation of this sort has three basic intentions.

The first intention is to help us to become more in touch with, and not in denial of, the reality of the present moment; this is called mindfulness. The second intention is to help us strengthen our ability to *concentrate or focus* our attention on a *single* thing. The third intention is to help us to become more compassionate, caring, and kind. In Sanskrit this last kind of meditation is called metta meditation. In English, metta is translated as lovingkindness.

In learning to meditate to increase our mindfulness, we are not trying to achieve some special state of mind—relaxed, blissful, calm, happy, or any particular state of mind at all. Rather we are learning to simply be aware of *whatever* might be arising in this moment. We are training ourselves to pay attention to our actual experience in each moment as it arises. So in any given moment we may be experiencing a rustling sound, feeling an itching sensation above our left eye, or have a strong feeling of anger arising within us. None of this is good or bad when we are meditating, it is just what is present for us in this moment and we are learning to pay attention to it. We are learning to *simply be there along with what is arising* and be consciously aware of it. We are not trying to make anything that is present stay longer, and we are not trying to push away or ignore anything present that might be unpleasant. We are not trying to *make* our experience into anything at all other than just what it is.

We begin our practice of Buddhist meditation with simple things, training ourselves to pay attention to the present moment, and to bring our attention back to it each time we are distracted. In training ourselves to maintain our attention on something as simple as the physical sensations of our own breathing, or sounds arising around us as we sit quietly, we are also training our ability to stay present and really notice what is happening at other times when someone one is "in our face," yelling at us and blaming us. Having a mind trained in this way will enable us to see clearly what is going on even in this difficult situation, and thus be in a better position to *consciously choose* a constructive response rather than just *reacting* out of habit and lashing out or running away. We lay a foundation of learning to pay attention by practicing in an easy and safe meditation environment, and when our abilities have increased we will then find that we are better able to stay present in the really difficult situations that come up so that we can begin to behave in ways that ease suffering rather than increase it.

Closing Summary and Suggestions

A good place to start a meditation practice of this type is with four basic sitting meditations: Basic Breathing Meditation, Hearing Meditation, Body Sensations Meditation, and Sense Perceptions Meditation. After trying them all out, most people find that one or two of them work especially well and become what they use most of the time they are doing sitting meditation.

Choosing from among the four basic sitting practices described below, make it a daily habit to meditate twice a day for five to twenty minutes each time. It is best to do this every day. If you decide, for example, to meditate only three days a week it will be easy to forget and soon find yourself not doing it at all. Simply make it part of your life —something you naturally do every day without having to debate with yourself whether you are going to do it. Making it a daily habit will also increase the benefits experienced. If you have an extremely busy day, still make it a point to sit and meditate. Even if you only sit for one minute, it is extremely helpful to do so because it keeps the habit going. You may also find that once you have overcome the initial mental resistance to sitting that you end up sitting longer than a minute.

Ironically, the days that we say we are too stressed or busy to meditate are the days that we really *need* to do it. We can learn to consciously notice that internal feeling of stress or anxiety and to view it as a *message* letting us know that we need to re-ground ourselves. A favorite Zen proverb says "You should sit in meditation twenty minutes every day, unless you are too busy. Then you should meditate for an hour."

Many people find it very valuable to do very short "micro-meditations" at various odd moments during their day: while standing in line at the store, waiting for a bus, or sitting at a desk at work. Just take a few seconds to connect to the sensations of breathing or sounds arising and become grounded in the present moment.

Some people find that it is helpful to keep a personal meditation journal. This could include aspects of personal meditation experience that seem revealing or significant: repeated patterns in the distractions that arise during sittings, mental resistance to doing meditation, or spontaneous insights about your life that arise when your mind becomes quieter, as well as signs of positive change in one's daily life. Sometimes, in the beginning, people feel like their new meditation practice is causing anxiety, fear, or anger. Almost always, meditation is *not the cause* of these things. Meditation simply provides a quiet, open, and safe *space* in which things that were there all along—perhaps for years—finally have a chance to surface and come into conscious awareness. This is beneficial, because once we are fully aware of these repressed things, the process of change and healing can finally begin.

We need to remember to be patient with the process. Meditation is a lifetime practice like eating well or exercising—if you want to be healthy you don't just eat one healthy meal or eat healthy food for a week. *Commit* yourself to doing the work. As time goes on you will notice more and more benefits in how things are going for you during the times that you are not meditating. We meditate not to get good at meditation, but to fundamentally change the way in which we respond to life each day.

In later chapters, we will be examining several other forms of meditation practice: walking meditation, practices for stopping ourselves when we are in the grips of a harmful habit, using meditation to work with troubling emotions, and using lovingkindness meditation to strengthen our ability to be caring. But for now, our primary focus is to create a good foundation of mindfulness for ourselves using the basic sitting practices outlined below.

Four Basic Sitting Meditations to Increase Mindfulness

In what follows there are four basic sitting meditations that we can learn and try out: Basic Breathing Meditation, Hearing Meditation, Body Sensations Meditation, and Sense Perceptions Meditation. All four meditations have the intention of increasing our ability to focus and pay attention to the present moment.

In practicing these meditations, it is important to begin by sitting comfortably in an upright but relaxed posture. There is no need to sit in the lotus position, or sit on the floor at all if you don't want to. Sitting upright, but not tense, is important because it will help us to stay awake and alert. If it is not possible to sit comfortably on the floor, then sit in a chair. If you have injuries that cause pain, you may need to lie on the floor—but do not do this unless really necessary because it will increase your chances of falling asleep. If you decide to sit on the floor, it is very helpful to sit on some type of firm cushion four to eight inches high to raise your hips higher than your knees. This will open up the angle between your legs and torso and prevent your internal organs from being uncomfortably compressed.

Using a timer for your meditation sessions is highly recommended. Decide before you start how long you are going to meditate and set the alarm on your timer to go off when that time is elapsed. Doing this will prevent you from being distracted by glancing at a clock periodically to see how long you have been meditating. It will also help prevent you from stopping when you are tired of it, bored, or restless. This will give you a chance to experience these states fully and get to see what they really are. Staying until your predetermined time is good practice in learning to open to difficult experiences rather than running from them as soon as they arise.

Choose a place to meditate that will not have people walking in on you and which is not overly distracting. When you are first learning these meditations it is a good idea to review the instructions each time before starting. If you would like a voice-guided meditation, you can make your own by reading the accompanying meditation script—with silent places between the paragraphs of instruction—into a recording device. Include enough silent pauses in your recording so that playback time is about fifteen minutes when you play it for guidance in your meditation session. Feel free to shorten the script if you feel you need less verbal guidance and if that seems to work better for you. Once you are familiar with how to do the meditations, having this kind of guidance will be unnecessary most of the time.

Reading the entire script before starting can be a good idea until you become familiar with doing the meditation. Once you are seated in your meditation spot and have started your timer (and your voice recording for a guided meditation if you are using it), begin by closing your eyes and taking four or five deep relaxing breaths and then begin. If you are uncomfortable closing your eyes, meditate with your eyes open and looking slightly downward at a spot four to six feet in front of you. Maintain your gaze on the spot throughout your session. You may wish to play back your recorded script during your session for voice guidance.

The structure for all four basic sitting meditations presented here is exactly the same. An object is chosen to place the attention on. Depending on the meditation chosen this is either the physical sensations of the breath, sounds arising in the environment, sensations arising within the body, or sense perceptions. The thing we choose to place our attention on is called the *Primary Object of Attention*. Inevitably, we will be distracted from our chosen focus and find that our attention has gone elsewhere. When this happens, we simply *notice* that the mind has wandered away from the Primary Object of Attention, and *gently bring it back* to our chosen focus. This typically happens over and over during the course of a meditation session.

The crucial element here is the *repeated process of bringing the attention back* to our chosen focus. This is the real work of meditation. *Each time* the attention is brought back to the chosen focus, *the mind's ability to concentrate and stay present gets stronger* as a result of this training using meditation. This is very similar to what happens with physical exercise and the increases in physical strength that is produces.

In addition to strengthening the ability to focus and be present, you are also strengthening your ability to *start over* again—every time you notice you have been distracted, you simply bring the attention back to where you want it to be and start over again. The ability to drop the past and start over is a very useful *life skill* that assists us in not getting stuck in the past, letting go of grudges, forgiving ourselves and others, and letting go of habits and beliefs that are not serving us well.

58

Basic Breathing Meditation

The Basic Breathing Meditation uses the physical sensations of breathing as the object upon which we rest our attention. For this meditation, you will be using the physical sensations of your breathing as what is often called the Primary Object of Attention—the place where you are choosing to place your attention in a particular meditation. In paying attention to the breath, simply be aware of the physical sensations of breathing wherever you happen feel them most strongly: perhaps at the nostrils, maybe your abdomen, or possibly your chest. Just feel the sensations without thinking that you need to comment on them, analyze them, name them, or make them into anything special. Just allow the breath to be whatever it wants to be and pay attention to it.

We are basically using the sensations of breathing—which are always right here right now—as an anchor to hold our attention in the present moment. In the other basic sitting practices, sounds arising, sensations present within the body, or sense perceptions arising in the immediate environment serve the same role of anchoring us in the present moment and taking us out of our compulsive thought stream.

In starting with the Basic Breath Meditation, you will very quickly discover that your attention does *not stay* on the breath—it may go to fantasizing, or planning what you will do later, or worrying about the future. This is normal. *Anything* that your attention goes to that is not the breath is viewed as a *distraction*. Each time this happens, simply notice that you have been distracted and then gently bring your attention back to the primary object of attention for the meditation—in this case, your breathing. You may find yourself being critical and judging yourself: "I'm terrible at meditation. I'll never be any good at this." Just notice you are judging yourself rather than paying attention to the breath, and then bring your attention back to the breath. Over time, you may notice a pattern as to where your attention goes when you are distracted—perhaps it goes to a problem that needs to be

59

solved, or reliving some experience from the past, or negative judgments about yourself. Information about this pattern can be very useful to you in achieving a better understanding about how your mind tends to work, and can be a starting point for retraining the mind.

Typically, when we are breathing there is no awareness of it on our part—it all just happens automatically on its own. So another aspect of what we are accomplishing here is learning the skill of making what is normally an *unconscious process* (breathing) into a *conscious process* (mindful breathing). This is useful because once we develop it, this skill can then be used to help us become more conscious of other normally unconscious processes, such as the working of our own internal thought processes. It is these thought processes that are frequently the root cause of or our distorted perceptions of people and events, as well as our reactive behavior that causes so much suffering. So learning to observe the breath may seem insignificant, but the potential benefit of learning to be consciously aware of our inner and outer processes and then change them is enormous.

Script for Voice Guidance with Basic Breathing Meditation. This should take about 15 minutes, so if you are recording the script to listen to while meditating, be sure to build silent pauses into it between the bullet points so it takes about 15 minutes.

- Sit comfortably. Keep your back straight, but without becoming tense or arching unnaturally. What you are about to do is not strange or unnatural. Be relaxed, but also awake and alert.

- Close your eyes (if you are comfortable with doing that). Deliberately take 4 or 5 deep breaths, feeling the sensations of air entering your nostrils and the stretching sensations in your chest and abdomen. Now let your breathing become whatever it wants to be, without trying to make it into anything special.

Just breathe naturally, and observe the sensations of breathing as they arise.

- Notice where you feel the breath most strongly. It could be at the nostrils, or in the chest or abdomen. Allow your attention to rest very gently on that area.

- Focus your attention on the actual sensations that are present. If you are feeling the breath at the chest, you may feel a lifting sensation, some stretching, followed by a falling sensation. The breath at the nostrils may produce a cool or tingling sensation on the in-breath and perhaps some vibration on the out-breath. Just feel what is happening without trying to name or describe the sensations.

- See if you can experience each breath as a separate and complete event, including the time at the end of a breath cycle when you are not breathing. Your job here is only to pay attention to this one breath right now. Then pay attention to the next breath that is happening, and then the next one... one breath at a time.

- To help maintain an awareness of the breath, you might try saying silently to yourself "in" with each in-breath and "out" with each out-breath. If you use this practice of silent mental noting, it should be done very gently. If using silent noting consistently draws you into thinking, it is best to discontinue using it.

- It's normal to be distracted many times—your attention may be pulled away by something hurting in your body, or a thought, or a memory, or an emotion. Simply notice that you have been distracted and bring your attention back to the feeling of your breath.

- Continue to breathe and be aware of your breathing. If you find yourself thinking "I'll never be any good at meditation," simply notice that your attention has been drawn away by harsh self-judgment, and bring your attention back to the breath. Whatever distracts you, just continue to start over each time and return to the breath.

- What we are doing here is very basic, simply being there with the breath—it's a little bit like you are sitting on a park bench and the breath is sitting there next you. All that is needed is to be there with the breath in a relaxed and alert state.

- When you notice that your attention is not on your breath, notice what has distracted you, and refocus your attention on the physical sensations of breathing. Each time you bring your attention back to the breath, you are strengthening your mind's ability to focus and pay attention.

- Being distracted a lot is normal. If you have to let go of distractions and start over again a hundred times, that's ok. That is not an *obstacle* to doing the practice, that *is* the central practice of meditation.

- Continue following the breath, and starting over each time you need to.

- **End of Meditation.** (A bell on your meditation timer or on your recorded guided meditation can be useful here as an ending device.)

  After your meditation session, make it a point to bring some of the qualities of concentration you just experienced—presence, calm observation, willingness to start over, and gentleness—to the next activity that you have coming up in your day.
  Remember: The purpose of meditation is not to become better at meditation, but to become better at life. This is central.

Other Basic Sitting Practices

The preceding script can easily be modified for use with the Hearing, Body Sensations, and Sense Perceptions Meditations. The only real difference in these four basic sitting practices is that each meditation has a different primary object of attention. In the **Hearing Meditation**, we use sounds arising in the immediate environment as the primary object of attention. Each time we notice that we have been distracted from hearing sounds, we gently bring our attention back to sounds arising. Distractions will be *anything* that is not sound: thoughts, internal body sensations, itches, memories, fantasies, problem solving, and so on. Keep bringing your attention back to hearing sounds arising. Simply hear the sounds that present themselves to you without trying to search out sounds or attempting to hear everything.

Typically, the mind's habit will be to try to figure out what a sound is, or label it in some way. Our task here is to simply *hear* each sound as it arises without trying to interpret it. Just be receptive to what presents itself and let the sounds come and go as they will. There is nothing that you need to do about any of these sounds—just hear them. You can view what you are doing as being *a receiving station for sounds*. If you pay attention carefully, you may notice that what seems to be single sound, like the hum of a refrigerator, may have several layers of sound to it. Some sounds you may like and others you may dislike. When that happens simply notice that there are two things present—the sound itself and your emotional response to it—and then bring your attention gently back to just the sound itself and starting over again each time you are distracted.

The **Body Sensations Meditation** uses physical sensations arising in the body as the primary object of attention. These sensations will be things like aches and pains, buzzing, tingling, warmth or cold, pulsing, vibration, tension, itches, movement in the digestive tract, and so on. We begin by taking four or five deep mindful breaths. Let the

63

breath then become natural, and use the breath as the primary object of attention *until* some physical body sensation arises that is strong enough to pull your attention away from the breath. When that happens, simply let go of being aware of the breath, and let your attention rest fully on the body sensation that has distracted you. Let that body sensation *become the new primary object of your meditation*. Maintain your attention on the body sensation, coming back to it each time you are distracted. If the body sensation fades and is replaced by a new body sensation, make that new sensation your primary object of attention. If it fades and there is no new body sensation, simply return your attention to the breath until the next body sensations arises—it then becomes the new primary object of attention.

As you observe each new body sensation that arises, notice that there may be several things going on at once in what seems like one sensation. Also notice how the feeling of the sensation changes over time, perhaps shifts position, or even leaves completely for a few seconds and then comes back.

If a body sensation is particularly painful and hard to stay with, you may want to return the attention to the breath for a while as a safe temporary "resting place." Meditation is not some sort of contest to see how much pain you can endure. If something is extremely painful or possibly injuring you, by all means shift your position so that you are more comfortable.

Remember to gently bring the attention back and start over each time a distraction occurs. In a Body Sensations Meditation, distractions will be *anything* that is not a physical sensation in the body: thoughts, emotions, sounds, memories, fantasies, problem solving, and so on.

The **Sense Perceptions Meditation**, works in exactly the same way as the Body Sensations Meditation—the awareness is simply *expanded* to include sense perceptions of any kind: touch, pressure, sounds, heat, body sensations, smells, and visual perceptions. Visual perceptions often happen even if our eyes are closed—there may be blackness, or more frequently, moving patterns of color and texture visible "behind the eyelids."

After we have some experience with the four basic sitting meditations, typically we will find that some of them work better for us than others and may become our typical "go-to" meditation. It can also work well, when we have more experience, to simply let our attention shift easily from breathing to hearing to perception or even to mindfully observing thoughts or emotions as they arise.

Moving Forward

The Buddha taught that when we are being mindful, four basic things will reveal themselves to us. First, it is *not events* that make us unhappy, but *our way of responding* to events that makes us unhappy. Second, we begin to see clearly *how* the mind's response to events *creates* suffering. Third, once we begin to see what the mind is doing, we have the ability to *change* the mind's habitual responses to things. Fourth, when we have learned to work with the mind in this way, *we can be content and at peace no matter what our external circumstances may be*. At this point, the four preceding points may just sound like empty words. However, when we have actually worked with the meditation practices for a few weeks or months, the truth of the words will eventually become real to us. The mindfulness that we acquire through meditation has the power to produce very deep and very positive changes in our lives. *This is the central reason that we meditate.*

In the beginning, when we are just starting out, we start by training the mind by using very simple objects such as the breath or sounds arising. Eventually, we can broaden that out to include whatever is arising, whatever is in front of us or inside of us in each moment: sense perceptions, thoughts, emotions, physical reactions, and so on. Whatever is happening, we are more and more able to *open to experience* and see more clearly whatever it is that is arising in the each moment. We are easily able to see what responses from us are wise and necessary in each situation. Meditation becomes more and more simply our way of being in the world. At some point, it can simply become how we normally experience life. Satish Kumar has stated this quite eloquently.

> Meditation is to pay attention to... all that
> passes through your mind and the mind itself;
> whatever is going on within you and between
> you and the universe. Meditation is not just
> sitting for an hour here or an hour there;
> meditation is a way of life. It is practiced all the
> time. There is no separation between
> meditation and everyday living. (2)

Notes for Chapter 4

1. Tolle, Eckhart, *The Power of Now: A Guide to Spiritual Enlightenment*, Novato: New World Library, 1999, p. 28

2. Kumar, Satish, *The Buddha and the Terrorist*, Chapel Hill: Algonquin Books, 2006, pp. 64-65.

CHAPTER 5

The Nature of Happiness and Suffering

Let's begin our examination of the Buddha's approach to understanding suffering by looking at a story from Korean Zen Master Seung Sahn.

> In Korea, people use grass cuttings to make compost. Cutting the grass with a sickle was a job for children. When I was eight years old I liked the job, so one day my friends and I went out and I cut a lot of grass. Then we gathered it all in a bag, and we all went to school together...very happy... I had already walked half a mile [when]... one of my friends said to me, "You cut your leg!" Then I looked at my leg and saw the blood. I was bleeding very badly, and blood was making squishing sounds in my rubber shoe as I walked. As soon as I saw this, I fell to the ground in great pain and couldn't move. The other students all came around to see what had happened, and they ran to get my mother and helped me to the hospital. (1)

This is a good example of someone who is really suffering. Let's ask ourselves a question: "*Why* is eight year old Seung Sahn suffering?" We all *know* the answer: he has cut his leg with a sickle, he is bleeding badly and is in a lot of pain, and he cannot move and must be helped to the hospital.

But are we *sure* that this explanation of Seung Sahn's suffering is really accurate? Go back and read the story again, very carefully this time, and see if we aren't missing something hugely important. What is it?

How Suffering Is Created

If we look closely, we will notice that even though he has a cut leg, he has managed to walk a half mile without any suffering at all—he is not in pain, he is able to walk normally, and he is enjoying the company of his friends. It is only *after* being told he is cut and seeing the blood and noticing it squishing in his shoe, *only then* does he fall to the ground in great pain and unable to move. As Seung Sahn goes on to point out, the real source of his suffering is not what has *actually happened* to him, it is caused by his *mental response* to what has happened to him. Once an injury such as this occurs, our minds are likely to instantly produce upsetting thoughts such as: "I'm very badly injured, this is horrible, I might not be able to play in my soccer game tomorrow, maybe they'll have to amputate my foot, maybe I'll bleed to death..."

So when we look closely, we discover that there really are *two* things present: the first one is Seung Sahn's *actual situation*. He is walking to school, his leg is cut and bleeding, and he is having a good time with his friends. These are all *facts*. It is also a fact that his cut leg needs medical attention. But, as we have seen, *all of this can be true without any suffering being present*. The second thing that is also present is a *mental story* that the mind is producing about how awful things are and what the future holds. None of this is factual or real. Nonetheless, it is this mind-created fictional story that is the *real source* of all his suffering.

The mind is constantly interpreting and adding on to events in our lives. However, we typically do not see what is going on because we are not yet skilled in observing how the mind works. Furthermore, we very regularly see the contents of the mental story *as facts*. Let's look at another example. Suppose my friend John, shortly after arriving at work, says to me "Is that everything you did this morning?" I instantly become angry and lash out at John: "Listen, I work harder around here than you ever have the whole time you have worked here!" If someone were to ask me what the anger is all about, I quite likely would say "John made me angry when he accused me of being a shirker." And I would view what I just said as *a statement of fact*.

This is pretty much how things seem to go most of the time when we become angry. The simple event described above is a good example of getting angry in a conditioned and reactive way with no element of mindfulness. Some event happens, anger arises, and then *all of my attention goes out into the external world*: John did this, John did that, he made me angry, he is to blame for this. The mind is focused entirely on the *external triggering event* for the anger: John's statement. But what if I make the revolutionary choice to *turn my attention inward* to look at my own anger process as it unfolds? What may I see when that happens?

With more mindfulness, it is possible to slow down the process and take a closer look at the chain of events going on inside me that I normally just don't see at all. The sequence of events typically looks something like this.

Anatomy of Reactive and Mindful Anger Responses

First, there is some actual event that takes place. In this case John has said to me: "Is that everything you did this morning?" This is the external triggering event.

Second, and happening very quickly, there is some sort of thought or perception or interpretation that arises such as: "He thinks I don't do enough," "He is criticizing me," "He is attacking me," "I need to defend myself." With some training in meditation, it becomes possible to be consciously aware of this thought stream.

Third, anger arises. *When I am mindful*, I know that anger is present and I am in touch with it in the body: heat in my face, pounding sensation in my chest, rapid breathing, and tense posture. I am aware of the tone of my own voice as I verbally react to what John said. Many times, however, there is *no conscious awareness* of the presence of anger and I do not really become aware of it until later when I look back on my behavior.

Fourth, because I do not yet know how to skillfully recognize and experience anger, my anger takes me over and I lose my ability to choose how to respond: I act unskillfully and lash out at John: "You're the one who is really lazy and trying to get me to do your work for you!" I blame my anger on John.

Fifth, at some point later on I may find myself judging my reaction harshly: "I behaved terribly."

Sixth, I may then move on to *globalize* my behavior—that is, I make it into something larger than just this *specific* episode of angry behavior. My thoughts become "I *always* get mad when someone says something that sounds like a criticism."

Seventh, things may go even further off the rails and I may make what has happened into a *personal identity*: " I'm just an angry hostile *person*. I'm such a jerk." I make my reaction into a *definition* of who I am. Obviously, if I think this behavior is who I am as a person, this is going to make it much harder for me to change than it would be if I simply viewed it as how I behaved in this particular situation.

The mind is almost always functioning in this way, but typically we do not *see* it. Mindfulness allows us to *see* the whole process and recognize that it is our *unskillful response* to what is happening that is causing all the suffering. Just in seeing what we are doing, the process of change has already begun. When we see this process clearly enough times, at some point we simply don't *want* to go there anymore—and we realize we don't *have* to go there anymore. Life can be much simpler and less painful. The question "Is that everything you did this morning?" can be answered with a simple "Yes."   No problem—done! How much easier that is!

We can learn to simply feel the anger fully, notice the mental stories we are running that keep it going ("She did this and she did that, she always does... It's all her fault") and allow the anger to simply be there and then wash through. We begin to see that the mental stories are what set the whole process of suffering in motion and provide the fuel to keep it going. We can also learn that there is no need to *believe* a story in our mind just because it is there.

Each step in the evolution of becoming angry and lashing out provides a place to see what is happening and *put a halt to the process*. I can notice that I am making the anger that is present into a definition of self and choose not to do that, which reduces my suffering. I may become mindful and in touch a little sooner in the anger process and consciously notice the heat and other sensations arising in the body, know that I am angry and have an *impulse* to lash out, and then *choose not to act* on that impulse, thereby reducing even more of my suffering (and John's suffering as well). If I am being very mindful, I may notice that my mind is interpreting John's statement as a personal attack when it is not, and therefore cut off the process right at the start before it really gets rolling. When mindfulness is well established, the strong habit of my attention going straight to—and solely to—the external triggering event has been replaced by what is now a natural inclination to look inward at my own internal response instead. At this point, life is getting much, much easier and less fraught with difficulty and suffering.

We can learn to *be there with* the anger (mindfulness) but not let it "hijack the car" and take us over so that the anger is now in the driver's seat and we are just along for the (very rough) ride. When we don't know that we are angry it can take us over. When we *know* we are angry and know how to deal with it mindfully, we can consciously *choose* how to respond and create less suffering. Furthermore, the anger itself at the time I am feeling it does not have to create suffering —it is just a sort of vibration in the body and some accompanying thoughts that we can learn to experience fully but not have the feeling sweep us away. In a later chapter we will look at some practices that will help us learn *how to* relate to anger and other difficult emotions in a more positive way.

Remembering what was investigated in Chapter 2, we know that there will always be pain and difficulty in life. But suffering is different from this. Suffering is an extra and unnecessary layer of discomfort that is added on by how we respond to the events of life. Even our attempts to find happiness often create suffering for us.

Our Ideas About Happiness Often Create Unhappiness

Indeed, it is often *our very idea* of happiness which *prevents us* from being happy. This happens because we put conditions on our happiness and say "I'll be happy when I graduate from college," or "I'll be happy when I become a partner in the law firm." Sometimes in Buddhism this is called "if-only mind." It can be very basic. I'm sitting in meditation at a retreat center and the mind says "If only I had a donut I'd be happy." But basic or not, there always seems to be something that we do not have that must be in place *before* we can be happy: lose ten pounds, look "just right," win our lawsuit, find the ideal life partner, start a family, get the kids out of the house and on their own, get divorced, reach retirement. It is literally endless.

Some of us may look at this and think, what's wrong with striving for things to make us happy? The problem is that we are putting *conditions* on our happiness. We believe that only certain conditions will make us happy. We are essentially saying that certain conditions must be fulfilled *before* we can be happy. The upshot of this way of operating is that it virtually guarantees that we will *not* be happy during the time those conditions are *not* fulfilled. *This limits our ability to be happy with what is here right now.*

If we are paying attention, we will notice that actually the conditions for happiness are *always* present. There is no need to wait to be happy. It is not wisdom for me to say "I will be happy when I finish writing this book," because that prevents me from enjoying the way my mind is working while I'm writing, from enjoying the white clouds when I look out the window, and the feeling of the cool breeze in my hair and the warm sun on my face when I go outside and walk to take a break from writing. If I say, "I will be happy when I finish this book," I make the present moment a mere stepping stone to the future, something to be finished with as quickly as possible and not something to be savored and enjoyed. We can enjoy *both* the destination—if we actually arrive there—and also always enjoy the moment-to-moment journey of getting there, even if the journey is sometimes hard. And if we don't arrive at the destination—or don't find it satisfying—then all there was to enjoy was the journey. Why throw away the opportunity for happiness now when there is no need to?

I have seen many of my students over the years do this precise thing. Perhaps a student wants to become a medical doctor. However, they hate the pre-med science courses they are taking and have to force themselves to study in order to get good grades so they will be accepted into medical school. They then go through the same process in medical school—finding what they are doing uninteresting and boring, but enduring the work and "getting it over with," so they can move on to their internship where they must also force themselves to "get it over with," so that they can finally get to the end destination of being a doctor. Literally years of "putting up with" and "getting through" the present moment are spent in hopes that somehow becoming a doctor will give them happiness. I actually had a 43 year old student in one of my philosophy classes who had been a doctor for 15 years and quit. He finally realized that he *never* liked studying medicine and that he *never* liked working as a doctor, either. He quit and went back to school to study Spanish literature because that was what he had always wanted to do and he was finally doing it and loving it.

The Unhappiness Gap

Most of us grow up with a huge blind spot in regard to where our suffering originates. Try asking almost anyone who is unhappy what it is they are unhappy about. They will say they are unhappy because they don't have enough money in the bank, their apartment is too small, or their boss at work doesn't appreciate them enough. Or they may say that their best friend moved away, they lost their job, or that they live in a city where it rains half the days of the year. What do these examples all have in common? In each case, someone is seeing *the cause of their suffering as residing in their external circumstances*—it is always something *outside themselves* that is making them unhappy. Though this *seems* an obvious truth, it is an illusion.

Two thousand years ago Epictetus, a Greek philosopher who had no knowledge of the Buddha's existence, came to the same realization about suffering that the Buddha had five hundred years before him. Epictetus, who was born a slave and then achieved freedom and became a teacher, clearly stated that our external circumstances do not, by themselves, cause anyone to suffer. He said that our suffering is caused by a *gap* between what we *expect or want*, and what we *actually have*. So far, this sounds like something we already know: when we don't *have* what we *want*, we are unhappy.

But what we typically *miss* here is that in any situation where we are unhappy, there are actually *two* things in play. First, suppose it is a *fact* that I live in a city that gets 45 inches of rain a year. This is my *external* situation, it is *what I have*. Second, there is my *wanting or expecting* that it should not rain this much. This is my internal situation. So my unhappiness is simply the gap between "What I actually have" and "What I expect or want."

Our social conditioning, of course, tells us that the way to *close* this gap and become happy is to try to *change the external world* and make it *conform to what we want or expect*. We try to try to *get* what we want in order to be happy, and virtually every message we have received about happiness reinforces this perception. In some cases we can do this and it makes sense to do this. In the example above, I *could* change my external situation by moving from Seattle to San Diego, though undoubtedly this could easily create new dissatisfactions for me: housing is more expensive, weather is monotonous, and so on. What we almost *never see*, however, is that there is something else going on here besides our external circumstances and that *always* trying to *get what we want* is not our only option. It is simply not possible for this gap, between wanting and having, to exist without the internal component. Instead of always seeing our suffering as coming from external circumstances, we can learn to *turn our attention inward* and recognize that a huge part of our suffering is generated in our own minds: our beliefs and expectations about what we *should* have.

I was angry with and resented my parents for many years because I believed they were bad parents: they were very poor listeners, controlling, never admitted mistakes or apologized, my father angered easily, and they didn't seem to want to know who I really was. I was very angry and unhappy about this. After many years, I finally realized that I was comparing my parents to some *idea of perfect parents* that my mind had created. So there was a gap between what I expected or wanted from my parents and the reality of what they were able to do. And at that time, the only way I saw to remove this gap was to try to *make* my parents conform to my mental idea how they *should* behave. This simply did not work. However, my failed attempts to make them bend to my ideas of how they *should* behave certainly did cause a lot of extra suffering for myself and for them.

At some point, I saw the foolishness of what my mind was doing. I realized that they were human beings with their own issues and insecurities and gaps in their knowledge, and that my unrealistic expectations were simply causing suffering. Yes, they were deeply flawed in their parenting and as human beings. Instead of insisting that they change, I changed my expectations of them to something that they were actually able to do. When I also started to see that their previous "failures" were coming out of their own pain and confusion, my suffering ended, and I could be more compassionate toward them. Our relationship then became much better. I had been expecting something of them that they did not understand, found frightening, and that they were incapable of doing. The gap between my mental parenting ideal and my actual parents had been eliminated.

In some cases of course, the behavior of the parents is so objectionable that the only satisfactory option is to leave the relationship entirely. But even in this case, suffering can be greatly reduced by dropping the mental story line that life should always be fair.

We often rail against something as uncontrollable as the weather and get upset because it is cloudy and cold for our July picnic. We do not easily see that our desire for the world to bend to our mental idea of what the weather *should be* is the real cause of our suffering, rather than the weather itself. We do essentially the same thing when we suffer horribly over all the injustice in the world. This does not mean that we should not do the things we can do to reduce injustice, but if we *expect* injustice not to ever happen, we will suffer as a result of this choice. And this additional unnecessary suffering on our part will not help one bit to correct a single injustice in the world.

Some of our unhappiness "gaps" are astounding: "I've done everything right to take care of my health and now I have cancer—this is totally unfair; I feel so angry and totally betrayed!" It's as though we believe we have entered into a *contract* with the universe and the universe is in breach of it. We seem to think we have agreed that "I will do such-and-such and the universe promises to do this-and-that in exchange." But being entitled to good health is something that exists only in the mind—and the "contract with the universe" is something that the universe never signed. Clearly, there is a huge mind-created gap between what I expect and what I actually have, and my suffering is greatly increased because of it. Having cancer is bad enough—why add the suffering of having been "betrayed" to it?

We also suffer due to our desire that things never change. One morning I came to work at the college where I teach and found a new computer on my desk; this seemed to happen every two or three years. I was happy with the old computer, and now I had to learn how to use the new one with its new software. I could either become upset and curse the college and suffer, or *turn my attention* inward and notice that my unhappiness gap is best addressed by seeing that I have an unwise desire that things should always stay the same. In this case, the external reality is that everything changes. The impermanence of all things was a central teaching of the Buddha.

Our difficulty with impermanence and change is widespread. We seem to unconsciously want jobs, friendships, a house, a favorite piece of land, or season of the year, to go on without change indefinitely. This simply results in our suffering more severely than necessary when things eventually and inevitably change or end. As the Buddha would point out, the central problem with most of the situations we have looked at here is that they involve *wanting* permanence in a world that is *in fact* impermanent. It is not the fact of impermanence that causes us to suffer, but rather our desire for permanence in an impermanent world. The Greek philosopher Epictetus grasped this idea very well.

> In everything which pleases the soul, or supplies
> a want, or is loved, remember to add this: What
> is its nature? If you love an earthen vessel, say
> it is an earthen vessel which you love; when it
> has been broken, you will not be [so]
> disturbed... take care of it [any blessing in your

77

life] as a thing which belongs to another, as travelers do with their inn... [or as you would do with a fine book on loan to you from the library]. (2)

Being Careful Not to Misunderstand

The idea of creating our own suffering is an alien and tricky one for many people. I have seen students in classes react to the idea that we create our own suffering by saying: "Life is even worse than I thought. Not only am I suffering but it's *all my fault*—I'm being *blamed* for my own misery. Now I'm *really* unhappy." But to react this way is to misunderstand the teaching. If suffering just dropped on us from the sky at random intervals, or if it were caused by external factors over which we have no control—now that really *would* be disheartening. But the real message here is that "Yes, I'm suffering but since I am the one creating it, I can do something about it—I can stop doing the things that are creating suffering for myself and others." This is hugely *empowering*, and truly good news for us.

I like to think of it this way. Suppose I am taking a long hike in the mountains and at some point I take my backpack off to find something to eat. While I am rummaging in the pack, I am stunned to find a ten pound rock: "How in the world did that get in there?" I toss the stone out, have something to eat, and resume hiking: "What a relief to have that rock off my back! This feels so much lighter and better!" Discovering the various ways in which we create suffering in our lives is very much like this. We become more mindful about what is going on in our lives and start really looking into what is present in the mind—our mental backpack, so to speak. We are often surprised at what we find: "No wonder life was so hard! I had no idea that there was such a huge boulder in my mental backpack. What a relief to discover it was there and get rid of it!" At some point, finding and removing these mental boulders becomes enormously exciting, and we get motivated to really spend some time using our newly found mindfulness to look for what else might be in there.

Happiness Is Bigger Than Pleasure

It is important to recognize that pain is not the same thing as suffering, and pleasure is not the same thing as happiness. We tend to think that happiness consists of banishing pain and difficulty and having one pleasurable experience after another: an enjoyable dinner accompanied by pleasant conversation, a great night's sleep followed by a wonderful run through the woods on a springy layer of decomposed bark, followed by... But life is not like that all the time, and might perhaps be boring if it were. Doing something very difficult, even painful, can be extremely meaningful and satisfying—for example, running five miles to get medical help for an injured hiker you came across on the trail. And endless rounds of entertainment and wonderful meals can, as the Buddha as a young man discovered, end up feeling hollow and unsatisfying. Happiness is bigger than both pleasure and pain. Jack Kornfield put it this way.

> Happiness is a profound sense of well-being, which includes both being connected with ourselves and the world. That's different from pleasure. Pleasure comes and goes. You can have a good meal and it's great—but then it's over. Pain and difficulties also will come and go. Happiness—true happiness—is a quality of well-being in the midst of pleasure and pain and gain and loss... Happiness is the capacity to open the heart and eyes and spirit and be where we are and find happiness in the midst of it. (3)

Another contemporary teacher, Lorne Ladner, has pointed out how trapped we often are in some rather narrow ideas regarding what makes for a good, happy, and meaningful life. As Westerners, we typically see happiness in one of three ways. Some see a happy and good life as being determined by external accomplishments such as business success, comfort, status, popularity, or lots of sensory pleasure. Others see a happy life as having deeply satisfying personal relationships. And still others believe that what is essential is making some significant contribution to make the world a better place. But Ladner points out that there is another way of seeing the question of what makes for a happy life.

> It's extremely rare for anyone...to answer this question *psychologically.* The Buddhist response to this question is deeply psychological: Buddhism asserts that a good, happy life is determined not by anything external but rather by the quality of our minds and hearts in each moment of life... Regardless of what we do or don't do externally. (4)

This is a radically different perspective from what we are used to. No matter what I might possess or might have done, *what does my life actually feel like* moment-to-moment? We are often so busy trying to obtain the things we have been taught will make us happy that we rarely ever take the time to actually get in touch with how this life we have actually *feels.* In this very moment, what is the state of my mind? Is my mind agitated and racing out of control? Is it full of thoughts of revenge, harsh criticism of self and others, or plans to get more for myself at the expense of others? On the other hand, perhaps my mind is focused and calm, with thoughts about helping a friend through a crisis or connecting with family later in the day, or thinking about how I can best honor my commitment to being there for my students.

And in this very moment, what kinds of *emotions* are in my *heart*? Am I angry, tense, anxious, or fearful? Perhaps I am full of guilt and shame, or maybe I am feeling conflicted and torn? No matter what successes I may have achieved in life, how can I be truly happy in such circumstances? Contrast this with the condition of another person's heart that is full of contentment, gratitude, love, and a feeling of joy because someone else is doing well in life. To have such a heart is essential to happiness, and it is possible to have it no matter what someone has or does not have in other areas of life.

What Comes Next?

Much of what robs our lives of happiness is the suffering created by our own minds. And typically, we have not yet realized that it is ourselves who are causing our suffering. Fortunately, with improved mindfulness we can get better and better at spotting, and interrupting, the multitude of ways the mind tricks us and causes suffering. In the chapters of *Part II: Nuts and Bolts*, we will examine a number of the major ways that the mind's response to what happens in life causes suffering and what can be done to change this. This suffering is created in many ways. It happens when we are swept away by strong emotions such as anger or fear, or anxiety. It also happens when we are in the grips of some false definition of self, or when we are overpowered by some very strong habit. We will examine how these causes of suffering, and many others, can be reduced or even eliminated. As we shall see, even the suffering caused by our discomfort with death can be transformed by seeing through the mind's delusions in regard to death. A fitting end for this chapter is a short Zen story from Pema Chodron.

> A big, burly samurai comes to a Zen Master and says, "Tell me the nature of heaven and hell." The Zen master looks him in the face and says, "Why should I tell a scruffy, disgusting, miserable slob like you? A worm like you, do you think I should tell you anything?"
>
> Consumed by rage, the samurai draws his sword and raises it to cut off the master's head. The Zen master says, "That's hell."
>
> Instantly, the samurai understands that he has just created his own hell—black and hot, filled with hatred, self-protection, anger, and resentment. He sees that he was so deep in

hell that he was ready to kill someone. Tears fill his eyes as he puts his palms together to bow in gratitude for this insight.

The Zen master says, "That's heaven." (5)

Notes for Chapter 5

1. Sahn, Seung, *Only Don't Know, The Teaching Letters of Zen Master Seung Sahn,* San Francisco: Four Seasons Foundation, 1982, p. 79.

2. Epictetus, *Enchiridion*, New York: Prometheus Books, 1991, translated by George Long, Sections 3 and 11.

3. Kornfield, Jack, "Finding My Religion," an interview with David Ian Miller, November 28, 2005, published at SFGate.com.

4. Ladner, Lorne, *The Lost Art of Compassion*, San Francisco: HarperSanFrancisco, 2004, page 8.)

5. Pema Chodron, Pema, *Comfortable With Uncertainty: 108 Teachings on Cultivating Fearlessness and Compassion,* Boston: Shambhala, 2003, pages 61-2.)

PART TWO

Nuts and Bolts

CHAPTER 6

Getting Off the Horse: Breaking the Grip of Habit Energy and Reactivity

There is a useful Zen story that Thich Nhat Hanh tells about a man on a horse.

> The horse is galloping quickly, and it appears that the man on the horse is going somewhere important. Another man, standing alongside the road, shouts, "Where are you going?" and the first man replies, "I don't know! Ask the horse!" This is also our story. We are riding a horse, we don't know where we are going, and we can't stop. The horse is our habit energy [our conditioning] pulling us along, and we are powerless. (1)

This indeed seems to be our story all too frequently. When something happens, our strong habit of reacting in a certain way simply takes over and causes us to act in the same unskillful way that we have done hundreds or thousands of times in the past. It often looks something like the following. You disagree with something I have said, I immediately feel attacked and become angry, and I then start verbally attacking you and defending some belief I have staked out as "mine." My intention is not to find the truth, but to "beat" you in an argument—some sort of personal contest—and emerge victorious. No one changes their mind or learns anything from the discussion, and there are hurt feelings and grudges created. There is also a *pattern* here that may well be familiar to me, and I know that acting this way has never worked well in the past. Despite that fact, I find that each time I am simply swept away yet again by my habit energy and act out the pattern for perhaps the ten thousandth time. How can I change this and get off the horse?

We need to, as Thich Nhat Hanh says, "...learn the art of stopping—stopping our thinking, our habit energies, our forgetfulness, the strong emotions that rule us." (2) And lest we misunderstand, we need to realize that this last part is not saying to stop *having* strong emotions, it is only saying that we need to stop allowing them to *rule* us —to *take us over*. There is nothing wrong with having strong emotions. But what we do need here are some specific practices to help us break the grip of our habits and reactivity so that we can actually *choose* wisely how to respond. We will look at, and build upon, four stopping practices suggested by Thich Nhah Hanh.

Four Practices for Stopping Habit Energy

The first suggestion is **Mindful Breathing**. The only difference between mindful breathing and regular breathing is that when we are breathing mindfully we are *aware* that we are breathing. We *are in touch with the sensations of* breathing in and breathing out. These sensations are always right here and right now. Consequently, when we shift our awareness to breathing it connects us to the present moment and takes us out of the habitual thought stream that is driving our harmful behavior pattern. It is a way of *stepping out of* the strong energy wave of our conditioned habits. Once that has happened, we can then reclaim our ability to *choose* how to respond.

This stopping practice can be done anywhere, even when in a stressful situation in front of a group of people. We just shift most of our awareness to the physical sensations of breathing right where we are. This can break the spell of habit. Shifting our awareness to the breath may also cause us to notice that our breathing is rapid and shallow. We can then consciously choose to breathe more deeply and slowly, while still being mindful, which will help to relax the body and the mind. Mindful breathing takes us out of our anxiety-causing thought stream and anchors us to something real in the present moment—the breath.

In my own practice I have found it useful to think of consciousness as being like a room in a house—it is basically an open space in which various objects of attention can arise. When we are upset by something, it is as though the upsetting event and accompanying thought stream and emotions expand to the point where they totally fill the entire room from wall to wall and floor to ceiling. My thoughts and feelings about whatever has happened have completely taken over the room, pushing absolutely everything else outside my awareness. My anger and agitation is all that exists for me in that moment. Stopping practices are essentially a device for making the room bigger. If I notice how upset I am and remember to place my awareness on the breath, it puts another object into the room. I then can begin to realize that life is much bigger than just my reaction to this one event. Many things besides the breath can serve this function: I can remember to look up at the sky and see the clouds or look out the window to see the trees. In that moment, my room becomes larger and I am not totally engulfed by my mental and emotional reaction to an event.

The behavior patterns that we have that are controlled by habit can be thought of as similar to gullies that have been cut into a hill by water erosion. The gullies start out very shallow, but each time water runs down a gully it cuts it a little deeper. The deeper the gully becomes, the easier it is for water to run down the same gully the next time it rains, and the harder it becomes for the water to take a different path down the hill. Our habits are a lot like those eroded gullies in the hill. The more we react in a specific way, the easier it is to simply flow down the same habit-response path the next time, and the harder it becomes to do something different. However, every time we successfully interrupt the energy of habit and do something different, we start to carve new "gullies" of response patterns and allow the old and dysfunctional channels to start to fill in. Over time, the old destructive habit gets weaker and weaker and the positive response pattern starts feeling natural and easy. This applies with equal relevance to all four of the stopping practices we will be considering here.

The second and third practices for stopping habit energy are **Mindful Walking** and **Mindful Smiling**. These work essentially the same way as mindful breathing. I am walking mindfully when I choose to become aware of my walking: the pressure of the ground under my feat, the feel of my clothing moving against my body, taking each step and placing my feet, and so on. I smile mindfully when I choose to be aware of smiling: my facial muscles, my feeling state, and all that is involved in the activity of smiling.

Mindful smiling may sound silly and foolish, or even impossible to do when extremely upset but: *try it out anyway*. It is amazing how this simple practice can shift emotional energy in the moment. A person's emotions and whole body can soften and their perspective on what is happening can shift dramatically. Just as with mindful breathing, mindful walking and smiling bring us out of reactivity and into the present moment.

The practices of mindful breathing, walking, and smiling can be *combined* with the fourth practice, **Acknowledging Habit Energy**. Acknowledging habit energy is one of the most powerful stopping practices. If we can begin to see our reactivity arising, we can simply acknowledge its presence in us. We can say silently "Hello, habit energy of anger, I know you are there," or "Hello guilt, I know you are there." We can simply smile to it and acknowledge its presence without judging it or ourselves for it being there. When we can remember to do this, our habit energy loses much of its control over us. If we know that anger, fear, defensiveness, or resentment is there, it can no longer "take us over" in quite the same way.

Acknowledging habit energy can be combined with mindful breathing and smiling by simply saying silently to myself: "Breathing in, I am aware of anger; breathing out, I smile to anger." As we continue to acknowledge habit energy and breathe, It can be shortened to "Anger... smiling" on each in-breath and out-breath. Shortening it also makes it easier to use repetitively for ten or twenty breath cycles when something longer is needed to "get off the horse." These are not *theories* about stopping habit energy, they are *practices*: things we can choose to actually *do* when difficulty arises. We can then *experience for ourselves* how they actually help us to shift our energy and engage life differently. The more we make use of these practices and see that we are benefitting from them, the more easily they will come to mind when we need them.

Our Difficulties Are Wonderful Teachers

Rather than view difficult times when we are seized by habit energy as failures or something to dread, we can recognize that they are ideal opportunities to transform our suffering into peace. Pema Chodron, who is from the Tibetan Buddhist tradition, puts it this way.

> [The teachings] ...show us how to transform difficult circumstances into the path of enlightenment; what we most dislike about our lives is the meat and potatoes of the mind training practices... What seem like the greatest obstacles—our anger, our resentment, our uptightness—we use as fuel to awaken... (3)

Often in life we find ourselves upset by something that has happened, and we start to react by doing something we have done thousands of times before, even though it has *never worked*, and we have always regretted our action later. Why do we continue to do this? In many cases, we do it because *we literally do not know what else to do*, and so we end up doing what we have always done. How can we finally *change* our behavior and stop making the same mistake? Pema Chodron describes a three step process based on a Tibetan Buddhist practice called "Train in the Three Difficulties."

The first step is to *notice* that we are agitated and upset, and catch ourselves in the early stages of some habitual piece of reactivity. We notice that we are all churned up and about to take the plunge into some habit-driven and harmful behavior. We may not know what to do about it, but we do know what is going on and that we are about to take the plunge. This awareness is a huge positive step, because without seeing clearly what is happening in us, the process of change cannot get started.

The second step is to do something *different*. Ideally, what we do differently is to turn our attention inward, drop the mental stories, and feel the emotion in the body. Ordinarily, our habit when we are upset is to send all of our attention out into the external triggering event: what someone did or said that upset us. Instead, we can turn our attention to our own inner response. First, we can notice a mental story running in the mind about the external triggering event: "Sam didn't show up to give me a ride like he said he would. He's so selfish and inconsiderate; he's always doing things like this." Once we notice this mental story, we can acknowledge that it is there and then put all our attention on the emotion present. Where do we actually feel the emotion in the body? What does it actually feel like? What are the actual *body sensations* that are present? We can *get curious about it*. Taking our attention to the body in this way grounds us in something real in the present moment and takes us out of reactivity.

However, many of us will not be able to turn our attention inward, drop the mental stories, and simply feel the emotion in the body. This is especially true in the beginning when our mindfulness is not very well developed. But the good news is that we do not have to turn our attention inward in this way in order to do something *different*.

Instead, we can simply do *anything* that is different from what our habit energy is pushing us to do. *Anything we do that is different will break the grip of habit*: we can take a walk, recite a poem or sing a song (either silently or out loud), or do a little dance. When we do this it will divert the flow of habit energy from going down that same old "mind gully" that is so deep and wide. This has the effect of *weakening* the old channel and simultaneously *strengthening* our ability to send our behavior where *we choose for it to go*. This is very freeing. In a stressful situation, I don't have to think up some wise or clever response, I only need to do something simple and *different*. Just do anything that is different that does not make the situation worse.

The third step is to commit ourselves to *keep doing the practice*. We recognize that we will need to continue to respond with the three-step process each time this particular habit energy comes up again. Doing it once is a start, but we need to do this practice repeatedly to eventually establish a new way of responding. Pema Chodron states our situation very concisely.

> Ordinarily, we are swept away by habitual momentum and do not interrupt our patterns even slightly. When we feel betrayed or disappointed, does it occur to us to practice? Usually not. But right there in the midst of our confusion, is where [our practice can produce the most benefit. We can make it a habit] ...to ask, "How can I practice right now, right on this painful spot, and transform this into the path of awakening? (4)

It's Never Too Late

The key to success with all of the above practices is catching ourselves about to go down the path of harmful habit energy again. I like the mental image of a toboggan perched at the top of a very steep, snowy hill. The toboggan is balanced very precariously, requiring only a slight breeze or a little nudge from its occupant to slide very quickly down the steep hill and crash hard into the tree at the bottom of the slope. That's me in the sled, and the force of gravity is my habit energy. Once the toboggan slips and it starts to move, it is very hard to stop it. And then there is cleaning up the mess and bandaging the wounds afterward.

Even those times when we are unable to successfully use any of the stopping practices and take the toboggan ride and crash again, there is still one more powerful tool we can make use of to weaken our harmful habit energy. We often mistakenly think that we only get one chance to deal with a particular situation that has arisen, and that if we haven't practiced well we have lost our opportunity. We may be left feeling remorseful. But that remorse can be used as a message that we are still in a position to reduce the power of our habit energy. No matter how unskillfully we may have reacted to some event, it is almost always possible to return to what has happened and do it over. No, we cannot turn back the clock, but we can revisit the situation now and respond in a different way.

Let's see how this works. Jane says something to me about our work loads, and I become extremely agitated and completely taken over by habit energy. As a result, I accuse Jane of lying and trying to push her work off onto me. My accusation is extremely unskillful and creates suffering. Sometime later I see this very clearly. At this point I can go back to Jane for a "do over." I can then say to her what I really feel in this moment when I am free of habit energy: "The last time I saw you I was really upset and I said something accusatory about workloads. I'm very sorry that I said that. Now that I am calmer, I know that what I really want to say to you is 'We have different recollections about what we actually agreed to as far as workloads. Let's see if we can reach a new agreement that works for both of us so that we can move ahead together on this project.'"

91

Doing this not only helps to weaken the old habit of blaming, it helps to establish or strengthen a new habit through practicing a new behavior pattern. It also helps to heal my relationship with Jane. It's great if I can do this only fifteen minutes or an hour later, but even if unable to do it for a day or two (or longer) it still has great power to change a habit and heal a relationship. Isn't it a nice surprise to discover that it really is possible to get a second chance in life? With continued practice, the time interval between acting on a harmful habit and recognizing the need for a "do over" typically gets shorter and shorter. Eventually, it becomes possible to see the unskillful habit response as soon as it occurs. Then, a "do over" can come almost immediately.

Notes for Chapter 6

1. Nhat Hanh, Thich, *The Heart of the Buddha's Teaching*, New York: Broadway Books, 1999, p.24.

2. Nhat Hanh, Thich, *The Heart of the Buddha Teaching*, p.24.

3. Chodron, Pema, *The Places that Scare You: A Guide to Fearlessness In Difficult Times*, Boston: Shambhala, 2002, p. 31.

4. Chodron, Pema, *The Places that Scare You: A Guide to Fearlessness In Difficult Times*, pp. 32-33.

CHAPTER 7

When Strong Emotions Arise

Many people have an uncomfortable relationship with their emotions, particularly strong or difficult emotions such as anger, fear, hatred, grief, and sadness. Over the years, I have heard many comments from students expressing a troubled relationship with their emotions. Here is a small but representative sample.

- "I just do such crazy things when I get all emotional and upset. It's like all my good sense just goes right out the window."

- "Strong emotions can be very inconvenient and always seem to happen when I would rather they weren't there."

- "Powerful negative emotions like anger and fear seem overwhelming and there is nothing you can do about them except shove them down or else just give in to them and act out."

- "I'm afraid to know what I'm really feeling because if I ever did get in touch with my emotions I'd find out how messed up I am."

- "Even good feelings like excitement or being in love overwhelm me and I end up doing something foolish."

How We Usually Relate to Our Emotions

Often, our emotions are a mystery to us and we are not very good at talking with ourselves or anyone else about them. In addition, our emotional vocabulary is often quite limited. We can say we feel great, good, pretty good, ok, so-so, pretty bad, and horrible. However, if we look closely, we will notice that these descriptions are not emotions at all, they are *evaluations* of what we are feeling. "Horrible," for example, is not an emotion. It is only a *judgment* that someone has passed on what they are feeling. The actual "horrible" emotion could be hurt, rage, anxiety, fear, sadness, grief, guilt, or a whole host of other emotions that someone would prefer not to be feeling.

Typically, our discomfort with emotions stems from two things: fear of strong emotions, and an unrealistic set of assumptions about how life ought to be going. Let's look at each of these in turn.

First, why do we tend to be afraid of our own emotions? This fear can have many causes. Sometimes there is the perception that if we actually allow ourselves to feel what we are feeling, we will feel worse. Our unpleasant feelings will just get stronger and last longer. Sometimes we are afraid of being overwhelmed if we open to our feelings and that we will lose control and never be able to regain it. Other times we are afraid that we will wallow in emotion and never be able to drag ourselves out. Worse yet, we may fear that our emotions will explode out of us and we will lash out and hurt others and create havoc in our lives. There is also the fear that if we get to know our emotions we will find out that we are "bad and worthless" or that there is something horribly wrong with us. This last one is similar to the person who is afraid of getting checked out by a doctor because they might find out that they have cancer. Surprisingly, we can even fear "good" or "happy" emotions like being in love because we believe they can sweep us away, cause us to make foolish decisions, and we will end up being badly hurt.

Whatever, the cause of being afraid of our feelings, it creates much unnecessary anxiety and suffering. Because we are often afraid of strong emotions, we tend to repress or "stuff" them in a variety of ways. This, as we shall soon see, also causes suffering. When we are afraid of our emotions and repress them, we stay stuck in a dysfunctional relationship with our feelings because we never learn how they actually operate. This is compounded by a second factor.

The second cause of discomfort with emotions is several, often unconscious, assumptions regarding our emotions. The primary culprit here is our belief that there are "bad" emotions and "good" emotions. Furthermore, we also seem to think that the ideal to shoot for is to successfully banish all "bad" or unpleasant feelings, and to try to feel "good" all of the time. We see any deviation from this ideal as being not ok. We see having certain emotions, the "difficult" ones, as a "problem," an abnormality that is not supposed to be happening and that needs to be gotten rid of as quickly as possible.

We try to make emotions go away by "stuffing" the emotions down, repressing, or ignoring them. It may come as a surprise, but acting out, the opposite of repression, is also a means of not feeling our unpleasant emotions. Our acting out, yelling and attacking other people for example, provides a *distraction* from actually *feeling* the emotion that is there. If we stay narrowly focused on "getting even with the person who hurt us," our plotting and actions distract us from the pain and sadness we are feeling.

We may also distract ourselves from what we are feeling by throwing ourselves into nonstop activities—continually finding ways to "stay busy" with work, social activities, recreational shopping, video games, and so on. The list of possible distractions is a very long one! People often distract themselves with food or various drugs, and even meditation can be misused as a means of avoiding difficult emotions.

However we may try to get rid of inconvenient emotions, the *results* are always the same—our being out of touch with our feelings always *comes at a very high cost*. For starters, being out of touch deprives us of important information about how our lives are unfolding. If we repress that feeling of anxiety and dread we feel every morning as we arrive at our job, we may keep working for years at a job that is literally killing us. *Numbing* ourselves in one or a few areas of life can become a pervasive habit that spills over into *all of our life*, robbing us of the joy and richness of living. Equally harmful, being out of touch with our feelings prevents us from really *connecting* with other people and sharing ourselves with others on a deep level. And, as most of us have experienced, when we are out of touch with our emotions they can blindside us and quickly "take us over" so that we act very unwisely before we even know what is happening.

Nearly everyone has tried arranging their lives such that they never experience heartbreak, fear, anger, or grief. But do we know of even a single person who has *ever succeeded* with this project? As hard as we may try, things change, sickness happens, jobs are lost, loved ones die or move away, and injustice occurs. Wisdom would indicate that since difficult emotions *will* come up with regularity, our best option is to learn how to be at peace with them when they do. Buddhist teachings on mindfulnesss offer us a radically different way of experiencing our emotional life.

Mindfulness and Emotions: A Radically Different Approach

All too often, we only see two ways of dealing with difficult emotions: we can either repress the emotion in some way and try not to feel it, or we can be overwhelmed by it and lose our ability to choose how to respond to events. Buddhist teachings attempt to provide a third and radically different alternative: we can learn to *feel all our emotions fully* without our emotions becoming some sort of *problem*. We can learn how to allow the emotion to *simply be there* and not be swept away by it, all the while keeping our ability to choose wisely how to act.

We may even find that the so-called difficult emotions can be savored as part of the richness of life and that they will naturally and easily wash through us if only we learn to stop doing the things that prevent them from doing so.

From a Buddhist perspective, there is nothing wrong with having strong emotions. We don't need to get rid of them, we just need to have a different kind of *relationship* with them. In this country many people suffer from coronary disease, diabetes, and cancer caused, at least in part, by their food choices. However, this certainly does not mean that food is the problem and that we should get rid of it. It only means that we need to have a healthier *relationship* with food. That same is true of our emotions.

We can learn that strong emotions cannot harm us if we come to know them for what they really are. We start simply by laying a foundation of learning how to experience some of the less powerful emotions—boredom, restlessness, annoyance—in a completely safe meditation environment. But the process we are about to learn is the same one we can use when really intense emotions come up when we are "off the meditation cushion." As we shall see, our thoughts and perceptions fuel our emotions, so we will also need to spend some time understanding how this works and how to have a different relationship with thoughts.

The RAIN Method

The Buddha taught a form of mindfulness meditation practice for working with emotions. Many contemporary Buddhist teachers have presented these teachings as a practice involving four elements: Recognition, Acceptance, Investigation, and Nonidentification.   This process has come to be known by the acronym RAIN. The RAIN format for presenting Buddhist teachings on working with emotions was first formulated by Michele McDonald, a teacher with the Insight Meditation Society. Let's look at how it works.

The RAIN practice is aimed at teaching us a new way of being with our emotions. It is very useful as a ten to twenty minute sitting practice, and it can also be done as a short "micro meditation" during the activities of a normal day.

As a sitting practice, we begin the same way we would begin the Basic Breathing Meditation from Chapter 4. We sit comfortably, upright but relaxed, and take three or four deep and mindful breaths. We then let our breathing become natural, and maintain our awareness on the physical sensations of the breath for several minutes. We can then notice if there is some emotion present. The emotion might be a strong feeling of anxiety or a slight feeling of boredom. Whatever it is, it becomes the primary focus (primary object of attention) for the meditation.

Recognition of what we are feeling is the first element of the practice and it is crucial. It is not possible to deal with an emotion effectively if we are not consciously aware that it exists. We begin by asking "What am I feeling right now?" Perhaps we notice that there is a good deal of resentment and also some anger present. It can be a good idea to acknowledge this silently in words: "I'm feeling some anger and resentment." Just a simple acknowledgement is all that is needed. There is no need to justify or explain the emotion that is present: "I'm angry *because* so-and-so did such-and-such." It doesn't matter. What does matter is that *the emotion exists in this moment and that I know it exists*.

It can be a good practice to get in the habit of checking in with ourselves periodically throughout the day: "What am I feeling in this moment? What emotions are present?" We often get out of touch with what we are feeling and may be surprised at what we discover—fear, for example. If there is judgment—"I shouldn't be feeling this" or "I'm wrong to be feeling this"—just notice the judgment and silently note what you are feeling with the word "fear."

Recognizing what we are feeling is a way of getting ourselves out of denial. As Thich Nhat Hanh explains, being in touch with our emotions is the first step in freeing ourselves from their domination and the suffering it causes.

[Every time an emotion arises] "...we can practice... recognition. When we are agitated, we just say, "I am agitated," and mindfulness is already there. Until we recognize agitation as agitation, it will push us around and we will not know what is going on or why. To practice mindfulness... does not mean [we never become] ... agitated. It means that when we are agitated, we know that we are agitated. Our agitation has a good friend in us, and that is mindfulness." (1)

Once we recognize that a strong emotion is there, its grip on us is loosened. The emotion is still there, but my relationship with it has shifted. This is true of other feeling states such as fear, anger, hatred, envy. Like it or not, whether I *should* be feeling it or not, whether I deserve it or not, the *fact* is that the emotion is present in me now. It is a fact. I know that it is there. I am not in denial. I am not oblivious to the emotion. I am not numbed out.

Acceptance, the second step, becomes possible once an emotion is recognized. To accept an emotion is to drop our mental resistance to it being there. Mental resistance is an attitude of "No; this shouldn't be here now, I don't want or deserve this." Saying "I accept it, but I *hate* it," is *not* accepting it. This is a form of mentally pushing away and rejecting the reality of its presence. Mental resistance is saying "No" to the *reality* of the present moment.

When we accept an emotion, or anything else, we say "Yes" to it, and we become willing to *open* to it and fully *experience* whatever it might be. A very simple but useful practice is silently saying "Yes" to whatever is real in this moment: "I say yes to the reality of anger in this moment." Try it, and see what happens. Acceptance means *relating to an emotion as if we had chosen it*. When I drop the mental resistance —"I don't want this, this shouldn't be happening now, I don't deserve this"—then there can be a sense of relaxation arising. "Ok, anger is here now. This is anger." We are no longer at war with the reality of the present moment.

Let there be no misunderstanding here. Accepting what is real in this moment does not mean we are saying it is *good*, nor does it mean that we are saying it is *bad*. It just *is*. And acceptance of what is real in this moment does *not* mean that we cannot take steps to *change* it.

Investigation comes third, and it is the part of the process that really allows us to make peace with an emotion. This is *not an intellectual investigation*—it is not trying to figure out why I am experiencing these feelings, looking at my childhood or earlier relationships, or painful events in my life in order to find a *cause* for them. This is an *experiential* investigation. What is the actual *experience* of grief? What does it actually *feel* like? This is like investigating the flavor of a new herbal tea. We are not trying to figure out anything about the tea: how was it grown and processed, what are the ingredients, is it grown in the United States? We just want to taste the tea and experience what drinking it *feels* like.

Frequently, we have a tendency of *pulling back* from difficult emotions or distracting ourselves from them. When we investigate an emotion we "lean into it," move closer, and really observe what it is. We get *interested* in it. We become *genuinely curious* about it. Our intention here is simply to *observe* the emotion as it presently exists in us.

In order to help us open ourselves and experience the emotion fully, we can ask ourselves some very simple but powerful questions. First, how do I even know I am angry? I know it because I notice that something is going on inside me. I can ask myself "Where do I actually feel the emotion *in the body*?" Perhaps what I call "anger" consists of heat in my face, a sensation of pounding in my heart and ribcage, some tight muscles across my back, and some very shallow breathing. How do these sensations shift and change as I observe them? These questions take us out of the thought stream and into the actual feeling of anger. Altogether, there are at least *four useful questions* we can keep in the back of our minds: 1) Where do I feel the emotion in the body? 2) What does it actually *feel* like? 3) What accompanying thoughts do I observe in the mind? 4) What other feelings are there besides the primary one? These questions are used from time to time during the practice of RAIN to continually bring the focus back to the feeling of the emotion itself.

Getting in touch with emotions in this way is the *core of the practice* to move us toward a different and healthier way of engaging our emotions.

Our usual response when we are upset is to focus our attention on what *triggered* the emotion: "I can't believe so-and-so did that, he's such a jerk, I'm going to get back at him every way I can." We are like a District Attorney, building our case to convict the person whose behavior triggered us. Instead of this, we can cultivate the habit of *looking inward at the emotion itself* as it exists inside of us.

A key point here is that when loud and unpleasant emotions show up at our front door, our usual response is to not let them in. The practice of mindfulness says to invite them in and *get to know them*. We can also recognize that these feelings are *just visitors*—they don't live in us as permanent residents.

Nonidentification is the final component in this form of practicing mindfulness with emotions. Identification with a feeling occurs when I see that feeling as part of who I am, part of my personal identity, something that *defines me as a person*. I see the emotion as a "me," rather than as a visiting condition. When we really begin to pay attention, we notice that emotions—and thoughts—are constantly arising and then passing away. I may think that I am an "angry *person*" but on closer examination I will notice that there are many stretches of time—some short, some long—when anger is not there. I can remember times when I was very sad, but in the middle of it, something funny came up and I laughed and felt happy and relaxed for a while. There is no single emotional state, or combination of states, that is an accurate description of who I am. It all comes and goes.

Emotions are a *temporary state or vibration in the body accompanied by thoughts*. Suppose you had a very physically demanding day working outside. Later that evening you are sitting in your favorite chair reading and you notice a muscle twitch in your calf that comes and goes every few seconds. Would you say that muscle twitch was who you are as a person? Is it somehow a definition of self: "I *am* that muscle twitch." When we really look at it, we recognize that it is simply a *passing condition* in the body. It is a *temporary visitor*. Emotions—always coming and going—are essentially no different.

The language that we use can be important here. We can begin to alter our habit of making emotions (or thoughts) into a personal identity by changing how we talk about feelings. Instead of saying "I am angry" or worse "I am an angry person" (both of which makes anger into a "me"), we can say "Anger is present now" or "I'm feeling some anger now." This applies to everything we do, not just emotions. When we trip over something we may say "I'm really a clumsy person," which creates a rigid definition of self. Instead, we can say "I had a clumsy moment there," which is accurate and does not create a personal identity. "I'm so stupid" creates an identity; "That was really a stupid choice" does not. Instead of saying "I'm a bad parent," we can say "I made some mistakes as a parent." This may seem trivial, but it is not. We are talking about *a fundamental shift* in how we see things.

Working With the Thought Stream

It is very useful to observe any thought stream that might be present along with the emotion itself. Frequently there is sadness, and then there is the *mental story of sadness*: "I'm always going to be sad. Nobody will ever care for a sad person like me. I'll probably die sad and very alone." Noticing the mental story as a separate event from the emotion is useful for several reasons. We can notice that it is the thought stream that energizes the emotion and keeps it going. We can also notice that the mental story is typically a work of fiction—the sadness is a *fact*, the story of sadness is not. When the story of sadness says "I'll probably die sad and alone," it is saying something about a *future* of which we really *have no knowledge*. When we pay close attention, we will also frequently notice that the *real suffering* we are experiencing is coming more from the mental story about sadness rather than the sadness itself. Once I become more skilled at opening and relaxing into emotions I learn that sadness is not really a problem—it's just sadness and it's what I'm feeling now and it's ok for it to be there.

As we get more skillful at working with the thought stream, we can notice that there is a certain impersonal aspect to it—thoughts just arise on their own without our *asking* for any of them. They seem to bubble up almost randomly and have a life of their own. We can learn to simply *observe thoughts arising* without getting caught up in them. When we do this, we can realize that there is no need to do anything about these thoughts—no need to chase after them or try to make them stay, and no need to try to push them away. Since we didn't choose them, there is no need to judge ourselves for having them. We can also practice nonidentification with thoughts, just like we learned to do with emotions. A thought is simply a temporary mental event, essentially no different than that muscle twitch that arises in the body under certain conditions. Neither the twitch nor the thought needs to be made into a definition of self. When thought is seen in this way, our relationship with it can be much freer and easier.

Lastly, there is no need to *believe* a thought just because it has arisen. It's just a thought—who knows where it came from? I find it useful to view thoughts as being like billboards along the highway. I am driving along and some billboard comes into view and it says "Visit Magic Mountain theme park and you'll have the time of your life." There is no need for me to believe this or not believe it—it's just a bunch of words that have somehow popped up on a billboard. Likewise, if a "mental billboard" pops up in my mind that says "Dale, you're a jerk and a loser and will never amount to anything," there is absolutely no need to attach any special significance to it or believe it. It's *just a thought*. The RAIN teachings on nonidentification can just as easily be applied to thought as they can to emotion, and doing so produces the same result of freeing us from a great deal of unnecessary suffering.

The Practice of Meditation on Emotions

Our usual response when we are upset is to focus our attention on the external event that *triggered* the emotion—an event that happened, or something that someone did or said. Instead of doing this, the practice of meditation on emotions trains us to *look inward at the emotion itself*.

Meditation on emotions can be used as a formal ten to twenty minute sitting practice, or as a practice we enter into spontaneously during the day when some strong emotion comes up. As a spontaneous practice, it could be as short as a few seconds, a minute, five minutes or longer—depending on circumstances. Since we are training ourselves in a new skill, it will usually work best to start with a formal sitting practice. The idea of "baby steps" is useful here—we start in a quiet and safe environment where we can focus on learning the skill without having to deal with other people or events. The concluding sections of this chapter provide step-by-step directions for both kinds of meditation on emotion.

As a **formal sitting practice**, Meditation on Emotions starts by sitting and focusing on the sensation of the breath for a few minutes. When an emotion arises, we then shift our attention to the emotion that is present—the emotion then becomes the primary object of attention for the meditation. Each time we are distracted from the emotion we simply bring the attention back to feeling the emotion in the body. If there is no emotion present, we bring the attention back to the breath and keep it there until another emotion arises. When that happens, once again, the emotion that is present becomes the primary object of attention.

In doing this meditation, when an emotion arises, we silently and gently note it as "anger" or "sadness" or "love" or "boredom" or "restlessness" or whatever it happens to be. If it's not clear what to call it, that's fine. There is no need to search for just the right word.

Next, see if it is possible to locate the emotion in the body. Where are the actual physical sensations of the emotion being felt in the body? What do these sensations feel like? Is there a nervous feeling in the stomach or a racing heartbeat? Are the eyelids heavy, or the shoulders drawn up? Notice how these sensations change as they are being observed. Are there times when they get weaker or are even absent? If no emotions come up that are strong enough to distract us from the breath, we just stay with the breath.

There is nothing that needs to be done about any of these emotions. Just be there with the emotions as an observer.

There may be a mental story-line that is going along with the emotion: "I'm always going to feel this way... I hate so-and-so for making me feel this way because they did such-and-such." Just notice the existence of the story-line and that it is a *totally separate thing* from the emotion itself. Keep bringing the attention back to the feeling of the emotion in the body. Simply observe the feeling without struggling against it in any way.

If observing an emotion starts to feel overwhelming, return the attention to the breath as a safe and comfortable home base. This provides a rest and also a *reminder* of what it feels like to just be with and observe something easy to be with—the breath. Then bring that same quality of awareness back to the emotion that is present.

If there is self judgment in connection with a feeling, just *notice* the judgment, and then remember that whatever you are feeling is just a feeling and that it is ok for it to be there.   Always come back to the direct experience of the moment: What am I feeling right now?

A good time length for this type of meditation is about ten minutes when first attempting it. After getting more used to it, the meditation can be expanded to fifteen or twenty minutes. Remember to determine the length of the sitting ahead of time and use a timer. This will help lessen the temptation to quit if things become difficult.

There is a **second type of formal sitting practice for emotions** that we could call Meditation on Difficult Emotions. In this case, rather than waiting for an emotion to arise on its own, we deliberately summon up the emotion by recalling a past event which was heavily charged with difficult emotion. As a formal sitting practice, we again begin by centering the attention on the feeling of the breath for a minute or two.

Next, we consciously bring to mind a difficult or troubling feeling or situation from the recent or distant past, some event or time when there was a lot of intense emotion—sadness, fear, hurt, pain, or anger. Take a moment to fully remember the situation. Doing this may not feel comfortable, but try to stay with it. If needed, we can always return our attention to the breath as a safe resting place. Returning to the breath can be a good way of getting reacquainted with how it feels to just be with something and observe it. With practice, that same "just-being-with-it" kind of awareness can then be transferred to the strong emotion arising.

Keep returning the focus to the sensations in the body that makeup the emotion that this particular memory has brought up. Where in the body are these emotions felt? Perhaps the mouth is dry. Is there shallow breathing, clenching of teeth, or a lump in the throat? Whatever is happening in the body, just notice it. There is no need to provide a verbal description of any kind.

Next, try bringing the focus to that part of the body where the sensations are the strongest. Remember that there is no need to do anything about these sensations except to be aware of them. It may be very helpful to say silently: *"It's ok, whatever it is, it's ok. I can feel this without pushing it away or getting caught up in it."* Just stay with the awareness in the body, accept what is there, and gently be there with the sensations. There is nothing wrong with whatever emotion that is present, no matter what it might be. We are in a safe place, learning how to be with our feelings in a different and wiser way. If at any time it seems too intense, simply let the attention rest comfortably on the breath again.

If there is an attempt to make an identity out of what is being felt—"I'm just a sad person"—simply notice the thought and let it go. Whatever emotion is arising is only a temporary visitor, not who you are.

It's good to always keep in mind that the intention here is *not to get rid of* the emotions being felt, but to have a *different and healthier relationship with whatever emotions might arise in life*.

Continue with the practice for ten to twenty minutes, remembering to determine the length ahead of time, and to use a timer so there is less temptation to quit when some difficulty arises.

Working With Our Emotions Can Bring Up Resistance

Once, after explaining the Meditation on Difficult Emotions, a student asked me: "Why would we *want* to deliberately bring up and then experience emotions that are unpleasant and 'yucky'?" This is a natural enough question. The answer is that it is a form of training. We begin to learn a different way of experiencing strong emotions by practicing in the safe environment of a meditation session. Later, we can learn to transfer that skill to our everyday life and become less likely to repress or be swept away when a strong emotional reaction pops up. After enough practice, we will find that we are much more likely to respond wisely even when we are feeling something very intense.

A personal story is useful here. When I was about seven years old, I had a small pimple or blocked pore on the back of my neck. It got infected and swelled into a good sized lump about the size of large grape. It became what is called a boil. There was a lot of pressure in it and it was very painful. My parents took me to the doctor and the doctor "lanced" it, which is a fancy way of saying that he stabbed it with a very sharp surgical instrument. When he did, the boil exploded and shot a mixture of blood and pus about three feet into the air—very "yucky" stuff! But, getting that yucky stuff out of the place where it was stuck was absolutely essential for healing to take place. Working with unpleasant emotions in meditation can help to heal us psychologically in much the same way.

In this connection, I am also reminded of a story I once heard about a boy who was terrorized by a very large and snarling bull dog. The dog chased him every day for weeks on his way home from school. One day, in desperation, the boy turned and faced the dog. When he actually looked at the dog carefully and up close, he saw that it was a very old dog and that it had no teeth! That dog is like our emotions— before we *look at them very carefully*, we think our emotions can harm us and we fear them. It is very freeing to find out that they cannot.

In working with our inner world of emotion and thought, we often like to proceed in a protected mode and only work with thoughts and feelings that are comfortable and not too distressing. As soon as we get into stuff that is messy, unpleasant, or scary, we back off and become unwilling to experience and investigate what is actually there. The problem with doing this is that the places where we are comfortable are *not* the places where our personal issues lie. They are *not* the places that we are "stuck" in our lives. Each time uncomfortable feelings arise, we can view them as a message from the deepest part of our being saying "You are approaching something very important—this is an area where you need to work in order to really change yourself at the most fundamental level." Each of us can learn to do this. "*Work at the level of your obstruction*" can be our guiding principle here.

It is important to remember that emotions are visitors. *They don't live here.* When they come knocking at our door, rather than barricade the door against them, we can invite them in and get to know them. We can make friends with them. We can also learn to allow them to leave rather than unknowingly continuing to do the things that encourage them to stay longer than they otherwise would. The RAIN approach is a very powerful practice for accomplishing this.

Micro Meditations on Emotions "Off the Cushion"

In addition to the formal sitting practices for emotions that we learned about, it can also be very useful to spontaneously do a shorter version of the practice when strong emotions arise during the course of our day. Simply remember the four step RAIN process. *Recognize* the feeling that is present as anger or fear or whatever it is, and then *Accept* it by saying "Yes" to the reality of its existence in this moment. At that point, *Investigation* can take place by turning the attention strongly inward to experience the feeling of the emotion as it exists in the body. There probably is a thought stream driving the emotion which can be noticed and then de-energized by maintaining focus on the emotion in the body. Lastly, check to see if the mind is making the emotion into a definition of self or personal identity, and practice *Nonidentification*. This whole process can often take place in as little as a half minute. Other times it may be necessary to take five or ten minutes with it.

Notes for Chapter 7

1. Nhat Hanh, Thich, *The Heart of the Buddha's Teaching*, New York: Broadway Books, 1999, p.74.

CHAPTER 8

Working with Harmful Desires

At its fundamental core, what the Buddha taught was a program for *changing* ourselves. Toward this end, he wanted to understand deeply the things that facilitate personal change and the things that block it. One of the major obstacles to changing ourselves is the fact that desires often arise that conflict with the changes we know we need to make in ourselves. Here's a simple example of how this often goes.

Suppose I say to myself, "I *know* I should eat healthy food," and I really believe this is true. But at the same time it is also true that I *want* a donut from that plate on the table. This situation creates an inner struggle between "I should" and "I want." My strong desire for the donut is pulling me away from what I know is in my best interest. When this sort of thing happens we typically try to deal with the conflict by *controlling* our wants. We believe we need something called "will power" in order to succeed in changing to healthier eating habits. If we just had enough will power we could resist eating that donut. During the times that our will power is strong, we eat the way we should and don't eat the donut. At other times, our will power is weak, and "I want" wins out over "I know," and we cave in and eat the donut.

This is a difficult way to live. Whether my will power is strong and I resist the donut or not, I am in a constant state of conflict, inner struggle, and turmoil. This uses a tremendous amount of energy and causes very real suffering. And in the end, there is typically no success in producing deep and lasting personal change. We succeed for a little while, and then there is backsliding and perhaps feeling defeated, demoralized, or guilty. This approach always involves *forcing*—we are trying to force an "I should" over the top of an "I want." This is actually a form of violence directed towards ourselves.

A Deeper Approach to Change: Making Peace with Desire

The Buddha taught a deeper approach that is based on mindful awareness. I can ask: "What if I *changed what I want*?" If I know I should eat healthy food and I also *want* to eat healthy food, all of a sudden life becomes very easy and simple. There is no more inner conflict or struggle because what I know to be right and what I want are exactly the same thing. I may say to myself "This is great! Why didn't I think of this before?" And it is great, but it also raises a very large question: *"How do I actually change what I want?"* I can't simply decide that, as of right now, I will only want healthy food. I want what I want, and *I want a donut!* Desires simply arise, and sometimes there is a very strong desire for a donut. What can I do?

There is no need to get rid of desires. We need desires—the desire to understand what is going on in our lives, for example, is necessary and useful. Furthermore, desires will always arise—even the Buddha had desires. So there is not a realistic hope of getting rid of unwanted desires. What we need is a different kind of *relationship* with desire. The Buddha taught that if we truly *understand* something, then we free ourselves from its domination.

The way that we change our wants is by really understanding our wanting, why we want something, and the consequences of wanting it. Let's see how this works in our example of no longer wanting to eat junk food.

First, I can investigate the actual *experience* of wanting. As was learned previously, this is not an intellectual investigation into the possible *reasons* for my having this desire. It is rather, an investigation of the actual *experience* of desiring. I can just sit with a desire that has risen, making it my primary object of attention. Where do I actually feel this particular desire *in the body*? What does it *feel like*? What is the thought stream that accompanies the desire? It may be helpful to silently note the desire while it is there as "wanting...wanting...wanting." This is essentially part of the practice of RAIN, used either as formal sitting practice or as the short spontaneous version. In this case, it is brought to bear on a desire that has arisen.

When we do this, we will notice several things. First, perhaps we will notice that very often *desire is actually a form of suffering*. It creates tension, agitation, and a general lack of ease in the body and mind. Second, it is possible to notice that desire is just a collection of sensations in the body and thoughts in the mind. We can notice that it is not really any sort of a *problem* for the desire to simply be there and for us to be there comfortably with it. The third thing that we are likely to notice is that *all desires eventually go away*, and they do it without any help from us. They may not go away on our timetable, but they do go away. They may come back at some point but, if we pay attention, we notice that they go away again. We can easily try this out for ourselves and discover first hand that it is true.

These three observations are total game changers in our relationship with desire. Our typical conditioning tells us that if a desire persists, we have to *do something about it*—we have to either act to fulfill the desire, or else try to get rid of it. But the lesson we can learn here is that there is *absolutely no need to do anything about a desire simply because it is there*. This is empowering! Desires can simply arise, we can feel them and know that they are there, but we also know how to peacefully co-exist with them. We now have the ability to *choose* whether to *act* on them or not. So even if unwholesome desires arise, they no longer have the same grip on us. This is a huge step forward. Even if we have a desire arise that conflicts with what we know is best for us, the sense of inner struggle is now gone. We know we can still act the way we know we should. Just as we learned with emotions, watching desire operate in this way is very much like watching billboards arise and then fall away as we travel down the highway.

Each time that we choose not to act on a desire, the desire becomes weaker. Additionally, each time we choose not to act on a desire, it strengthens our ability to simply say no to desires that arise that we know are not good for us. Over time, our unhealthy desires lose their strength and come up less frequently. They may even cease to come up at all. At this point, life becomes much freer, easier, and happier. All of this is good news, and there is more still to come.

A Deeper Approach to Change: Changing Our Desires

Here is how the process of changing desires begins. After getting in touch with the experience of desire and learning to make peace with it, I can then learn to ask, "What is *underneath* the desire for the donut?" Perhaps I want a distraction: but distraction *from what? Am I trying to fill a nonmaterial hole with a material thing?* How well does this really work? If I have a very real nonmaterial need, such as for deep personal connection with other people, no amount of donut eating is going to fill that hole. Really seeing this clearly erodes the donut desire's power over me.

Or perhaps I'm reaching for a donut because I am bored. Perhaps my present job is tedious, meaningless, and harms other people and the Earth. My nonmaterial need for meaningful work is quite real. The fact that this need is not being met is causing me distress, and so I reach for a new wardrobe, a cigarette, or a donut. Mindfulness allows me to experience the whole process. When I become a careful observer of my experience I *notice:* 1) feeling distressed about my job, 2) a desire to relieve the stress by "medicating" the anxiety with a donut, 3) a feeling of temporary pleasure and distraction and relief while eating, then 4) a sugar crash and depression, and then 5) the anxiety arising again. When I really *see all of this mindfully*, I find that *the desire for the donut starts to go away*. I see the utter futility of trying to take care of my need for meaningful work by eating a donut—or a dozen donuts. This kind of noticing is how mindfulness meditation helps us.

If I become consciously *aware of my internal and external behavior while it is happening* then *I can free myself from it.* When I really see that I am craving a new car *because I feel worthless and empty*, and I also *see* that *having the car will not change that emptiness*, I *no longer crave it in the same way.* I recognize that I will still have exactly the same issue of worthlessness but will now be sitting in a new car and owning a large car payment. I see the *absolute futility* of trying to address my feeling of worthlessness and emptiness by acquiring a new car. When this happens, the desire begins to drop away—in fact many times it drops away immediately. Other times, I need to engage multiple times in the process of looking deeply at what is going on before an unwholesome desire starts to drop away.

Seeing Clearly and the Lesson of the Hot Coal

The following story helps to explain why we often continue engaging in behaviors that harm ourselves, and also makes clear what is needed to stop engaging in those behaviors. Imagine that you are walking down a street near where you live, and a man comes up to you in a very agitated condition. He says to you "Please, please help me! I have this terrible, searing pain in my right hand. I don't know how I can endure this for another moment. Please help me! Tell me what to do." This man is obviously suffering greatly, and you are moved by his plight. You look down, and you notice that the man is gripping a red hot coal very tightly in his right hand. What do you say to him?

I think anyone would tell the man to simply *release the coal* from his hand. The only reason the man has not already released the coal is that he *has not seen the connection between what he is doing and his own suffering*. Once he sees clearly that gripping the hot coal is the *cause* of his suffering, he no longer *wants* to grip the hot coal. Releasing the coal does not require thirty years of prior meditation practice, or some special technique, or a superhuman amount of will power. When the *connection* between the *behavior* and the *suffering* is seen clearly, the desire to continue with the behavior evaporates and the gripping of the coal stops.

This is our situation precisely in regard to our own behaviors that we continue to engage in even though we are suffering greatly because of them. We simply have not seen the connection yet. Once we see clearly that our lifestyle choices are causing us to suffer, we no longer *want* to make those choices anymore. Seeing clearly totally transforms our situation. Once we see the connection between our opulent lifestyle and the suffering of working long hours at a stressful job to pay for it, our desire to continue with the opulent lifestyle starts to drops away. When *we are able to see what we are doing in its entirety, we simply do not want to do it anymore.*

This connection must be seen at a very deep level. It cannot just be an intellectual or verbal understanding. This means that there must be total clarity about the knowing of what the right thing to do is—it cannot just be something that others have said, or something we have read, or something we are "supposed to think" is true. And it also means that there is total clarity in seeing the real suffering that is generated by the act. *We need to know these things in "every cell of our body."*

When this level of clear seeing is achieved, will power simply becomes irrelevant. A simple example can serve to make this clear. Imagine that you are standing on the curb of a busy street in a large city. You want to cross the street but there is a bus approaching at a high rate of speed in the lane nearest the curb. Do you step off the curb in front of the bus? No, of course not. Is it necessary to debate this question in your mind: "Should I step in front of the bus or not? This is tough, there are good reasons on both sides of this issue. Sometimes I think it's and good idea and other times..." No. It's not like that at all. Debating the issue never even occurs to you. Do you need strong will power in order not to step in front of the bus? No. This is a very *easy* decision. And why is this? It is because you *see very clearly the connection* between the behavior being considered—stepping in front of the bus—and the great suffering that will come as a result. There is no *desire* to step in front of the bus to cross the street, therefore no will power is required at all. All that is needed is seeing clearly *the connection* between what you are about to *do* and the *suffering* that will be experienced as a result.

Preventing Trouble Before It Starts

We can deal with desire *after* it has arisen but we can also prevent much of it from arising in the first place. Thich Nhat Hanh makes an observation that is very relevant to this in his analysis of the actions of a Thai sea pirate who has raped and killed a twelve year old refugee girl. We can and should capture the sea pirate so that he cannot continue to rape and kill. But there are "...many babies born along the Gulf of Siam, hundreds every day, and if we... do not do something about the situation, in 25 years a number of them will become sea pirates. That is certain." (1) He is saying that if we do not change the *conditions* that are *creating* sea pirates who are capable or raping and killing, the sea pirate that we captured today will soon be replaced by another one. Our situation with desire is the same. It is important to identify and then remove or modify the conditions that are *creating* unhealthy desires—whether it is for junk food, for drugs, or for excessive possessions when others are starving.

We can deal with desire after it has arisen, but we can also stop exposing ourselves to conditions that *promote* unhealthy desire in the first place. Advertising messages have the sole purpose of creating desire for products and lifestyles, many of which cause great harm. Movies, books, magazines, music, and many other things can do the same. When we are being mindful, we can notice the effect these things have on us. Being in the presence of other people who are pursuing unhealthy desires like eating junk food or smoking can also help to create desire for these activities and products. So if we limit our exposure to these forces, we can help to create conditions in which unhealthy desires are less likely to arise. The Buddha often said that "This is, because that is," meaning that if we want to change something harmful, we need to first look for and then change the *causes* that create what is harming us.

It is crucial that we develop a healthier relationship with desire. The Buddha taught that "Desire blinds us, like the pickpocket who sees only the saint's pockets." (2) Because the pickpocket's desire to steal money is so strong, he can see nothing but opportunity for stealing money and is completely blind to the much more valuable wisdom that could be received from the saint.

Our desires can truly serve as filters that prevent us from seeing important parts of our situation. Suppose, for example, I am waiting at a train station, and I am eager to board the train and begin my trip. There are many sounds in the train station but my mind is focused on listening for *one* sound only—the sound of an approaching train. Because I *want* so much to hear the train sound, many other sounds around me go unnoticed or noticed only very superficially—I may, perhaps, miss the sound of my name being paged for an important phone call.

The same thing happens when I have adopted a personal stance on some issue and am involved in an argument trying to prove that I am right. Because of my strong desire to "win" the argument, any information that does not pertain to "proving my belief" tends to be cast aside, barely noticed, or not even noticed at all.

To be constantly and unmindfully desiring is to be consistently blind on a regular basis. If our objective is wisdom and deep personal change, clearly this blindness is not a good thing.

Notes for Chapter 8

1. Nhat Hanh, Thich, *Being Peace,* Berkeley: Parallax Press, 1987, pp. 61-64.

2. Kornfield, Jack, *Buddha's Little Instruction Book,* New York: Bantam Books, 1994, p. 55.

CHAPTER 9

Mindfulness for Dealing with Anxiety and Depression

"Buddhist teachings are not a religion, they are a science of mind."

--Dalai Lama (1)

Using Mindfulness to Reduce Anxiety

When I discuss anxiety with a class, I always begin by asking the students if they have anything they are presently feeling anxious about. I write the answers on the board and I always get a list that looks something like the following.

- I won't pass my chemistry test on Friday.

- Can I make enough money to cover this month's rent?

- I'll get in a fight when I meet with my ex-husband when we get together to discuss custody.

- My family is coming for a visit this month and I'm really stressed about it.

- I'm afraid I won't have what takes to make it when I start at a big university next term.

I then ask, what do all these things have in common? Can you see it? Yes! Every single one of them is about something that *may happen* in the *future*. Friday will arrive and I will not do well on my test. The end of the month will arrive and I won't have enough money for rent. But if we ask, "Is there any problem in the present moment?" the answer is almost always "No." Yes, I have a test in the future but right now I'm sitting in a safe environment, nothing is threatening me, I'm not in any pain, I haven't flunked anything and I'm still in good standing with the school. It's all fine.

"Anxiety" says Thich Nhat Hanh, "is the illness of our time, [and anxiety] comes from our inability to dwell in the present moment." (2) This is very important. When we are fearful or anxious, we are living in the future. We think that something will or may happen in two minutes, two weeks, or two years: we will lose our job, someone will get mad at us, we will say something clumsy, the wrong politician will get elected, it will rain on our picnic tomorrow, nobody will like me when I start at my new job.

When anxiety starts to arise, it is a good mindfulness practice to ask ourselves: "Is there anything wrong in the present moment?" We can all try this out in our own lives! This question brings us back to the present moment and, almost always, the answer to this question is "No." Our fear and anxiety come because we are not present. A very simple example: I start for a morning run, and my mind says "I'll never make 3 miles, this is awful, I can't possibly run that far, I'm too tired..." This is in the future. "Is there any problem in the running that is happening right now?" No, I'm ok. All that is necessary is to simply do the running I am doing right now—no mental story about how I may be feeling a mile down the road. There is only a problem if I create one by not staying present.

During a time in the hospital being prepared for surgery, staying present with each moment as it arose helped me reduce or even eliminate fear and anxiety. If I said "This is what I'm doing now, I'm having blood drawn," it was ok. But if the mind started jumping off into the future and saying things like "Life is never going to be the same again after my surgery, this is going to be really painful, I've got weeks of difficult recovery time ahead of me"—suffering was created. When I remembered to ask myself "Is there any problem in (anything wrong with) the present moment?" the answer was always "No." At another time just prior to the surgery, I was in a room talking with the anesthesiologist: I was comfortable, not in any pain, what I was doing was not difficult, it was all fine. When the mind went into "They're going to be cutting on me in about thirty minutes and there is a lot that could go wrong," there was increased tension and anxiety. If I stayed present, then I was able to focus on doing the things I actually could do in the present moment to improve the situation and mentally let go of everything else that I could do nothing about. Perhaps what I could do was ask a question about what is coming next, or request a sedative, or hold hands with my wife.

The meditation practices introduced in Chapter 4 can be very useful in bringing the mind to rest comfortably in the present moment. Breathing, hearing, and body sensations are good places to place our attention to anchor us in the present moment and take us out of any thought-stream about the future. The mind cannot be forced to be at peace. Alan Watts observed that "To try to control the mind forcefully is like trying to flatten out waves with a board and can only result in more disturbance." (3) We must leave the mind alone. The mind settles when we allow it to rest, in the same way that muddy water naturally settles and becomes clear when we stop disturbing it. Meditation can be an effective means of quieting a mind that is already disturbed. But we can also work to get in touch with the ways that we are *causing* the anxiety to be present in the first place. Let's look at some useful practices.

Creating Anxiety: Excessive Attempts to Control

Having the goal of getting to some ideal of "calm person" in the future doesn't work because the idea of "calm person" isn't real, and the future is not real, either.

What is real is the present moment and our focus needs to be on *understanding the ways that we bring anxiety into existence* moment to moment. When we look in this way we are likely to see three important things that we are doing that create anxiety: 1) excessive attempts to control things, 2) attachment to outcome, and 3) indulging in comparison and competition.

Zen teacher Charlotte Beck tells a story that is very useful in reflecting on the issue of our excessive attempts to control things.

> ...sometimes pilots are accidentally caught in hurricanes, subjecting the plane and themselves to terrible stresses... Many of us are like... the pilot in the plane, just holding on, hoping we'll make it out of the storm. We feel ourselves caught up in the buffetings of life... severe illness... difficulties in relationships, which can seem quite unfair. From birth to death, we're caught in this swirling of winds, which is really what life is... Our aim is like that of the pilot: to protect ourselves and our plane... hoping to make our way through without being hurt.
>
> Suppose that instead of being in a plane, we were in a glider in the middle of the hurricane, without the control and power than an engine provides. We're caught in the sweeping winds. If we have any idea that we're going to get out alive, we're foolish. Still, as long as we live within that enormous mass of wind, we have a good ride. Even with the fear and terror, it can be exhilarating and joyful—like riding a roller coaster... [The] mind that thinks, pictures, gets

122

excited, gets emotional, blames other people, and feels like a victim is like the pilot in the airplane [with an engine] who's trying desperately to make his way through the hurricane. In such a life of tension and constriction, it takes everything we have just to survive. All of our attention is on ourselves and our control panel; in trying to save ourselves, we don't notice anything else. But the man in the glider can enjoy everything—the lightning, the warm rain, the scream of the wind. He can have a great time. What will happen at the end? Both men die, of course. But which one... knows joy? (4)

The story of the two pilots is about controlling things, and it is also *our* story. Obviously, there are times that it makes sense to try to influence the direction of events if we can. But it is also true that the more things that we try to control, the more anxiety and stress we will experience in life. Obsession with strategies of control prevents us from fully experiencing life and all its richness and creates suffering instead of appreciation and joy.

Our attempts to control things can seem endless. A friend once had a dinner party and assigned people where to sit, served all the food in order to control portions, and had conversation topics prepared ahead of time—instead of just letting things unfold naturally. Other people try to create "the perfect wedding" and create huge amounts of anxiety and stress through trying to micro-manage and control everything.

We even try to control the contents of other people's minds when we try to get them to see us the way we would like to be seen. We do not and cannot control another person's perception of us. We do control our choices of how we will act. Instead of trying to *look* honest to others, we can simply focus on *being* honest and let go of how anyone might see it. We control our character but we do not control our reputation. When we forget this, we suffer.

Creating Anxiety: Attachment to Outcome

When we observe the mind carefully, we notice that it has a tendency to attach itself very strongly to getting a specific outcome from an action. Suppose Susan is applying for a job she wants. She has been wanting a job just like this one for months, and believes getting the job is crucial for her future happiness. She just *has to have it*. The getting of this job is nonnegotiable. *Not* getting the job is *totally unacceptable—she must have it.* Being in this mental state of attachment produces high levels of anxiety, and it also undermines Susan's ability to do her best.

There is an alternative to this, which is called nonattachment. Nonattachment to outcome does not mean not caring about the outcome. It means not *having to have* a specific outcome in order to be ok with it; or put differently, it means being ok—at peace—with the outcome *whatever it may be*. What would it look like for Susan to approach her job application in a nonattached way?

A nonattached approach begins with *noticing* the parts of her situation she actually has some control over. Susan controls how much research she does to prepare for the interview: locating and then practicing with typical interview questions, finding out about the company she wants to work for and what they need, and so on.

She also controls whether she reminds herself to stay present! Each time the mind starts creating a "mental movie" of future disaster, she can bring it back to the simplicity of breathing in the present moment. She can remind herself that her actual task here is simply to *answer questions* at an interview. It is *not* her task to actually *get the job*. Whether she gets the job or not is controlled by other people, not by her.

Lastly, if she has a job now and the job she is applying for is an upgrade, Susan can *practice gratitude* for her present job and the other blessings presently in her life. She can also practice gratitude for the *opportunity to apply* for the new job. By focusing on what is real in the present moment, and on what she actually *does* control, the sense of pressure and anxiety can be lessened enormously.

The ancient Taoist teacher Chuang Tzu described how a very skilled woodworker explained his approach to his art:

> When I am about to make [something]... I guard against any diminishment of my vital power. I first reduce my mind to absolute [stillness. I remain three] ...days in this condition, and I become oblivious of any reward to be gained. Five days [from when I start] ...I become oblivious to any fame to be acquired. Seven days [from when I have started] ...I become unconscious of my four limbs and my physical frame. Then, with no thought of the Court [who hired me] present in my mind, my skill becomes concentrated, and all disturbing elements from [the outside] are gone. I enter some mountain forest. I search for a suitable tree. It contains the form required [already in it]. I see the [finished form] in my mind's eye, and then set to work [removing the excess wood from the form I see]. Otherwise, there is nothing. I bring my own natural capacity into relation with that of the wood..." (5)

The woodworker is not concerned about the final product, nor is he concerned with whether he wins fame or recognition. He has a preference for a good outcome for his sculpture, but he is focused on bringing his best effort to the actual task in front of him. Then, even though there is a preference for something, there is no pressure; then there is just pure doing, letting the activity flow through him. There is no anxiety.

Gandhi was once asked about his efforts to free India from British rule. How could be possibly hope to be successful against an adversary as powerful as England? How could he keep his hopes up after many years of being unable to expel the British from India? His reply was simple. *"I do not want to foresee the future. I am concerned with taking care of the present. God has given me no control over the moment following." (6)* Gandhi saw quite clearly the wisdom of not being attached to the outcome of his actions.

Creating Anxiety: Making Comparisons

In the movie *With Honors*, Simon, a penniless person, says to a Harvard student named Monty: "You try too hard. Winners don't even know they are in a race. They just love to run." We can look at how we are doing and compare it with others: do we have less status, less money, fewer accomplishments and awards, fewer friends. But we can do something else instead. We can let go of how we are doing compared to others and simply enjoy the experience—the "running"—or whatever it is we might be doing in our life.

There was a time when I had a part time teaching job but badly wanted a full time position which paid more per class, provided reassurance of a job from year to year, and came with medical insurance and retirement benefits—all things that I didn't have. I felt I was better qualified than most of the people who had full time jobs at the college where I worked and I felt angry and resentful about my situation. I was suffering. One day John, a full time colleague and friend, was telling me about some French doors he was looking at while in a home improvement store and lamenting the fact that he couldn't afford them.

126

I was suddenly jolted by a realization. Although John made a lot more money than I did for doing the same work, the fact was that I *could* afford to buy those doors if I wanted them. I realized that it did not matter whether someone else had more of something than me. What mattered was whether I was happy with what I had. I started asking myself a completely different set of questions. Did I have enough money to buy the things that I actually wanted and needed? Yes. Did I enjoy the work I was doing as a teacher? Yes, very much so. Did I like the fact that, as a part time teacher, I was not required to go to departmental and other committee meetings? Yes, absolutely! Did I have some very good friends at the college? Yes, again. I no longer had any complaints about my job!

I realized I was making myself unhappy by viewing how I was doing in relative terms—comparing myself to other people. I began *turning my attention inward* to look at what I actually needed, and whether those needs were being met. This is basically utilizing an "inner yardstick" to see how I am doing, a yardstick that is not dependent in any way on how others are doing. When I applied this inner yardstick to my job at the time, I realized I had an absolutely wonderful job. I was now just running and loving to run!

How Mindfulness Can Help With Sadness and Depression

Chronic sadness, low energy, and depression are as prevalent as anxiety. These various related states exist on a continuum from chronic sadness, to low energy, to depression, to severe depression. Can meditation and mindfulness help with these states? Yes, in at least three ways.

First, when depression or sadness arises we can sit in mindfulness meditation and begin *to see what our depressed state really is*. When we do this we discover that depression, sadness, and related conditions are collections of constantly changing body sensations and thoughts. There may be some heaviness in the chest

127

area, a knot in the stomach, some tension in the muscles of the upper back, or a heavy sensation in the eyelids. Along with the body sensations we can notice a thought stream: "Everything is messed up, I'm always going to feel this way, there's no hope for anything, why should I even try, I'm a hopeless mess." The intention with this practice is simply to *observe* what is present in ourselves without self-judgment or criticism. If criticism arises, we can remember to recognize it as thoughts arising and simply note it as "self-judgment" or "thinking." Making friends with depression or sadness in this way helps to create some space around it so that it no longer fills up the entire "room" of our awareness. We can simply be there, along with the sensations and thoughts, in a "room" that is large enough to contain more than just our unhappy condition.

Along with this, we can also watch the mind's tendency to make this collection of changing thoughts and sensations into a solid identity: "I am a depressed person." Making a collection of thoughts and feelings into a fixed definition of self makes it harder to move through these states and not stay stuck in them. If we observe our experience very carefully we can see the truth of our situation more clearly. The statement "I am a depressed *person*" is not an accurate description. "I am someone who is *experiencing unhappy feelings on a regular basis*" is accurate and makes things much more workable.

I knew someone once who was actually delighted when she got an official diagnosis of clinical depression. In talking with her about it, I discovered that she actually reveled in her identity as clinically depressed because it 1) made her unique and special, 2) gave her a reason not to do anything that she found hard or didn't want to do, and 3) provided a bullet proof excuse for not having done anything with her life. Those three underlying ideas, if not acknowledged and uprooted, will make it extremely difficult or impossible for her to not stay stuck forever in her depressed state.

A second Buddhist practice for working with depression is one of the Five Mindfulness Trainings examined previously: *Cultivate mindful consumption*. In Buddhism, *consumption* means all the forms *of taking things in* that exist in our lives. We can commit ourselves to ingesting (taking in) only items that produce peace, health, and well being, in our body and mind. This includes food, drink, drugs, TV programs, movies, conversations, friendships, books, magazines, video games, recreations, hobbies, music, activities, writings we create, and more.

Do we really need to watch two hours of news every day? How is this affecting our state of mind? Do we really need to spend time with co-workers who exude negativity and complain about everything constantly? How is this affecting how we think and feel? Is the food we are eating keeping us energetic and healthy or making us sick and giving us a junk food hangover in the morning?   It can be a very useful practice to make a list of all the *toxins* we are taking in—things that do not enhance our sense of well being or even tend to destroy it. This will provide an excellent starting point for making positive changes in our lives. A key question to ask about each of these toxins might be: *"Is what I'm getting from this item really worth the price I'm paying in the form of personal toxins and damaged outlook on life?"* Paying careful attention to our moment to moment experience will enable us to answer these questions and then make the necessary changes.

A third important practice for working with depression is to use mindfulness to expose the gaps between what we *believe* is the right thing to do and what we are *actually doing*. This gap has sometimes been given the acronym PIG, which stands for Personal Integrity Gap. If someone deeply values caring for the environment but works all day at a job that contributes heavily to environmental degradation, this will cause internal conflict and likely contribute to feelings of self-loathing. The bigger the gaps of this type, and the more of them that we have in life, the more likely we will fall into a chronically unhappy and depressed state.   It's a painful way to live, though frequently we are not in very good touch with this pain or its real cause. Mindfulness in general and meditation in particular can help us connect with our deepest values and then begin to act on them.

These mindfulness practices can be extremely useful in working with sadness, low energy and depression. These states are on a continuum of intensity. In more severe cases, it may also be very useful and even necessary to add the use of counseling and even medication. Medication can sometimes correct a chemical imbalance but it comes with some serious risks.

Drugs frequently only help to reduce the symptoms somewhat but do not get at the underlying problem. If someone is chronically sad, there is usually a very real *cause* for it. Eliminating the underlying cause produces a deep form of healing rather than only reducing symptoms. If someone has a headache they can be given a pain killer, but it is so much better to eliminate what is causing the headache in the first place. I remember talking to a student who was taking medication for depression and he reported that the drugs did take the edge off his depression, but they also numbed him to all his other feelings as well. This may well be a case in which the "cure" is worse than the disease.

An important upside of mindfulness practices is that they often help significantly and they don't have a downside. In any given situation, even if the practices prove less than helpful, it is extremely unlikely that they will make the situation worse. Unlike drugs, mindfulness practices seem to generate few if any negative side effects.

Notes for Chapter 9

1. Kornfield, Jack, *The Wise Heart: A Guide to the Universal Teachings of Buddhist Psychology*, New York: Bantam Books, 2008, p. 7.

2. Nhat Hanh, Thich, *The Heart of the Buddha's Teaching*, New York: Broadway Books, 1998, p.78

3. Watts, Alan, *Tao: The Watercourse Way*, New York: Pantheon Books, 1975, p. 118.

4. Beck, Charlotte Beck, *Nothing Special: Living Zen,* San Francisco: HarperSanFrancisco, 1993, pp. 68-69.

5. Watts, Alan, *Tao: The Watercourse Way*, p. 110-111.

6. Edberg, Henrik, "Gandhi's 10 Rules for Changing the World," *Dailey Good News that Inspires*, http://www.dailygood.org/story/466/gandhi-s-10-rules-for-changing-the-world-henrik-. Piece originally written June 28, 2013.

CHAPTER 10

Mental Resistance: Arguing with Reality

Life presents us with a regular stream of events and happenings that are sometimes difficult for us to bear. At the personal level, we get sick, we lose jobs, we have financial setbacks, and we lose friends. At the global level, on a daily basis we hear about war, starving children, destruction of the environment, climate change, prejudice and bigotry, cruelty to animals, trafficking in human slaves, and people defrauding others out of their life savings. It seems endless and it is easy to feel overwhelmed. Can Buddhist teachings help us here? Yes, they can. It begins by being mindful and *noticing* how *our response* to these events, not the events themselves, is at the root of our suffering.

Mental Resistance

Unfortunately, all too frequently our response to such events is what Buddhism calls *mental resistance*. Let's start with the simple case of getting sick and having an important job interview tomorrow. If I am behaving the way many people do, my response may run something like the following. "This is terrible. I've been so careful about taking care of my health and now this happens. Why is this happening now when I have that important interview tomorrow— I hate this! This is so unfair. I don't deserve this."

This is mentally resisting the *fact* that my illness exists. I am essentially complaining about, fighting with, and objecting to the *fact* that I am sick. All of this amounts to the thought that "This *should not* be happening, I *wish* that this had never happened, I don't *want* this."

To most of us, this seems quite normal and natural. But mentally rejecting that this is the way things are right now puts me in a state of opposition, struggle, and conflict with the reality of this moment. Whether I deserve to be sick or not, whether it is my preference to be sick or not, whether it causes harm or not—the simple truth is that I am sick. Saying that it should be otherwise puts me *out of alignment* with the reality of *this moment*. It does nothing to *change* the present reality, and it adds a layer of unnecessary personal *suffering* to the experience.

I can get mad at an illness or I can see it as just a part of life that people get sick. If I am sick I can still do the things available to me to improve my health, but when I get mad at God or the universe for the existence of illness, I create additional suffering. I can get mad at a rabid animal, or a destructive hurricane, or a person who is destroying the natural world, but it is much more skillful to view all of these things as "just part of what happens on this planet" and not put any energy into outrage against the *fact* that these things happen. It's like getting furious with President Trump: it doesn't make him behave any better and all that fury and hatred I'm carrying around inside certainly does not help me in any way, either. A useful practice here is to very carefully observe how I feel when I am railing against the universe, and then ask myself if this doesn't seem like suffering.

Our habit of going into opposition to reality when we don't get what we want is a strong one. Very frequently, the last word to escape a person's mouth before their airplane crashes into the ground is "No!!!!" or an expletive. If you are going to die anyway, why fill your last few minutes with resistance, negativity, and rage?

It is possible to mentally resist almost anything: a thought or emotion arising inside us, a bodily sensation or injury, another person, or a small or large event in our immediate environment or the global environment. In each case, however, the process is exactly the same: we are rebelling mentally against what is true in that moment.

The True Cause of Our Suffering

In the question and answer section of his dharma talk "What Is Being?" Zen teacher Adyashanti frames this issue by means of a very useful cooking metaphor. A member of his audience, call her Sarah, is feeling anguished and overwhelmed by the extreme pain and suffering inflicted on animals here and worldwide. Sarah states that there are things she can do about it, and she does those things, but there's a vast ocean of suffering that she cannot do anything about. It's overwhelming and she feels terrible.

In the situation with abuse of animals, there are many components present. Which component is crucial in order to create Sarah's suffering? We can think of it as being like putting ingredients into a pot to make a soup. At what point is the crucial ingredient added into the mix that pushes us over into suffering?

The *first ingredient* in Sarah's situation is that there is a huge amount of animal suffering in the world. Many companion animals are neglected, homeless, and euthanized every day. Billions of animals are kept in tiny, filthy spaces, and then killed for their flesh, skins, and milk every year. These are *facts*. *Secondly*, there are some things that Sarah can actually do to help and she is doing those things. She volunteers at an animal shelter, eats a totally plant based diet, gives talks in the community to help educate people about the issue, and so on. These things are also *facts*. *Third*, no matter how much she does, she can't take all the suffering away. She can only do her piece. Once again, these things are *facts*. *Everything stated above is absolutely true*. And when *only* these ingredients—these facts—are present, Sarah has no suffering about any of it. It's just the way things are right now. So the question is: What must be *added* to this mix to push Sarah into a state of suffering? Adyashanti offers the following analysis:

> Anything that would cause you to suffer over it
> is not real...if you think a thought that is not in

alignment with truth [with reality] you will
suffer, like "It shouldn't be that way," then you
feel discord. Why? Because reality shows you
it is the way it is, like it or not, say it should be
or it shouldn't be, right or wrong, none of that
matters to reality. The animals still go though
pain. We can say that people shouldn't starve
or shouldn't be cruel or there shouldn't be
torture in the world... But reality at any given
point says "But there *is*." So your "shouldn't" is
not in accordance with reality.

If you want to suffer, go into opposition with
[reality]... As soon as you think something
shouldn't be [the way that it is], you are in
opposition to the way it is. And I'm not saying
the opposite, I'm not saying things are the way
they *should* be. Both should and shouldn't have
no basis in reality. And if *it is* [if it *exists*] if
you're open, there will be a *response* to what is.
It's not like "Everything just is and I'll go crack a
beer and watch TV and eat popcorn while the
whole world goes down the tubes, what do I
care?" That's not a true understanding. (1)

The suffering is created when *we add on something that is not a
fact, not real, not true.* This occurs when we rebel against the truth and
say "It shouldn't be this way" and "I should be able to take all this
suffering away." So it is our mental *resistance to the truth* that is the
crucial added ingredient that causes us to go into overwhelm mode and
to suffer.

If there is simply a knowledge and acceptance of the various
facts about animal suffering, then we can operate from a place of clarity
and peace, and put *all our energy into doing the things we can do to*

help. And we will not suffer over what we cannot do, such as make the whole problem go away quickly. The truth is that Sarah's *suffering over the abusive treatment of animals simply does not help the animals in the slightest, and it does not help Sarah in any way, either.* In fact, feeling overwhelmed typically leads to feeling exhausted and giving up. When we stop resisting reality, then *all of our energy* can be liberated and can go directly into our *response* to the problem, and none of it goes into creating suffering for ourselves.

Sometimes no matter what we do, the amount of suffering we are confronted with breaks our hearts. But even this does not have to be a problem if we do not resist it. Adyashanti puts it this way:

> ...the key is to *let your heart break*; let it break...
> If you really let it break, it opens into love [and]
> ...opens you into a response [of doing
> something]... Just let it break all the way, don't
> protect yourself. (2)

Not protecting yourself means surrendering to the *reality* of heartbreak. If we open to heartbreak—say yes to it—even heartbreak is just part of life to be experienced fully and savored. It does not have to be a problem and it does not have to be incapacitating. If we open to it and are willing to experience it without resistance, it will wash through, not become a permanent emotional resident, and we can get on with our lives.

As the Dalai Lama once said in explaining his lack of hatred and anguish over the Chinese murdering thousands of monks and destroying much of Tibetan culture, "They have taken so much. Why should I also let them take my peace of mind?" (3) How could losing his peace of mind possibly *help* anyone?

To sum up, psychological resistance—objecting to the truth—is an unskillful response which creates many unnecessary problems. Mental resistance creates unnecessary suffering in ourselves, and it makes it harder to respond to problems effectively because it drains our motivation and energy. Additionally, the negativity of our mental resistance energy often blinds us to creative solutions to problems, and also tends to drive away people who might help—after all, hardly anyone finds this kind of energy appealing.

A Better Alternative: Surrender to the Present Moment

Since our habit of mental resistance is clearly dysfunctional we need a more effective alternative. How can we meet these kinds of difficult events more skillfully using Buddhist teachings? The Buddhist alternative is the practice of surrender.

The word "surrender" has many negative connotations for most Westerners: it suggests giving up, throwing in the towel, not trying to do anything about a bad situation. But surrender means something different here. Surrender means total *acceptance* of what is real in this moment. It is *surrender to the truth*. In surrender there is not a single part of me that says "This may be the way things are but it shouldn't be this way." To put it in terms of Western religion, it could be called surrender to God's will. Some examples can help to give a sense of what surrender of this sort feels like.

Suppose I am walking down the sidewalk taking care of some errands. At some point it starts to rain and I have no rain gear. At first there is agitation and tension: "I've got to get out of this rain, I'm going to be drenched, this is terrible." But there is no shelter anywhere, and it rains even harder. I become frantic, looking for a way to avoid getting soaked. At some point, I say to myself "Ok, I'm going to get really drenched and that's just the way it is. I can be ok with that." In that moment, there is a great relaxation of the body and the mind. I've stopped fighting with the reality of the present moment. I have surrendered to the reality of getting wet. I can and should do the things I actually can do to minimize the damage, but I can now do those things while in a peaceful and centered mind state. I might even enjoy the experience the way that children sometimes have fun getting drenched in the rain!

Most of us have had the experience of driving to get to an appointment on time and getting more and more upset as we begin to realize that there is very little chance of arriving on time. When I finally say to myself "Ok, I'm going to be late. It's not my preference but this is how it is. I just need to do the things I can do to help soften the consequences of my lateness." In that moment of acceptance, of surrender, there is a sense of peace. This is surrender to the reality of being late. And again, it does not mean that I don't act to remedy the situation as best I can. Being in a more relaxed and present state of mind will often help me to easily see the best action to take.

Eckhart Tolle has explained surrender quite elegantly. " … [Surrender means that] you allow the present moment to be… Accept— then act. Whatever the present moment contains, accept it as if you had chosen it." (4) There have been many instances when I have been astounded by the power of surrender.

Several years ago I was diagnosed with cancer and chose surgery for treatment. At first, my mind rebelled against the diagnosis —it was not possible; I had no symptoms and had taken excellent care of my health for many years. I felt fear and foreboding welling up inside me. At some point, I sensed that I was resisting—pushing away—the truth of my situation and was able to let go into acceptance. I have cancer; it is a *fact*. In that moment of acceptance, there was peace and the ability to determine exactly what steps to take next. Sometimes the rebellion against the facts would come back again, but I would again recognize the resistance and let go of it and there would be peace again.

Dealing with a serious medical issue and having major surgery provided many opportunities to learn about surrender. Once I had agreed to the surgery and was being prepared for surgery with a drip needle in my arm, I likened it to taking an airplane trip. Once the plane has lifted off, there is absolutely nothing I can do; my life is entirely in the hands of other people: pilots, air traffic controllers, jet mechanics, etc. All there is to be done is to meet each moment as it arises, let go of trying to control things—I *cannot* control them—and experience the journey moment-by-moment. If I do not surrender and accept my lack of control of what is happening, there will be unnecessary suffering. My surgical experience was no different.

After the surgery came the realization that hospitals are great "equalizers." In the post-operative wing of the hospital, it does not matter how rich and famous someone is, how smart and educated they might be, how good looking or cool, what awards they have won— everyone on the post-operative floor is the same. Everyone is looking not-so-good, everyone is experiencing pain, it's not possible to do the things you can normally do, there is no privacy, everyone is walking around in a hospital gown with their rear end exposed for everyone to see. Strangers entered my room at all hours of the day and night and poked and prodded me, the food was terrible and even unhealthy, nurses didn't always come right away. It would be easy to fall into resistance: "This isn't the way it's supposed to be; this isn't my idea of how a hospital should be run." *But it's the way this hospital is run right now*. If I was unable to accept that this was the truth of that moment, I would suffer. When I let it all go and just surrendered to the moment— this is the way things are right now—there was peace and it was all ok. Additionally, there was nothing in accepting the reality of my situation that need have prevented me from clearly and firmly asking for changes that I wanted.

The experience of feeling stressed is very closely related to mental resistance. Eckhart Tolle explains this relationship in the following way.

> These days, many people have *stress*. What does that mean? It means that you are in conflict with this moment... Everyone is under stress, which means they are *in conflict with what is*. They don't want to be *here*, they need to be in the *future*. That's called stress... They can't be *here*, because they need to be *there*— urgently. ...You're in a fighting mode with life. You're in a fighting mode with the present moment, which is life. [The attitude is]: "Whatever it is, I'm against it." What do you

think about the present moment? "I'm against it. It shouldn't be." (5)

Another wonderful teacher, Indian philosopher Jiddu Krishnamurti, also taught the necessity of surrender. During a lecture he once surprised an audience by pausing and then saying, "Do you want to know my secret?" The audience became totally silent, and Krishnamurti continued—"This is my secret: I don't mind what happens." (6) Unfortunately for his audience, he did not explain. However, in light of what has been examined here so far we can recognize that he is talking about surrender. Tolle explains Krishnamurti's "secret" this way.

> The implications of [Krishnamurti's] simple statement are profound. When I don't mind what happens, what does that imply? It implies that internally I am in alignment with what happens. "What happens," of course, refers to the suchness of this moment, which always already is as it is. It refers to content, the form that this moment—the only moment there ever is—takes. To be in alignment with *what is* means to be in a relationship of inner nonresistance with what happens. It means not to label it mentally as good or bad, but to let it be. Does this mean you can no longer take action to bring about change in your life? On the contrary. When the basis for your actions is inner alignment with the present moment, your actions become empowered... (7)

Mental resistance is a deeply ingrained *habit*, but it is *only* a habit and it can be overcome. When that happens, any interest in complaining or cursing events simply drops away. We get real clarity on our situation and become very solution oriented. We also tend to stop other people who are complaining about something we have done and simply ask them "What would it take to make this thing ok for you? Is there something that you actually want from me here?" If there is

140

nothing that will make it ok, if the other person doesn't want me to do anything, then there is no point in our continuing to participate by hearing the complaining. Often when this point is reached, even the other person realizes their complaining is pointless if there is nothing that can be done that will satisfy them. If there actually is something that is wanted from us, and we are willing to do it, then we simply do it and the interaction is finished.

How to Let Go of Resistance: Some Practices

Understanding what surrender *means*, and knowing *how to actually do it*, can often be two different things. Fortunately, there a good number of mindfulness practices that can help us learn the skill of letting go.

Meditation is a primary tool for working with all mental/emotional states, including resistance. The practices are simple, but quite powerful. Several of Thich Nhat Hanh's practices for stopping habit energy can easily be modified to work with resistance. These can be used either as micro-meditations lasting only a few seconds to a minute, or as longer formal sitting practices.

Simply acknowledging the presence of mental resistance is one of the most powerful practices. If we can begin to see our resistance well up, we can acknowledge its presence in us. We can say silently "Hello resistance, I know you are there." We can simply acknowledge its presence without judging it or ourselves for it's being there. When we do this, our resistance loses much of its grip on us.

A second kind of practice is a modified breathing meditation. First, we catch ourselves going into resistance mode, and then begin breathing mindfully. It can be very helpful to combine the breathing with saying silently "Resistance is present… Smiling to resistance." The first half is said on the in-breath, and the second half on the out-breath. Another phrasing that is useful here is "Resistance present… Letting go of resistance," again coordinating the words with the in-breath and out-breath. After a few repetitions, this can be shortened to "Resistance…

Letting go." It may even be useful to emphasize the out-breath and to visualize the resistance leaving the body with each exhalation of air.

Another kind of practice involves making our resistance our primary focus in meditation. *Lean into* the resistance and *get curious* about it. Where do I feel resistance in the body? What does it feel like? What is the thought stream that is present? This is essentially the same method use in dealing with difficult emotions examined in an earlier chapter. In the same vein, we can also check in to see if we have made the resistance present into a personal identity: "I'm a very resistant person." Letting go of this definition of self helps loosen the grip of resistance.

Yet another type of practice involves first *noticing* that we are resisting some occurrence, and then consciously *shifting our attention* to discovering possible actions to do something about the situation and then doing it. We can say to ourselves; "Resistance is present. Resistance is futile. *What can I actually do?*" Eckhart Tolle puts it this way:

> If your overall situation is unsatisfactory or unpleasant, *separate out this instant* and surrender to what *is*. ...Then look at the specifics of the situation. Ask yourself, "Is there anything I can do to change the situation, improve it, or remove myself from it?" If so, you take appropriate action. Focus not on the 100 things that you will or may have to do at some future time, but on the one thing that you can do now. This does not mean you should not do any planning. It may well be that planning is the one thing you can do now. But make sure that you don't start to run "mental movies" [of the future] and lose the Now. (8)

Sometimes we cannot even plan. When my father was dying, none of us in the family had any idea what would happen next or how long anything would take. All we could do was respond to each moment as it arose. As long as we stayed present and continually practiced letting go of resistance to each new event, and letting go of

142

any idea of what any of this was "supposed to look like," everything was okay. There was sadness, exhaustion, and fear arising, but if there was acceptance of these things, they, too, were okay.

One last practice just asks us to silently say "yes" each time there is some situation that is causing us suffering because we are mentally resisting its existence. Tara Brach, a long-time Buddhist teacher and practitioner, describes her experiment with the practice this way:

> Nothing was going right... Tired of the aversion, I decided that instead of resisting everything, I would *agree to everything*. I began to greet whatever arose in my awareness with a silently whispered "yes." Yes to the pain in my leg, yes to [my] blaming thoughts, yes to the sneezes [of people around me], and the irritation and the gloomy gray sky.
>
> At first my yes was mechanical, grudging, and insincere, but even so, each time I said it, I could feel something relax in me... I intended not only to accept what I was feeling [and experiencing] but to actively welcome it. I began to offer the yes with a softer, more friendly tone. I even smiled from time to time— my whole drama started to seem silly. My body and mind grew steadily lighter and more open. (9)

Saying yes to what is in front of us is an enormously useful practice. Any time we are tied up in knots or furious over our situation we can remember this practice: I say yes to unhappiness, to flat tire, to a government that seems totally incompetent. Try it out, and see what happens—see for yourself how it can shift things.

It is important to not lose sight of the fact that saying yes or agreeing to everything does *not* mean agreeing to *do* everything. If a person asks me to do something I don't want to do, I don't need to agree to *do* it. But I do need to agree with the *fact* that this person is asking me and the *fact* that I need to respond in some way to the invitation.

The same thing applies to believing or agreeing with everything that anyone *says*. All that needs to be accepted is the *fact* that this is someone's belief. To agree with the belief itself simply because someone else believes it would be another misunderstanding of Tara Brach's practice.

Preventive Measures: Heading Off Resistance Before It Arises

While we need to deal with mental resistance when it has arisen, we can also learn to regularly engage life in such a way that resistance is much less likely to come up in the first place. Ajahn Chah, a forest monk in Thailand, explained this to a group of students with the following story:

> He picked up the glass of drinking water to his left. Holding it up to us, he spoke in the chirpy Lao dialect that was his native tongue: "You see this goblet? For me, this glass is already broken. I enjoy it; I drink out of it. It holds my water admirably, sometimes even reflecting the sun in beautiful patterns. If I should tap it, it has a lovely ring to it. But when I put this glass on a shelf and the wind knocks it over or my elbow brushes it off the table and it falls to the ground and shatters, I say, 'Of course.' But when I understand that this glass is already broken, every moment with it is precious." (10)

If we recognize from the outset that everything changes eventually, then when change happens it will be much easier to not respond by going into mental resistance against the new reality. What the Buddha taught about the impermanence of everything is not a theory. It is the *practice* of seeing the impermanence in each moment of our experience. When we do this, change no longer surprises us and we no longer need suffer because of it. This applies to death as well, an event that generates more resistance than almost anything we can name. Greek philosopher Epictetus, who was not a Buddhist, recognized this quite clearly:

> In everything which pleases the soul, or supplies a want, or is loved, remember to add this: 'What is its nature?' If you love an earthen vessel, say it is an earthen vessel which you love; when it has been broken, you will not be [so] disturbed. [Similarly] If you are kissing your child or wife, say it is a human being whom you are kissing; if the wife or child dies, you will not be [so] disturbed." (11)

There is a wonderful Taoist story, the parable of the pine and the willow, that captures very well the simplicity and power of surrender. Consider how two different trees respond when there is heavy snow.

> The pine branch, being rigid, cracks under the weight; but the willow branch yields to the weight, and snow drops off. ...the willow is not limp but springy. (12)

The pine tree *resists* the weight of the snow and breaks under the pressure. The willow tree *accepts* the weight of the snow without fighting against it, bending naturally with the load, thus allowing the snow to easily slide off without harming the tree.

Notes for Chapter 10

1. *Adyashanti, What Is Being? Satsang With Adyashanti*, produced by Open Gate Sangha (https://www.adyashanti.org), 2007; DVD of dharma talk given in Palo Alto, California, June 20, 2007.

2. Adyashanti, *What Is Being?" Satsang With Adyashanti*.

3. Kornfield, Jack, *The Wise Heart: A Guide to the Universal Teachings of Buddhist Psychology*, New York: Bantam, 2008, Dalai Lama quoted on p. 250.

4. Tolle, Eckhart, *The Power of Now: A Guide to Spiritual Enlightenment*, Novato: New World Library, 1999, p. 29.

5. Tolle, Eckhart, *The Flowering of Human Consciousnes: Everyone's Life Purpose*, Louisville, CO: Sounds True, 2004, DVD of public talk given in La Jolla, California, March 5, 2001, afternoon session. Originally produced by Namaste Publishing, Inc., 2001.

6. Tolle, Eckhart, *A New Earth: Awakening to Your Life's Purpose*, New York: Dutton, p. 198.

7. Tolle, Eckhart, *A New Earth: Awakening to Your Life's Purpose*, pp. 198-199

8. Tolle, Eckhart, *The Power of Now: A Guide to Spiritual Enlightenment*, Novato: New World Library, 1999, pp. 174-175)

9. Brach, Tara, *Radical Acceptance: Embracing Your Life With The Heart of a Buddha*, New York: Bantam Books, 2003, pp. 81-82.

10. Epstein, Mark, *Thoughts Without A Thinker: Psychotherapy from a Buddhist Perspective,* New York: Basic Books, 1995, pp. 79-81.

11. Epictetus, *Enchiridion*, Amherst, New York: Prometheus Books, 1991,Section III. Translated by George Long.

12. Watts, Alan, *Tao: The Watercourse Way*, New York: Pantheon Books, 1975, page 76.

CHAPTER 11

Drugs and Other Distractions and Addictions that Cripple Us

Over the years, I've had a good number of students ask me what the Buddha taught about using drugs. Traditionally, the Buddhist answer has been found in the Fifth Precept on Right Action which says: "Do not use intoxicants." (1) But this answer is too simple. It also says nothing about the Buddha's *reasons* for an apparent prohibition on intoxicants.

The Fifth Buddhist Precept

The Five Buddhist Precepts are all intended as guides for ethical conduct. We misunderstand them if we read them as *rules telling us exactly what to do*. In *Interbeing*, Thich Nhat Hanh provides an excellent explanation of this point.

> The Sanskrit word *sila* means precept as an *intention* of mind that manifests in body and speech. Buddhist precepts are not prohibitions. They *are guidelines for living mindfully*. The practice of precepts does not restrict our liberty. (2)

> In the Sutras, the Buddha often used the word *sila* (precepts), but he also used the word siksha (trainings). This latter term is more consistent with the Buddhist understanding of how to practice these guidelines, and so I have recently begun using "mindfulness trainings" instead of "precepts." (3)

So the Fifth Precept, or Mindfulness Training, is intended to provide guidelines for behaving mindfully in regard to drugs. But not *just* drugs. The Fifth Mindfulness Training is about all forms of *ingestion* or taking things into our body as well as our consciousness. We ingest when we consume or take in food, drink, drugs, sights and sounds, conversations, personal relationships, and much more. The things that we allow into our consciousness and our body have a profound effect on our happiness, health, and well-being. In *The Heart of the Buddha's Teaching*, Thich Nhat Hanh explains the real breadth of the Fifth Mindfulness Training.

> [The Fifth Mindfulness Training requires committing myself to] *cultivating* good health, both physical and mental, for myself, my family, and my society by practicing mindful eating, drinking, and *consuming*. I will *ingest* only items that preserve peace, well-being, and joy in my body, [and] in my consciousness... I am determined not to use alcohol or any other intoxicant or to ingest foods or other items that contain toxins such as certain TV programs, magazines, books, films, and conversations. ...a proper diet [regarding *all* forms of ingestion] is crucial for self-transformation and for the transformation of society. (4)

The Fifth Mindfulness Training does not require us to rigidly follow any specific rule for what we take into our body and consciousness. However, the Training does advise us to *cultivate* being *mindful* about what we take into ourselves.

What Makes Drug Use Unskillful?

Clearly, when we look at drug usage as a mindfulness issue, we may see that whether a drug is an intoxicant or not depends on how it is being used. The very same substance can sometimes be an intoxicant and sometimes be something that enhances health and well-being. Morphine is a good example. Morphine can be used to avoid awareness of what is happening in a person's life, in which case it is an intoxicant.

But morphine can also be used to anesthetize a patient for a lifesaving medical surgery, or to ease the pain of a person who is terminally ill.

Mindfulness and deep looking are central here. In Buddhism, *the key issue is whether something is being used to avoid awareness*. If we are using something to avoid being aware of our emotions, desires, thoughts, and general situation in life, then our behavior is unwise and will lead to suffering. Using something to avoid awareness is not limited to drugs. Applause, roller coasters, gambling, shopping, and numerous other things can all be intoxicating and used to blot out important parts of our lives.

In truth, almost anything that we engage in or use can be abused and work as a distraction in our lives. Even things we usually see as good and necessary can be used to addictively distract us from what is real and thus prevent our personal transformation. Working at productive employment is normally good, but it can become obsessive —workaholic—and a way of not seeing and not dealing with the suffering in our lives. The same can be true of eating, exercise, or reading one novel after another. They can all be used as distractions and as a means of avoiding experiencing what is present in our lives.

This is crucially important when we remember that *seeing reality clearly* is the first of the two central purposes of Buddhist practice. And seeing reality clearly strongly impacts the second central purpose of practice, which is *self transformation*, so that we can stop causing so much suffering for ourselves and others. In order to make wiser decisions that cause less suffering, we must first see clearly what is happening in our lives.

In *A Path With Heart*, Jack Kornfield has the following to say about this.

> How do we manage so consistently to close ourselves off from the truths of our existence? We use denial to turn away from the pains and difficulties of life. We use addictions to support our denial. Ours has been called the Addicted Society, with over twenty million alcoholics, ten million drug addicts, and millions addicted to

gambling, food, sexuality, unhealthy relationships, or the speed and busyness of work. Our compulsions are the repetitive attachments [behaviors] we use to avoid feeling and to deny the difficulties of our lives…. Our addictions serve to numb us to what is[real], to help us avoid our own experience… (5)

The Four Step Process of Reaching for Something to "Use"

When we are being mindful and in touch with what is going on inside of us, we will notice that there is a universal *process of "using something"* that is present in almost all instances of intoxicant use. Typically, we have the following relationship with an intoxicant, whether it is alcohol, marijuana products, nicotine, opioids, applause, misuse of food, or anything else we may be "using." When we pay close attention, we can notice that there are four steps involved.

1. At first, I am feeling more or less ok. Perhaps I'm having lunch in the staff room at work and there is nothing much going on in me or in my immediate environment.

2. Next, some sort of triggering event occurs: a memory, a thought, someone says or does something, an event happens. Suppose while sitting having lunch today, someone asks me to join an organization to help educate people about climate change. This feels like "sticking my neck out" and exposing myself to criticism from other people, and I start to feel some fear and anxiety about it, as well as some judgmental thoughts about myself: "I'm really a coward and a hypocrite; I'm a bad person."

3. The emotion, thought, or internal reaction that has arisen is something that I don't want to experience.

151

In general, this can be fear, anxiety, anger, agitation, sadness, nervousness, confusion, or even feeling too excited and happy and "about to jump out of my skin."

4. The next thing that happens is that I *reach for something* to make what I am experiencing go away (or at least tamp it down and make my awareness of it recede into the background). In our example perhaps I excuse myself to go back to work and throw myself into a frenzy of cleaning up my desk. If I am still having uncomfortable feelings and thoughts come up when I arrive home, I may reach for some marijuana to get stoned, or a have a few beers, or eat a dozen pieces of candy, or play video games, or go on a shopping spree to "put it out of my mind and feel better."

At this point in the story we may say, "But if I feel better as a result of reaching for something to alter my experience, what is the harm done?" Actually, there are numerous harmful internal results, or internal karmic consequences, that are produced by this process of reaching for something to avoid our experience.

Internal Karma: "Smoking Cigarettes Will Stunt Your Growth"

In Buddhism, the word karma has to do with the fact that all of our actions produce consequences. It is the same idea that is expressed in the Christian teaching that *you reap what you sow*. Karma takes two forms. Internal karma is the effect that our acts have on ourselves. If I drink fifteen cups of coffee, I will feel nervous and jittery. This is not punishment for drinking a lot coffee, it is simply the operation of cause and effect. If I regularly tell lies to people, I will experience the stress of having to remember which lies I told to which people so that I do not trip myself up and get caught. This is part of the internal karma of lying.

External karma is the effect that our acts have on the outside world. If I regularly tell lies, people in my community will eventually stop believing what I say. Additionally, they may also be more hesitant to believe anything that anyone says, thus undermining the level of trust in the community. Both of these effects are examples of external karma. Applying the Buddha's teachings on karma to the question of drugs and other intoxicants can be very useful.

As children, some of us may remember adults telling us that "Smoking cigarettes will stunt your growth." It turns out they were right, but perhaps not in the way that they thought. All drugs, including nicotine, as well as nondrug addictions such as shopping or video games, have a way of stunting our growth and keeping us in an immature state. Drugs and other types of addictive abuses stunt our growth and development in at least three important ways.

First, habitually indulging in this four-step process of using prevents me from *ever* learning how to simply be with my feelings and my experiences and make peace with them. I will, for example, always be uncomfortable with and afraid of my anger until I learn to open to it and just feel it without trying to repress it, numb myself to all emotions, act it out violently, or judge myself harshly for it and feel guilty. I can spend a lifetime always opting for some distraction that prevents me from ever learning a healthy way to experience my emotions and life.

Second, avoiding my experience prevents me from seeing clearly what is *underneath* my uncomfortable feelings. I am prevented from seeing and then working through whatever life issues lie underneath my fear, anxiety, agitation, or confusion. When I am depressed, there is likely a *reason* for it—perhaps my job is tedious and without meaning, I have no friends, or I regularly am judging myself harshly. Until I get in touch with this and learn to work with it, the best I can hope for is a little superficial management of my symptoms. Emotions—fear, anxiety, anger, depression—are like messengers who knock at our door with information about what is going on inside ourselves and in our lives. If every time they come we slam the door in their faces, we never receive those valuable messages about how we are responding to life and where we are struggling. As a result, we stay stuck and unhappy year after year.

If we don't get in touch with our fundamental life-issues, we often just trade one addiction for another. In many cases, the addiction is just a *symptom* of the real problem. So maybe I go to Alcoholics Anonymous and I stop drinking alcohol but I switch over to being addicted to the coffee and doughnuts they serve at the meetings. Or perhaps I become addicted to the AA meetings themselves, and attend seven or eight meetings per week. Or I may switch over to gambling, or shopping, or video games. Until I get at what is *underneath* all these addictive activities—first the feelings, and then the underlying life-issues—nothing important ever changes.

When we are not in touch with our own experience and life-issues, we are likely to find ourselves agreeing with or accepting what is considered a "normal" life as defined by our society. This is often a life of tedious and unfulfilling work that beats us up physically and psychologically. It is a life of shallow and unsatisfying or even toxic personal relationships. It is a life of hopelessness, resignation, and "settling" for things that are empty of any real meaning. And of course the worse we feel, the less we want to know about what is going on or what we truly feel, and the more we crave something to take the edge off.

Not being in touch with my own experience and feelings results in my living an alienated, numbed out life that is full of repressed internal conflicts and suffering. When this alienation and anxiety is "dealt with" by simply applying even more drugs, activities, and other distractions, the cycle simply continues—often for an entire lifetime.

The key question to ask ourselves here is: "When I find myself reaching for something to "use," *what is it that I am afraid to feel, experience, or be aware of in this moment?"* The answer to this question puts us in touch with our *deepest personal issues*. Once we begin to get clear answers to this question, we have made the first crucial first step toward profoundly changing ourselves and breaking old dysfunctional patterns

Third and lastly, when we are "using something," we never learn to do things that are difficult, scary, painful, sad, or unpleasant. And yet doing these kinds of things can be among the most meaningful, satisfying, beautiful, rich, and beneficial things we do in our lives. In order for this to happen, we must not allow our discomfort to stop us. I will always cherish the last three weeks of my mother's life that I spent caring for her as she went through the dying process. It was a beautiful experience from which I learned life-altering lessons. But it was also scary, sad, and physically exhausting. Had I avoided being fully present for this time, I would have missed something special, and my mother would have missed something as well.

Life is full of possibilities that are richly rewarding but also very difficult: working for an important social cause, being there for a friend going through a painful divorce, writing a book, completing a very challenging class, speaking out about an injustice at work, or confronting our own deepest wounds through meditation or counseling. If we take the easy road of constantly distracting ourselves, our lives, and the world itself, are poorer as a result.

Claude Anshin Thomas, formerly an American soldier in Viet Nam and now a Zen monk, has written a wonderful narrative of his journey toward healing. In his book, *At Hell's Gate: A Soldier's Journey from War to Peace*, he describes going to Viet Nam as an 18 year old and participating in horrific violence, returning home with deep psychological wounds, being berated by people in "the peace movement," becoming homeless and lost in drug addiction, and finally discovering the curative powers of mindfulness. Eliminating drugs and other types of "using" was essential for him.

> After I went through drug and alcohol rehabilitation in 1983, I stopped turning to intoxicants (the obvious forms). Looking back,

155

this is probably the single most important event in my life, because *it gave me the opportunity to experience my own life* [emotions, mental patterns, behavior] and to experience it directly —*the only place from which healing and transformation can begin to take place.* ...You can just feel whatever is there, exploring it, until you also discover the liberation that comes with stopping the struggle [to avoid your experience] and becoming fully present in your own life [even in times of pain or difficulty]. This is the real path to peace and freedom. (6)

Practices for Working With Addictions

Our habit of reaching for something to avoid experiencing the present moment keeps us stuck in our dysfunction. But our habit of reaching for something is also the way out. We can begin to pay attention to what is happening, and use each impulse to "reach for something" as an opportunity to pay attention, choose to respond differently to that impulse, and change ourselves profoundly.

Just becoming more mindful of what we are doing and *clearly seeing the four-step process play itself out over and over in our own behavior* can be of enormous benefit in bringing about change. When we clearly see the complete ineffectiveness and futility of our avoidance strategies, the *desire* to engage in them often drops away. Sometimes, it can drop away very suddenly.

In addition to being generally mindful about the four-step process, there are three specific levels of practice that can be used for working with the problem. The three levels of practice are: 1) learning to work with the desire to "use," 2) getting in touch and making peace with the emotions that underlie the impulse to "use," and 3) getting in touch and working with our deepest life issues that are driving our emotions.

The **first level of practice** involves learning to deal with the *desire or impulse* to reach for something to use so we don't immediately get swept away into using again. Eckhart Tolle suggests the following practice.

> If you have a compulsive behavior pattern such as smoking, overeating, drinking, TV watching, internet addiction, or whatever it may be, this is what you can do: When you notice the compulsive need arising in you, stop and take three conscious breaths. This generates awareness. Then for a few minutes be aware of the compulsive urge itself as an energy field inside you. Consciously feel that need to physically or mentally ingest or consume a certain substance or the desire to act out some form of compulsive behavior. Then take a few more conscious breaths. After that you may find that the compulsive urge has disappeared —for the time being. Or you may find that it still overpowers you, and you cannot help but indulge or act it out again. Don't make it into a problem. Make the addiction part of your awareness practice in the way described above. As awareness grows, addictive patterns will weaken and eventually dissolve. Remember, however, to catch any thoughts that justify the addictive behavior, sometimes with clever arguments, as they arise in your mind. Ask yourself, Who is talking here? And you will realize the addiction is talking. As long as you know that, as long as you are present as the observer of your mind, it is less likely to trick you into doing what it wants. (7)

Tolle's suggestion is a form of micromeditation, which we examined previously in Chapters 4 and 6. In reading Tolle's advice, we may find ourselves wondering what he means by "not making it into a problem" when we give in to an addictive craving and act it out. Basically this means not creating some huge *drama* or *fictional mental story* around what happened: "I always give in to my cravings, I'm just a bad person, I'll never free myself from this addiction." If you find that you have already created a huge and untrue mental story about your lapse, you can practice catching the mind in the act of doing this and recognize what is going on for what it is—the mind creating a piece of fiction which you can choose not to believe. The simple *fact* is that you acted on a particular craving *on this occasion*—this is real, and the rest is fiction. Simply continue to work with the addiction by doing the practice, and watch what happens over time.

This also ties in closely with the discussion of nonidentification from Chapter 7. The mind—the "little voice in my head"—may be saying "You've had a stressful day, you deserve something to help you unwind; go ahead and pour you're yourself a glass of bourbon." If you think this little voice is who you are, it will be likely to send you for the bottle. If you recognize that the thoughts produced by the mind are very much like the messages on impersonal billboards along the highway, then it becomes much easier to attach no weight to those thoughts. This is what Tolle means when he speaks of being "present as *the observer* of your mind," rather than believing that your mind is who you are.

Our impulse to reach for something comes from a desire to not experience the present moment. We may be out of conscious touch with what it is we want to avoid, so in many cases all we are in touch with is a sort of restless feeling. It is like opening the refrigerator door and looking at the various foods inside: "What do I want? An apple? No, that's not it. A piece of cake? No, that's not it. A roll with hummus? No... Maybe it's not food at all. Maybe I'll listen to music or play a video game or drink a few beers or go for a drive."

Some Buddhist teachers have called this condition "Wanting mind looking for something to land on," and we all have experienced it at one time or another, sometimes with great frequency. It is the state of feeling restless and wanting *something* but not knowing what it is we want. This is because *what we really want is to escape what is present right now.* This is a state in which "I don't know what I *want* but I know I do *not* want *this.*" This is saying no to the present moment. It is mental resistance to what exists here and now. The key feature here is that there is something uncomfortable or unsettling in this moment right now, and we want to make it go away. It is this restless, squirmy, "I-don't-want-to-be-feeling-this" sensation that we need to sit with, open up to, and explore, rather than always seeking some distraction. This squirmy feeling of restlessness can be *used as a red flag alerting us* to the fact that we are about to act on our addiction again, and that we are at a choice point.

When we develop some skill at spotting the impulse to reach for something to use, we can then employ some of the stopping practices from Chapter 6: acknowledging habit energy, smiling to our desires or emotions, and Pema Chodron's practice of doing *anything that is* different from what we usually do in order to break the chain of habit energy.

The truth is that everything we do either strengthens or weakens some tendency is ourselves. Each time we are uncomfortable and choose *not* to reach for some distraction or avoidance device, our habit becomes weaker.

The **second level** of working with our dysfunctional habit of using goes deeper. At this level, the focus is on getting in touch with, and making peace with, the emotions that are underneath the impulse to use. The desire to reach for something is frequently the direct product of some emotional state having arisen that we don't want to be experiencing: anger, guilt, fear, sadness, confusion, anxiety. Using the skills of meditating on emotions that we were introduced to in Chapter 7, we can learn to sit quietly, receptively, and nonjudgmentally with emotions, and experience them fully—just allowing them to be there. When we do this, we discover that no matter what we are feeling it is ok for it to be present. We can open to the emotions by sitting with them, asking ourselves "Where do I feel this emotion in the body? What does it actually feel like? What is the thought stream that accompanies this emotion?" When we learn to be at peace with these emotions, the desire to reach for some kind of "eject button" is undercut at the source.

By using the practices examined previously in Chapter 4, we can get skilled at taking a step back from all our thoughts and emotions and simply watch what is going on without getting caught up in any of it. We can just be a careful and nonjudgmental observer of our internal process. We may even want to sit with the emotions for ten or twenty minutes as a formal meditation practice. There is no need to try to force an understanding or figure anything out; we can just be receptive to *noticing* our actual experience moment to moment.

At the **third and deepest level** of working toward personal transformation, we can learn to sit with the question "What am I fearful and anxious about?" When we do this, perhaps we discover an important *life-issue*: We are studying business administration in college but have no heart-connection with it and get no sense of fulfillment from the prospect of a lifetime of chasing after money. No wonder it is necessary to literally force ourselves to study for classes! This issue of meaningful work, once surfaced, can then be addressed and resolved, and our fear and anxiety naturally begins to subside, along with the strength of our impulse to use distractions.

At this third and deepest level, a good meditation practice is to sit with the question: What is my fear and anxiety about? What is driving my anger? In doing this as a formal sitting practice we begin as we would in doing the basic breathing meditation described in Chapter 4. After we have settled in with conscious breathing and the mind has become a bit calm, we say silently, gently, and nonjudgmentally to ourselves every thirty seconds or so: "What am I angry about?" Then we just sit with an awareness of the breath, sounds arising, or body sensations and see what comes into our awareness. It is important not to try to *make* something happen or try to figure out an answer by thinking in words. We just sit, repeat the question, and are receptive to what presents itself. If nothing happens at the first sitting, we continue to practice the meditation a few times every day. This is working at the level of our deepest obstructions.

All three levels of practice can be implemented on an ongoing basis. First, work on practices to prevent being swept away by the impulse to use something. Second, get in touch and make friends with the emotions that we are trying not to experience by distracting ourselves. Third, get in touch with the underlying unresolved life issues that give rise to the difficult emotions, and begin the work of resolving those issues.

External Karma: Effects on the World at Large

Karma is the recognition that our acts produce consequences. In addition to the internal consequences of using drugs and other avoidance behaviors discussed earlier, there are also external consequences put out into the world outside us. Everything is interconnected, and our actions impact many things, some of them close to us and obvious and others a great distance away in miles or in time. When we see these external consequences clearly, it can help motivate us to change our behavior profoundly.   The following are a few of the external consequences involved in using drugs. With a little reflection and investigation, what follows can easily be applied to nondrug addictions as well.

The use of tobacco products is a good place to begin. Tobacco cigarettes are basically a system for the delivery of the drug nicotine. Our use of tobacco comes at a high cost in the external world. Smoking kills 7 million people a year.   Additionally, a recent study by the World Health Organization found that tobacco consumption causes a yearly loss of $1.4 trillion in health-care expenses and lost productivity worldwide. Commercial tobacco farming worldwide uses 10.6 million acres of agricultural land that could be used to grow food. Tobacco production also uses a surprisingly large amount of wood and is a major cause of deforestation: 12.5 million tons of wood are utilized annually for curing tobacco using wood fires. This works out to the equivalent of one tree for every 300 cigarettes (one and a half cartons). Not counting this wood burning, just the burning of cigarettes alone creates the greenhouse gas emissions equivalent to about 1.5 million vehicles driven annually. Secondhand smoke is particularly deadly: It contains twice as much nicotine and 147 times more ammonia than so-called mainstream smoke, leading to close to 1 million deaths annually. 28% of these deaths are children. (8)

Alcohol consumption also comes with a heavy load of external consequences. Excessive drinking in the United States was estimated to cost $249 billion in 2010. Most of these costs were due to reduced workplace productivity, crime, and the cost of treating people for health problems caused by excessive drinking. A shocking 88,000 lives are lost in the U.S. each year due to excessive drinking. (9)

Additionally, instead of using valuable farm land to grow grains, potatoes, sorghum, and grapes to make alcoholic beverages, this same land could be used to grow food for people or returned to forest. And the amount of farm land at issue here is huge. If we look only at the land needed to produce alcoholic beverages from wheat and grapes, we find that 54 million acres of land are required worldwide, and that the number of people whose total food needs could be provided by this same land is 176 million—more than half the current population of the U.S. And these are the numbers that come only from wheat and grape alcohol and do not include alcoholic beverages produced from corn, rye, rice, malt, barley, potatoes, honey, or fruit other than grapes. Additionally, growing crops to make alcohol uses enormous amounts of water for irrigation, fossil fuels for powering farm equipment, and also creates large quantities of greenhouse gases. (10) Even more energy and resources are used in the actual brewing process, shipping, refrigeration, and use of one-way containers.

Alcohol and cigarettes are only two examples of addictions. With some reflection and perhaps a little research, it is relatively easy to become aware of the negative impacts of other dysfunctional avoidance addictions as well: marijuana, opioids, stimulants, compulsive eating or shopping, video games, excessive working, and so on. Doing such reflection and research can be a useful "deep looking practice."

The external karma of addictions can be seen from another perspective as well. People frequently speak of things they would like to do or to have—things like better dental care, health insurance, better quality food for themselves and their family, a chance to go to college, safe tires on their car, music lessons for a child, filling their prescriptions—but conclude that they "cannot afford it." In reality, however, their inability to afford things is often simply the result of their having chosen to spend their money on something else: their addiction of choice.

One striking example of this is a woman I met while volunteering at a local food box agency. Her income was below the government-established poverty line so she was there to pick up her free monthly food box. It came out one day when we were talking that she dreamed of owning her own home but that she couldn't save any money for a down payment because her family had trouble making ends meet. At that point, we discussed the fact that she smoked, and it turned out that her husband also smoked. Between them, they were smoking more than three packs of cigarettes a day. When we did the math, we were shocked to learn that they spent $4920 a year on cigarettes that could have been saved for a down payment on a house.

The above example shows us how people's spending on their addictions of choice can prevent them from having money to do any number of positive things. This, of course, impacts others than just themselves. Many times it's our children who bear the burden of our addictive choice—either directly or indirectly.

While this applies to other addictions, it is relatively easy to see in the smoking example. Children can suffer directly by being exposed to secondhand smoke. In addition, they can suffer indirectly by not being fed properly because there isn't enough money left after the purchase of cigarettes for the purchase of good quality food.

This analysis of our *money* expenditures can be applied with equal force to our expenditures of our *time and energy*. Getting stoned, drunk, or bingeing on games steals our time and energy. We often say "I don't have time to help or volunteer in my community or make healthy food to eat." *But why don't we have time?* Very often, the simple fact is that we are compulsively spending our time and energy on some addictive distraction: drugs, television watching, shopping, and so on. The hours that we squander in this way could be put to much better use: quality time with friends and family, taking classes, learning new skills, volunteering in our community, or going to the gym. The extra hours of paid employment that are needed to *pay for* our addictions can rob us of even more time and energy.

Lastly, one of the components of the Buddha's Eight-Fold Path is something called Right Livelihood. Part of Right Livelihood asks us to become mindful about what kinds of jobs we are creating for other people through the purchases that we make. If I purchase intoxicating drugs, what kinds of jobs does that create for people? Are they jobs that endanger the employee's health, pay an exploitive wage, or treat people as commodities, or possibly involve them in unethical or criminal activity? If, on the other hand, I choose to purchase a locally grown box of organic apples, that is likely to create jobs of a very different nature. When I am mindful, I begin to see that the dollars I spend help to create and support the continuing existence of specific kinds of jobs and businesses. This is all part of the practice of looking deeply and seeing the interconnectedness of things.

We have only scratched the surface of the multitude of internal and external consequences of our addictive behavior, but perhaps this is just enough to give an inkling of the high cost of our unwise choices in this area.

Notes for Chapter 11

1. Smith, Huston, *The World's Religions: Our Great Wisdom Traditions, Revised Edition*, San Francisco: HarperSanFrancisco, 1991, p. 108.

2. Nhat Hanh, Thich, *Interbeing*, Revised Edition, Berkeley: Parallax Press, 1993, p. 7. Emphasis added.

3. Nhat Hanh, Thich, *Interbeing*, Third Edition, Berkeley: Parallax Press, 1998, p.7

4. Nhat Hanh, Thich, *The Heart of the Buddha's Teaching*, New York: Broadway Books, 1999, p. 96. Emphasis added .

5. Jack Kornfield, *A Path With Heart*, New York: Bantam Books, 1993, pp. 23-24.

6. Claude Anshin Thomas, *At Hell's Gate: A Soldier's Journey from War to Peace*, Boston: Shambhala Publications, 2004, pp. 153-154. Emphasis added.

7. Eckhart Tolle, *A New Earth: Awakening to Your Life's Purpose*, New York: Dutton, 2005, pp. 246-247.

8. All tobacco statistics are from Jacopo Prisco for CNN, "Study Reveals High Environmental Cost of Tobacco" May 31, 2017, https://www.cnn.com/2017/05/31/health/tobacco-environment-who-report/index.html Information in the Prisco article was derived from information contained in "Tobacco and Its Environmental Impact: An Overview," a study by the World Health Organization, 2017, http://www.who.int/tobacco/publications/environmental-impact-overview/en/ .

9. CDC. Excessive alcohol use continues to be drain on American economy. October 15, 2015. Information also obtainable from Collaborative on Health and the Environment, https://www.healthandenvironment.org/environmental-health/environmental-risks/chemical-environment-overview/alcohol.

10. Klimek, Oliver, "The Environmental Impact of Alcoholic Drinks Production," August 22, 2014 Dramming: Everything Whiskey, http://www.dramming.com/2014/08/22/the-environmental-impact-of-alcoholic-drinks-production/ . Accessed October 16, 2018.

CHAPTER 12

Mindful Speech: Language As a Tool for Personal Change

The Budhha put great emphasis on mindful speech. What has been traditionally called Right Speech is a prominent part of the Eight Fold Path, and the Buddha included Mindful Speech as one of the Five Mindfulness Trainings for guiding ethical and wise action. Buddhist teachings on mindful speech have often been presented as a collection of rules: speak truthfully, do not speak cruelly, avoid exaggeration, speak charitably, and speak kindly. But this is much too superficial. Huston Smith touches on a deeper aspect of Buddhist mindful speech in his classic *The World's Religions*, telling us that the Buddha urges us to become careful *observers* of our own speech for the purpose of *changing how we engage life*.

> [We must]...take hold of the switches that control our lives, beginning with attention to language. Our first task is to become aware of our speech and what it *reveals* about our character. Instead of starting with a resolve to speak nothing but the truth—one that is likely to prove ineffective at the outset because it is too advanced—we will do well to start further back, with a resolve to *notice* how many times during the day we deviate from the truth, and to follow this up by asking *why* we did so. Similarly with uncharitable speech. Begin not by resolving never to speak an unkind word, but

by *watching one's speech* to become aware of
the *motives* that prompt unkindness.

After this first step has been reasonably
mastered, we will be ready to try some
changes. The ground will be prepared, for once
we become aware of how we [actually] do talk,
the need for changes will become evident. (1)

It is this deeper aspect of mindful speech that will be the focus
in what follows.   Speaking mindfully begins by paying very careful
attention to the things we say. We do this for two reasons: to learn
about ourselves, and then to change ourselves.

**First Aspect of the Practice: Observing Our Speech to Learn
About Ourselves**

In this first aspect, we mindfully observe our speech because we
know that doing so will reveal important information to us about
ourselves. It provides us with information about our current beliefs,
attitudes, values, and mental response patterns. Our way of speaking is
a sort of *mirror* we can hold up that enables us to see things about
ourselves that are causing suffering and that need to change. This is
particularly true when our observation includes looking at our *motives*
for what we say.

Our observation needs to include *both* our *external* speech—the
spoken or written words we put out into the world—and also our
internal speech—our unspoken "internal monologue," "self talk" or
mental commentary on things. Most people find it easiest to start by
working with external speech. However, internal speech, the speech
that is not subjected to our mental "censor for social acceptability," can
be the most revealing of what is truly going on inside us. Both types of
speech can be very revealing of our present inner reality.

In carefully *observing* our speech we make no special attempt to
alter our speech in any way. We simply pay attention to whatever
words come out of our mouths, and what motivates them. Later when

more skill is developed, we can start to observe the words that arise silently within our minds. Let's see how this all works.

Suppose I begin to notice that I consistently refer to politicians as jerks, liars, evil, and monsters. It becomes clear that I have a strong habit of judging and condemning politicians, and not seeing them fully as people just like me who want to be happy and who suffer as a result of their unskillful actions. If I pay attention to how I actually *feel* when I am speaking this way, I may notice that I am filled with anger, resentment, and hostility, and that this anger and resentment is a painful and toxic load for me to carry around every day.   This is useful information about myself.

I can then ask myself about my motivation for these statements. Do I do this to feel smarter and superior? Is it to impress other people with my clever put-downs of those in political office? Maybe my motivation is to fit in with others who are doing the same thing. Perhaps I engage in this way of speaking to distract myself from feeling the fear or anger that I have in me in connection with their behavior and policies. What does looking at my motivation tell me about myself?

Practicing mindful speech can also help us to notice what kind of language we use when we talk about ourselves—either externally or internally. Do we refer to ourselves as "poor me" and a victim who "can't win for losing," or say "these things always happen to me?" Do we say, or think to ourselves, "Once again, I've done something stupid." If we are paying attention, this language may reveal to us a consistent pattern of seeing ourselves as victims, as powerless, or as incompetent. What motivates us to say these things about ourselves? Is it an excuse for not trying because we are afraid we might fail? Is it a form of punishing ourselves because we believe we are worthless? Once we are in touch with our underlying issues, we are in a position to do something about them.

We can also begin to look at our internal monologue, our silent commenting on things and judging them. It can be a bit shocking and even painful to see what is going on in the uncensored confines of our minds. However, we can simply learn to look at it in an open and curious way. Sometimes it seems that our silent habit of judgmental comments is endless: "That was a stupid statement," "Mike really just doesn't care about the environment at all," "Sarah is really a spineless person," "That's really an ugly outfit that person is wearing. How could anyone think it's ok to go out in public dressed like that?" Our central job here is simply to observe the words as they arise. We may wish to gently and silently note them as "judgmental thoughts." In addition to judging others, we may also find ourselves thinking "That is so judgmental of me; I'm really a horrible person." Then we can simply notice this new comment with curiosity and as just another additional piece of our internal speech. We may choose to silently note it as "self-judgment."

There is a wide spectrum of possibilities with this practice. We may notice that we spend a lot of time complaining about everything. What is our *motivation* for doing this? Is it a way of talking about things that are impersonal and "safe" and don't involve sharing our thoughts and feelings more deeply with other people? Could it be a way of showing others how idealistic and noble we are when we rail against the injustices of the world? How does this impact our outlook on life and decision making? Is it a way of unconsciously "training" ourselves to focus on the negative, resulting in making the world seem like a worse place than perhaps it really is?

Other times we may notice ourselves regularly making jokes that belittle or ridicule or criticize people. When we really sit with this, does it seem to indicate a certain level of hostility, anger, meanness, negativity, or lack of compassion on our part?

Some people even notice that their habitual way of socializing and interacting with others consists of "sparring" with them, trading insults, or jabbing at them verbally as a way of being "funny" or "friendly." Do we do this to keep people at an emotional distance because we are uncomfortable with affection or intimacy? What kinds of relationships does this tend to promote? Is that what we really want?

Second Aspect of the Practice: Changing Our Speech to Transform Ourselves

In many cases, simply *seeing* what we are doing and what it reveals to us about ourselves is *enough all by itself* to produce change in our speech and in our selves. This is the lesson of the hot coal from Chapter 8 on desire. When we see the *connection* between gripping the hot coal in our hand and the pain we feel, the desire to continue gripping the goal drops away and we effortlessly release it. Likewise, when we see the connection between our speech patterns and our behavior and suffering, we don't want to speak that way anymore. Our language and our underlying attitudes and behavior begin to spontaneously change. This can sometimes happen quite quickly.

In many other cases, however, something beyond seeing what is going on is needed in order to change—we need to make a *conscious effort* to deliberately change our speech. If we consciously and deliberately speak differently, eventually our beliefs, attitudes, desires, emotions, perceptions, and behavior will change.

Let's see how this works by looking at the earlier example of using harsh and judgmental language when referring to politicians. This language was helping to maintain a hostile and judgmental state of mind, and to create separation between self and others. I can begin to change this reality by deliberately retraining my speech. I can begin to say "President Trump" instead of "the jerk in the White House" or "Trump and his henchmen." We can still strongly disapprove of the President's actions but, over time, we will find that our level of hostility and personal suffering begins to subside. We can then take more productive action because our perceptions and thought processes are not clouded by hatred and hostility.

These changes that happen as a result of deliberately changing our speech typically unfold in *stages*. When we first start working with the second aspect of mindful speech, we may find that we only notice our harsh judgment *after* we have made it. Sometimes it happens several hours or even days after we have made it. Still this is progress, because we did, in fact, notice it. We can then reformulate our remark in our minds and say the new and less judgmental statement silently to ourselves. This begins the retraining of the mind.

An even more powerful practice might be to seek out the person we made the remark to, and say "I referred earlier to the President as a monster. That's not really how I want to be speaking about him. What I really want to be calling him is 'The President,' because I'm working on becoming less judgmental and hostile." This is the first stage: we discover *after the fact* that we have spoken in a way that strengthens negative tendencies, and we then do it over again in a way that will help us to change. A "do-over" is always possible, even if we have to do it silently and speak only to ourselves.

As the practice continues, less time will go by before we notice unskillful speech. Instead of two hours, it becomes thirty minutes, then five minutes, then right after we have said it. This is wonderful! At some point we catch ourselves right *in the middle of saying it* and stop, and then rephrase what we are saying. This is even better! After a while longer, we can notice the *impulse* to say something harsh arise in the mind, and then choose not to act on it. This is a profound shift! Each time we do this, we are withholding water from the seed of harsh judgment within us, and the impulse to say such things arises less and less. After a while, we simply have a new habit of speaking that feels quite easy and natural. This becomes our new default setting. *And*—we feel much different on the inside. We are beginning to radically change our state of mind and heart.

One more example may be useful here. Suppose while doing the first half of the practice—observing our speech—we discovered that we have the habit of talking too much. This is actually quite common. It seems that we feel that we have to comment on everything, and to fill all available silences with words. When we examined our motivation for doing this, perhaps we found that there was a need to appear smart or knowledgeable, or be the center of attention and liked by others. It could also be that we want to prevent ourselves from knowing what we are feeling, or perhaps to make sure the conversation never drifts into sharing our deeper self which is frightening. Perhaps also, we notice some of the external consequences of our speech pattern: people tend to stop listening, or excuse themselves and walk away from conversations involving us. What does the second half of the practice— changing my speech in order to change myself—look like in regard to talking excessively?

We begin by making a greater effort to continue to simply notice what is going on—this in itself can be very powerful in producing change. We can get curious about what is happening and observe it closely in all its details. This makes it possible to look deeply to see what our real issues are and where we are stuck.

Additionally, we can silently *acknowledge our habit energy* of talking a lot: "Breathing in I am aware of nonstop talking, breathing out I smile to nonstop talking." It can even be useful to acknowledge our habit out loud "I've been talking a lot. I really don't want to be doing that. Tell me how you feel about this issue and I'll listen very carefully." This can be followed up by making deep listening into a mindfulness practice.

It can be very useful to let friends know of our intention to change and then to ask them for help: "I'm working on being less of a compulsive talker. Would you help me by letting me know when I am talking a lot? Maybe we could work out some sort of hand signal." The idea of a "do-over," mentioned previously, can be quite useful with excessive talking. We can revisit the conversation hours or just seconds later and say: "When you asked me if I enjoyed the concert, I gave you the whole history of my experience of going to concerts. What I really want to be saying here is a simple 'Yes, I enjoyed it very much.'" The interval between the "do" and the "do over" tends to grow shorter and shorter over time until we begin catching ourselves in the act of, or only having the impulse to tell the story in three volumes. Then we simply choose not to go there.

It can also help to practice speaking in short chunks and then stopping to listen, thereby building breaks—spaces—into what we are saying. If there is a silence, we can practice just being with it or asking a question about others' perceptions and then really listening. Closely related to this, we can practice being mindful of how what we are saying is being *received* by others. Do people look bored, restless, frustrated, and as if they are trying to find some space to say something and participate?

Finally, we can get in the habit of asking ourselves when the impulse to speak pops up: Is this comment really necessary?

Deep Listening As A Part of Mindful Speech

Mindful speech involves more than just the words that we put out into the world or that arise within our minds. Our ability to listen to others, Thich Nhat Hanh tells us, is fundamental.

> "Deep listening is at the foundation of Right Speech. If we cannot listen mindfully, we cannot practice Right Speech. No matter what we say, it will not be mindful, because we will be speaking only our own ideas and not in response to the other person." (2)

What is involved in deep listening? Often what we call listening is simply remaining silent while planning how best to be able to insert our own opinion as soon as the other person stops talking. Deep listening is not like that. To listen deeply means to listen without agenda, without trying to extract something for ourselves or change the other person in some way. It is listening without needing to respond with something "sharp" to say or thinking you need to "fix" whatever the other person's "problem" is. It is just being *receptive* and taking in the words being said, the tone, the emotions, and the body language of another person. We listen deeply when we have the simple intention of *understanding* the other person. How does this person see things, and how do they feel?

Our intention is to listen without judgment or criticism. Even if what is being said is untrue or criticizes us, our focus remains on staying present and understanding the other person. If a desire to defend ourselves or argue comes up we can just notice it is there, and choose not to act on it and continue to listen. It may be helpful to say silently "Hello impulse to argue, I know you are there," and continue to breathe in and breathe out mindfully and keep bringing our focus back to understanding the other person.

It is also important to pay attention to our own internal signs that we are getting near the end of our ability to listen. Rather than trying to continue when we are feeling exhausted or very agitated, we can simply say "I'm glad to have a better understanding of how you feel, but I think I am at the end of my ability to listen attentively right now; let's pick a time to talk about this again tomorrow."

In the beginning, most of us are not very good at deep listening, but it is a skill that we can learn. *Listening deeply is crucial because it is what enables us to know what words will be useful to say to someone, rather than speaking only from our own preconceived ideas and personal agendas.* With deep listening, our speech can come from a real understanding of someone else's situation, perspective, and feelings and be much more likely to leave them feeling understood and connected. To listen in this way is a real gift of healing. Before we can speak in a way that is useful and kind, it is first necessary to understand the person we are speaking to. This seems obvious, and yet we often forget it.

When we have taken the trouble to understand someone first, we will also be much more likely to present our ideas in ways others will be able to understand and give their serious consideration. Deep listening helps makes all this possible.

The Buddha's Teachings In Regard to Lying

Right Speech in the 8 Fold Path has often been interpreted as being about avoiding lying, exaggeration, and unkindness in one's speech. But the Buddha's teaching is much deeper than a simple set of rules for speaking. The admonition against being untruthful is really about asking us to be mindful and notice when we are not being truthful, and then analyze our motives.

Interestingly, the Buddha taught that lying is not bad because it is morally wrong, but because it is unskillful. From a Buddhist perspective, there are at least three aspects to this unskillfulness.

First, the motive for lying is almost always the desire to avoid revealing our true selves, both to others and to ourselves. Huston Smith puts it this way:

> For why do we deceive? Behind the
> rationalizations, the motive is almost always

174

fear of revealing to others or to ourselves what
we really are. Each time we give in to [this
desire to "protect" ourselves by projecting a
false self]... the walls of our egos thicken to
further imprison us. (3)

In interacting with others we may be trying to present an image
of ourselves as always calm, or happy, or knowing what to do. Such
false images of self end up being things we must put much energy into
defending, protecting, and enhancing. We are constantly being vigilant
and trying to create and maintain a suitable image of ourselves in other
people's minds (and probably in our own as well). But of course,
because we have no control over other people's minds this behavior
leads to stress, frustration and suffering. Additionally, having a mentally
created image of self constricts our ability to respond authentically and
freely in each moment—instead, we believe that we have to respond
based on "the kind of person that I am:" "I'm a well educated person,
so naturally I don't want to watch action-adventure movies."

Second, not being truthful creates separation between
ourselves and others. This explains how two people can be co-workers
or friends for twenty years and still not really know each other or feel
connected. For twenty years they have been both trying to project a
favorable but false image of themselves to impress others.

Third, being untruthful with others undermines people's ability
to trust each other in the community in which we live. The more people
are lied to, the more likely they are to not believe anything that is said
to them and to be untrusting.

There are no general rules in Buddhism to tell us exactly what to
do. The basic instruction is to be mindful about speech—be present and
really see what is in front of you—and recognize that there may be
times when lying is what a situation requires. For example, sometimes
in order to protect a group of school children from a dangerous person,
it may be necessary to speak falsely to the would-be predator. Again,

motivation is a key factor here, along with issues relating to *what other alternative courses of action are open* in a given situation.

Mindful speech is a powerful method for retraining the mind. In the introduction to the *Dhammapada* the Buddha states the following:

> Our life is shaped by our mind; we become
> what we think. (4) ...As irrigators lead water
> where they want, as archers make their arrows
> fly straight, the wise shape their minds. (5)

Learning to be mindful about speech is a powerful method for shaping the mind because a great deal of our thought is based in language. If we change the language we use, we change our thoughts. If we change our thoughts, we change our feelings, perceptions, and behavior.

Notes for Chapter 12

1. Smith, Huston, *The World's Religions, Revised Edition*, San Francisco: HarperCollins, 1991, pp. 106-107. Emphasis added.

2. Nhat Hanh, Thich, *The Heart of the Buddha's Teaching*, New York: Broadway Books, 1999, p. 86.

3. Smith, Huston, *The World's Religions, Revised Edition*, San Francisco: HarperCollins, 1991, p. 107.

4. *The Dhammapada*, translated by Eknath Easwaran, Tomales: Nilgiri Press, 1986, Paragraph 1.

5. *The Dhammapada*, translated by Eknath Easwaran, Tomales: Nilgiri Press, 1986, Paragraph 80.

CHAPTER 13

Metta: Cultivating Our Ability to Be Caring

Most of us can remember times when we were consumed with resentment because someone treated us badly. Maybe someone we thought of as a close friend never came to visit when we were going through a health crisis. Afterward, we just were unable to let go of the resentment and blame that seemed to be eating us alive. We know, when we look at it deeply, that none of this is good for our health, and it also does not help the people who have hurt or disappointed us to behave better. Wouldn't it be wonderful if there were some method to help us let go of things like this, start over, and heal ourselves and our relationships?   The Buddha taught a powerful form of meditation called metta that can do just that.

The Buddha wanted to make use of every possible tool to help us change: mindfulness meditation helps us learn to see our present situation more clearly and make friends with our emotions. Being mindful about our speech helps us to change our attitudes and response patterns. Learning to stop seeing beliefs and preferences as defining who we are as a person makes it possible to not get caught up in arguments and power struggles.

Metta is a Sanskrit word that is usually translated as *lovingkindness*, and is another method for bringing about profound change in ourselves. Metta is a form of meditation that is designed to help us learn to open our hearts and be more caring, kind, loving, and compassionate. It helps us to be forgiving and to let go of grudges, anger, and animosity—mental and emotional states that lessen our quality of life, and prevent us from improving our relationships with others.

The Practice of Metta: Sitting Meditation

Metta involves the silent repetition of specific phrases that express the wish that various individuals, including ourselves, may experience peace, well-being, and happiness.   The intention is not to somehow make other people happy by expressing this desire, but to change ourselves, moving us in the direction of greater compassion, kindness, and caring. Metta can be done both as a formal sitting practice, and as a spontaneous practice at various times throughout the day.

The metta phrases used are short, and are recited silently while in a state of meditation. The phrases can be combined with an awareness of the breath: the first half of the phrase can be said silently on the in-breath, and second half on the out-breath. The following is a list of useful examples of metta phrases, and once we are familiar with metta practice, we can feel free to choose which ones work best for us. We can also make up our own phrases if we wish.

May I dwell in peace

May I manifest loving kindness

May I be happy

May I be healed

May I be whole

May I be filled with love

May I be free from suffering

May I be content

Metta as a formal sitting practice typically begins by saying metta phrases for **Self** first, and then moves on to others. It is a good idea to keep things simple. One way to do this is to decide on four phrases before starting that resonate with us, and then plan on saying each phrase four to six times before moving on to the next phrase. We say each phrase slowly, and say the first half of the phrase on the in-breath, and second half on the out-breath: "May I be... filled with love." After repeating this four to six times, we move on to the second phrase we have chosen: "May I... be happy," for example. After having worked through the four phrases focused on ourselves, we have completed the first "round" of the meditation session. After having read this, it is useful to stop reading for a few minutes and try out what was just described as a short metta meditation before moving on to the next section.

The idea in metta is to begin by trying to generate lovingkindness for ourselves, which most people find fairly easy (exceptions to this will be discussed later). In the second and following rounds of the meditation, we try to expand our circle of concern and caring outward to include more and more individuals. The second round focuses the same phrases on a person that has been a *benefactor* for us. This would be someone who has been there for us in times of trouble, performed acts of kindness and generosity toward us, and been a caring and wise presence in our lives. Before starting with the phrases, it can be very useful to imagine our **Benefactor Person** standing in front of us, and to call to mind various times when this person helped us and in other ways cared about us. We can then begin saying the exact same phrases in the Benefactor round that we used earlier in the round focused on self. If we have a friend named Gene who has always been a helpful and caring presence in our life, we begin saying the phrases for him: "May Gene be... filled with love," then "May Gene... be happy," and so on until each of the four phrases has been said four to six times. This completes the Benefactor round. Again, this would be a good time to actually do a short meditation for a chosen Benefactor before moving on to the next section.

The third round moves our meditation focus to someone who is more removed from our normal circle of caring. Our intention here is to expand the number of individuals that we are capable of caring about. In the third round, we say our same four phrases for what is called a **Neutral Person**. A neutral person is someone we don't know very well and don't have any particular feelings about one way or another. A neutral person could be the person we do our banking with, a neighbor down the street, the mail carrier, or a student in class that we have never spoken to. If we know the person's name, we should use it in saying the phrases. If we don't know the person's name, a short description can be used: "May the mail carrier... be filled with love." We then continue with our chosen metta phrases just as we did in the previous rounds. The particular persons that we choose to focus on in the various rounds in a metta session can, and often will be, different persons each time a metta session is done. The metta phrases can be the same for every session of metta, or different phrases can be chosen for a different session. Within, a given session however, the metta phrases should stay exactly the same for each round. This helps us to view all individuals as being equally worthy of our caring, with no one getting special treatment. Before reading further, take a few minutes to actually practice metta for a Neutral Person.

It is possible to learn to care about the well-being even of individuals who are difficult to be with, or perhaps have harmed us, or are causing harm for the world at large. In round four, we choose what is usually called a Difficult Person to use as the focus of our metta phrases. In some Buddhist traditions, this person has been given the label Enemy, which is not a particularly good choice since part of the intention in this practice is to learn not to view *anyone* as an enemy. Viewing someone as an enemy does not help that person to behave better, nor does it help us to develop more lovingkindness toward that person. The label of Difficult Person also has its own problems as it can carry a suggestion of blame. It might, therefore, be better to think of this individual as a **Person I Have Difficulty With**.

After choosing someone as our Person-of-Difficulty, we begin the fourth round by saying the exact same metta phrases, using the person's name if we know what it is. We may notice our mind rebelling at the idea of wishing this person peace and happiness, but it is important to simply note the mental resistance and then just continue to say all the phrases exactly as before. It can be a very good idea to reflect on the good things this person has done, or good qualities they have, before starting this round. A work supervisor may yell at employees, but may also volunteer regularly to take neighborhood kids camping, for example. A person is always much more than just their problematic behavior. In the beginning, it can also be a good idea to not begin the process of learning to do metta with *the very most difficult* person we can think of. Starting with a person who is fairly difficult might be a better choice. Pause for a moment right now, and give a good faith effort to say all the phrases for a chosen Person-of-Difficulty before reading further.

In the final round, we expand our circle of individuals we care about to include **All Beings Everywhere**. This includes not just all humans, but all living beings of every kind: "May all beings... be filled with love," "May all beings... be happy," and so on until all four metta phrases are completed. As a way of acknowledging that we are not fundamentally different from other beings, I often like to end a metta session by repeating the phrase "Just as I wish to be happy... all beings wish to be happy." When finished with the entire metta session, we can sit quietly for a few minutes in a relaxed and present state before getting up and returning to other activities.

For your next metta session, later today or tomorrow, try the entire metta meditation as a seamless practice through Self, Benefactor, Neutral Person, Person-of-Difficulty, and All Beings. This should probably take about fifteen to twenty minutes. At some point during a metta session, you may notice that you've been distracted from saying the phrases. This is normal. When it happens, simply acknowledge the distraction and gently bring the attention back to saying the phrases.

Over time, most people find that practicing metta will sometimes generate a lot of emotion and other times very little. This is not at all unusual. However, even if it seems like nothing is happening and we don't feel anything much, we can have faith that change is occurring in ourselves, and keep doing the practice. The place to look for results is in our *lives*, not in our meditation *sessions*. If we find that we are getting better at letting go of grudges, and being more caring and kind, then the practice is working.

Practicing Metta Throughout the Day

Metta is a formal sitting meditation, but it can also be something that we do spontaneously at various times during our normal day. Suppose you are walking down the street and someone on the other side is sneezing and coughing and is obviously ill. You can look at them and say silently "May you be healed" or "May you enjoy good health." If someone else looks angry and agitated you can say silently "May you be at peace." This is an easy practice, it requires no additional time from your day, and most people find it enjoyable. It also is very effective at strengthening the ability to care, even for people that we do not really know at all.

Another variation on metta practice involves shortening the rounds from five to only three, or in some cases to only one round. This can be very useful if we are lying awake at night fuming over what somebody did earlier in the day. Three rounds of metta can work very well here. We begin as usual with doing metta for self, then move immediately in the next round to metta for the person we interacted with earlier that left us upset and angry. We can try to call to mind some of the good qualities this person has, and perhaps remember that this person's behavior is coming from their own pain and confusion.

This helps us to make a good faith effort to say our phrases as sincerely as possible. To help see this "difficult person" as not so different from ourselves, it can be very useful to add the additional phrases "Just as I wish to be happy... John wishes to be happy," and "Just as I wish to be loved... John wishes to be loved." The same basic phrase structure can be used for "be at peace," "be free of suffering," and "be safe." After completing the Person of Difficulty round, we then move on to say the same phrases for all beings. This shortened practice of three rounds can go a long way toward releasing the anger and blame that is present in that moment.

A similar type of shortened metta meditation can sometimes be used right at the time someone is doing something that makes things difficult for us. Perhaps while sitting on a bus, another passenger is talking in a very loud and offensive manner. Right where we are, we can close our eyes and breathe mindfully, and then begin saying metta phrases for the person engaged in the loud behavior. This is essentially reducing a metta session to just one round, focusing entirely on the one person who is the source of difficulty for us in that moment.

In working with the three-round and the one-round version of sitting metta, a cautionary note is needed. Eating well is not just something to do to make an upset stomach go away, though that, of course, is an excellent idea. Likewise, *metta is not primarily intended as a sort of trick or gimmick to use to remedy a particular episode of being emotionally upset*. Its main value is to create *a greater ability to be caring all the time*. This is similar to going to the gym to exercise. If we are feeling stiff and sore from too much sitting and inactivity, it might help to feel a bit better to go get some exercise. But the principle value of exercising lies in its becoming a regular practice so that we have more physical resources *all the time*—better able to meet any emergency that might arise requiring some strength or stamina. Metta is exactly like that—it is intended to be done with regularity in order to increase our capacity for lovingkindness so that we have it constantly available to us as part of our way of engaging life every day. Yes, metta can provide "symptom relief" but more importantly it is a preventive measure or health practice to put us in a place where we can regularly respond to life in a caring way no matter what life might throw at us.

Answers to Frequently Asked Questions

The following questions have been put to me by various students over the years. The accompanying answers may throw some additional light on the ins and outs of metta practice.

1. *"It seems to me if I wish people well who are behaving badly, I am simply condoning their bad behavior and saying that it is ok. I really would rather see them suffer as punishment for what they have done. But at the same time, I recognize that walking around carrying a huge load of animosity is not good for my health. How do I resolve this tension that I feel?"*

Carrying animosity *isn't* good for our health, and it does nothing to improve the bad behavior of the person for whom we won't do metta. We sometimes have a tendency to confuse letting go of anger and resentment toward a person with saying that what this person did was right or fair. We may even feel that we are compromising our deeply held ethical principles. But that is not what needs to happen. We can clearly say that what this person did was wrong and take steps to prevent them doing it again, and at the same time wish them peace, wisdom, and happiness. It helps to remember that with greater wisdom, peace, and happiness, this person would be much less likely to behave so badly.

It is also worth questioning whether one or two actions of a person truly define the totality of who they are. So, yes, this person may have embezzled money from a bank when they were twenty years old, but they also have volunteered as a teacher's aide at a local elementary school and done a wonderful job of helping a younger brother cope with bullying at school. Clearly this person is more than just someone who embezzled money once. When we see this, we can open our hearts to them and at the same time release the heavy load of judgment and anger we are carrying toward them.

2. *"When I try to do metta for a particular Person-of-Difficulty, I feel an enormous amount of fear come up, I don't feel safe, and I feel like a phony when I try to say the metta phrases. This person really hurt me very badly, and I don't really want them to be happy. How can I open up and do meaningful metta for this person?"*

If we have trouble doing metta for a Person-of-Difficulty because we still fear for our safety when we think of the person, there are a number of strategies that may help. If we have not already done so, we can try *starting* our metta practice for difficult people by choosing individuals who are only slightly difficult and who don't frighten us. In this way we can start to build up our capacity to be caring in an easier and more comfortable arena. If we have never climbed a mountain before, it does not make sense to start with an attempt on Mount Everest. Instead, we choose a mountain that is easier and less scary. Eventually, we will become stronger and more able to take on harder tasks.

When we are ready to take on doing metta for someone who frightens us, we can try imagining them standing on the other side of a very deep canyon with rock cliffs so that we feel totally safe. Envisioning ourselves in this protected position may help to reduce our fear and increase our ability to have caring feelings toward this person. Another good strategy is to imagine the difficult person as an infant. None of us started life as murderers or dictators of a militant nation. Even Hitler was an infant once: small and very vulnerable, deserving of love and care, innocent of any malevolent acts, and absolutely no different than we were as infants. Seeing our person-of-difficulty in this way may make it easier to open our hearts to them and offer them metta.

Finally, many people find it very helpful to try to see the other person's difficult behavior as coming out of the difficult person's *own pain and suffering*. In the same vein, it might also be useful to see them as suffering from a kind of *blindness*, which causes them to hurt others because they do not see clearly the reality of their situation and have not yet learned to sense deeply the pain they are causing others.

3. "I don't really have any difficult people in my life right now, but I would still like to do all the rounds in a metta session to get as much benefit as I can. What should I do?"

There are at least two options here. First, we can choose a person that we knew earlier life—they don't even need to still be alive —that we still have some feelings of resentment or anger toward at times. This is good practice for developing a stronger ability to be caring, and it may also help us to release some deeply buried pain surrounding our relationship with this person.

A second possibility is to use public figures that we do not know personally but still have strong feelings of resentment or harsh judgment toward. Such a person might be a particular writer, a politician, or someone who has committed a horrible crime that has been in the news.

4. "I have a lot of trouble doing metta for myself because it seems wrong and selfish to wish good things for myself. In addition, I often feel that I don't deserve to be happy or at peace. Is this normal?"

Unfortunately, this situation is not that unusual. However, change is definitely possible. When we have trouble doing metta for ourselves, we can work with it in either or both of two ways. First, we can envision a cherished family member or a compassionate friend saying the phrases and directing them toward us. A second strategy is to not start the metta session with Self, but to start with Benefactor instead. Once some feelings of lovingkindness have been built up in the Benefactor and Neutral Person rounds, it then becomes easier to feel loving kindness for Self, which has now been moved to round three. Essentially, Self as been moved to the Person-of-Difficulty round.

5. *"I have a friend who is applying for law school and I started to do metta for her, saying "May Sarah be admitted to law school." But then I thought, maybe being a lawyer won't be a good thing for her. How do I know whether to do metta for her or not?"*

This question raises a very good point. We really *don't know* whether going to law school or getting married to a particular person or quitting a job will be good for someone. This is why the metta phrases need to be *very general*: "May Sarah be happy" or "May Sarah find meaningful work." Also, in doing sitting metta meditation, exactly the same phrases need to be used in each round. While Sarah, who may be the focus in the Benefactor round, has some interest in law school, what happens when we get to John the mail carrier in the Neutral Person round? Do we want to be wishing him admittance to law school, too? Surely in the round for All Beings we don't want to be saying "May all beings be admitted to law school!" So as a good guideline, we need to look for phrases that are both positive and that apply to everyone.

6. *"Isn't saying metta phrases basically the same thing as saying positive affirmations: "I am at peace," "I am happy," and so on?*

Metta phrases are different from affirmations. *Affirmations* are positive statements about what exists: "I *am* happy," "James *is* at peace," "the mail carrier *is* healthy," and so on. If I say these phrases and I am not happy, James is not at peace, and the mail carrier is not healthy, then I am simply practicing lying and some part of me will know that. In addition, saying that someone *is* happy is not going to help create a more caring outlook in ourselves. Metta phrases are like saying "happy birthday" to someone. In saying "happy birthday, Jim" we are not saying that Jim *is* having a happy birthday, we are *wishing* him a happy birthday: "May you be happy on your birthday." If the wish is heartfelt, it develops a greater capacity for caring in the person who has expressed it.

7. *"I find it hard to wish success and happiness to people I am in competition with at work, school, games, or personal relationships. If they are successful, then that means there is less for me. Can I still do metta?"*

Yes. Often the problem is that we tend to see the world in terms of what anthropologists call The Theory of Limited Good. This way of looking at the world is founded on the idea that there is only so much good stuff in the world and that if someone gets more of it that means there is less available for others. On the surface, this often seems plausible. If I am slicing up a pie to be served to eight people at a Thanksgiving dinner and I cut myself a piece that is half the entire pie, that does seem to mean everyone else gets less as a result of my getting more. Likewise, if two people apply for a promotion at the office and Jane gets it and Michael doesn't, that does look very much like Michael getting less because Jane got something good.

But while the idea of limited good seems true in some cases, when we look at the things that we care about the *most,* we discover that it is not true. My acquiring more wisdom, or happiness, or love, or peace of mind does not leave less of these things for others. In fact, if other people have more wisdom, for example, that actually makes it *easier* for me to acquire more wisdom, too. The more happiness and peace there is in the world, the better place it is for all of us to live.

8. *"I find metta sort of appealing but it also seems unrealistic. How can I ever be expected to like people who have harmed me and may harm me again?"*

The idea of *liking* everyone is unrealistic. However, it is not necessary to like someone or approve of them as a person in order to offer them lovingkindness. Liking is different from caring. I may not like my neighbor who yells at his children, but I can still care about his well being, suffering, and happiness. He probably is suffering deeply himself and, if he was happier and more at peace, he probably would yell at his children a lot less. He may never be someone whose company I enjoy, but I can still want what is best for him and support him in his good actions to the extent that I am able.

It is all too easy to see the world as made up of "Us" and "Them." Members of our "Us Group" are individuals who believe and act like we do and are worthy of being cared about. Members of our

"Them Group" are not like us and are seen as "less than" and not worthy of caring about, helping, or supporting. Practicing metta focuses our attention and caring on everyone and creates a powerful sense of connection that challenges the idea of an "us and them" world by giving us a way to see everyone as included in "us." If we are to survive as a species we must transcend our tendency to care for only a few. Astronomer and science educator Carl Sagan had the following to say about it:

> Human history can be viewed as a slowly
> dawning awareness that we are members of a
> larger group. Initially, our loyalties were to
> ourselves and our immediate family, next, to
> bands of wandering hunter-gatherers, then to
> tribes, small settlements, city-states, nations.
> We have broadened the circle of those we love.
> We have now organized what are modestly
> described as super-powers, which include
> groups of people from divergent ethnic and
> cultural backgrounds working in some sense
> together—surely a humanizing and character-
> building experience. If we are to survive, our
> loyalties must be broadened further, to include
> the whole human community, the entire planet
> Earth. ...the choice, as H.G. Wells once said in
> a different context, is clearly the universe or
> nothing. (1)

Notes for Chapter 13

1. Sagan, Carl, *Cosmos*, New York: Random House, 1980
    p.339.

CHAPTER 14

Reverence for Life: Making Peace with All Beings

We do the various practices that the Buddha taught in order to radically change ourselves, and we also do them for the benefit of all living beings everywhere. The *practice* of treating all life with reverence is both a practice for profoundly transforming ourselves so that we are kinder and more caring, and it is also a principle means by which we can drastically reduce the amount of suffering in the world at large. When we practice we practice for all beings.

Reverence for life is central to what the Buddha taught. The First Mindfulness Training, also known as the First Buddhist Precept, identifies reverence for life as the first of five principles for ethical conduct as described in the aspect of The Eightfold Program known as Right Action. The First Mindfulness Training is sometimes interpreted as the simplistic commandment: "Do not kill." However, the Fifth Training is not a commandment and is much broader in scope than simply not killing. The following is Thich Nhat Hanh's explanation.

> The First Training is about reverence for life: "Aware of the suffering caused by the destruction of life, I am *committed to cultivating* compassion and learning ways to *protect the lives* of people, animals, plants, and minerals. I am *determined* not to kill, not to let others kill, and not to *support* any act of killing in the world, in *my thinking*, and in *my way of*

life." We may be killing [unnecessarily] every
day by the way we eat, drink, and use the land,
air, and water. We think that we don't kill, but
we do. *Mindfulness* of action helps us be aware
so we can stop the killing and begin saving and
helping." (1)

As with all Buddhist teachings, *mindfulness* is absolutely
essential here. We must begin to look deeply and *notice* the ways in
which we contribute to the harming of life, and then take steps to
change our behavior. We cannot do this perfectly, which is why the
Training stresses that we are *committed to cultivating* ways to protect
life. So the intention here is to minimize the harm—both killing and
suffering—that we cause to life.

What the Buddha proposed here is quite radical. It is radical in
the sense that the teaching applies to all life, not just human life. The
Dhammapada, a very old and central Buddhist text, makes it crystal
clear that the teachings on reverence for life apply to *all living beings*:

One is not noble who injures *living creatures.*
They are noble who *hurt no one.* (2) ...They are
not following dharma who resort to violence to
achieve their purpose. (3) ...Him I call a
Brahmin [wise person] who has put aside
weapons and renounced violence toward *all
creatures.* He neither kills nor helps others to
kill. (4)

The Buddha's teachings on reverence for life are radical also is
that they ask us to look not just at our own acts of directly killing or
harming, but also at all the ways we lend support to and encourage the
harmful behavior of others. Much of the time we do this as a result of
our tendency to go through life in a half-conscious state of mind, never
really looking deeply at the repercussions of our everyday acts.

We may think that we do not kill or harm very much, but we must train ourselves to look at both the near consequences of our actions and the far away consequences. The near consequences take place immediately after our action and they take place at a very close distance. Near consequences are usually easy to see. For example, if we hunt and shoot a deer we cannot escape the fact that we have killed.

The far-away consequences of our acts take place quite a while after our action and may also take place at a long distance away. When the results are far away, we are unlikely to notice them unless we get in the habit of looking deeply. Almost always, it is in the far away consequences of our acts that we will find the vast majority of the harm we cause. In the example of shooting a deer, we probably don't see any harm caused beyond the death of the deer. When we look deeply however, we may become aware of the harm caused by driving our large truck at ten miles per gallon across three states to get to our chosen hunting spot. If we travelled a two thousand mile round trip, we have burned 200 gallons of gasoline, producing 3,920 pounds of carbon dioxide (5) which promotes global warming and climate change—a threat to all life on earth. Furthermore, in burning that 200 gallons of gasoline, we have unnecessarily depleted a nonrenewable and scarce resource, thus contributing to the likelihood of wars over petroleum.

Going along with this is a huge commitment of dollars and petroleum used to station U.S. military forces thousands of miles away to protect "our" access to oil. And all of this so that we can have the pleasure of hunting and killing an innocent animal in the woods and bringing home a small amount of meat to eat. And very expensive meat it is. At three dollars a gallon, just the gas for the trip is $600, and then comes the cost for lodging and restaurant food and purchase of a license to kill deer. Total cost for the trip could be a thousand dollars or more. This is money that could have been put toward education for children, health care, or donated to reduce famine in the world or fight climate change. These are all examples of the often unnoticed far-away consequences of our acts.

Personal Beliefs and Attitudes

> If you want *to have friends, you must be friendly*. If you want to make peace, you must be peaceful.   ---Peace Pilgrim (6)

Our first task, the Buddha taught, is always to change ourselves. With practicing reverence for life, this begins by carefully observing our own response to the events of life and beginning to notice the places where we are contributing to harm and death.

One of the ways we can practice reverence for life is by speaking out. When we see racist, sexist, unjust, or exploitive behavior and do not speak out, we help to enable these attitudes and acts which often promote violence and harm. Speaking out at the time something is happening can require both courage and also the wisdom to speak in a way that is not aggressive or condemning. I knew a student who complained to me about belittling and offensive remarks made in class by one of his current professors. When I suggested that he let the instructor know how these remarks cause harm, he would not do it— not even anonymously. He said "It's not my job to tell someone how to teach." In truth, it is everyone's job to address harmful behavior, and if no one says anything to this professor his behavior will simply continue.

Like it or not, being mindful requires that we recognize that our behavior sets an example and influences the behavior of others in at least three ways. First, when someone sees me doing something I may be creating a possibility and a choice for someone that had never occurred to them before: "Oh, look, one of my friends is putting grape juice on her breakfast cereal instead of cow's milk—what a great idea; I never thought of that." Unfortunately, this can also happen with harmful events. After a prominent person commits suicide, there is often a spike in the society-wide suicide rate. (7) Some unhappy person may have never even thought of suicide as an option until he read in the newspaper that a successful actor had just taken his own life.

Secondly, every time we do something, we make a *nonverbal statement* to the world (by the simple fact of doing what we are doing) that we think it is an acceptable or good thing to do. "Oh, Heather drives 80 miles an hour on the freeway, or laughs at racist jokes, or smokes cigarettes so she must think it's ok to do those things." In effect, Heather's action gives *permission* for others to do the same thing, thus making it a little easier for them to make the same choice she did. This is just as true of positive behavior as well as negative.

And third, if we are out in the world "living our truth," some people will notice and be curious enough to ask about it, providing an opening for a very useful conversation if we can both share what we know in a nonblaming way, and listen respectfully to each other.

Our actions influence people in ways we may never know about. A student named Josh came up to me after a philosophy class in which we had just spent two weeks questioning our cultural assumptions about killing and eating animals. He told me of a recent experience in which he was going through the line in the college cafeteria and was intending to order the chicken stir fry. Before he placed his order, the student right in front of him in line ordered the tempeh stir fry. He said to himself "I've been questioning how we treat animals and have been thinking about trying the tempeh stir fry—this guy's having tempeh, I'm finally going to try it, too!" And he discovered that he liked it and that he really *could* eat vegetarian and be fine with it. The student in front of Josh in line had a profound impact on Josh, and yet that student will never know it. Josh never saw his face, doesn't know his name—but his behavior changed Josh's life. It also changed the world, making it just a little bit less violent.

Many of us, including myself, can remember playing a board game called Monopoly as young children. For years, I saw playing the game as nothing more than a fun thing to do. But then one day many years later, I heard a lecture by sociologist Allen Johnson who raised the question: "What are my children learning from playing Monopoly with me?" The goal in the game is to win, and a person wins by absolutely bankrupting every other player in the game so that they have no money, no property, and are forced out of the game in disgrace. In playing this game, what are we being taught about what it means to be successful? It became clear to Allen that he was helping to foster an attitude of greed and ruthlessness in his children, and clearly these attitudes often lead to acts which harm life.

Once, when leaving to take a trip, Gandhi was asked if he had a message to leave for others. He replied, "My life is my message." (8) This is as true for each of us as well: The way we live *our* life is also *our* message to the world.

Another way we help to create harm to life is through our mental habit of tribalism. Tribalism means seeing events through the lens of being a member of a particular tribe: Americans, Republicans, Democrats, Socialists, Christians, Jews, environmentalists, conservatives, feminists, and so on. When we do this, we tend to think in terms of benefitting only "our side" or "our group." Thus we set ourselves up in opposition with other tribes and "their side." When we think of ourselves as Americans, we tend to believe that a foreign policy of "Protect American interests" is natural and right. But what this really means is that the U.S. is not in a region of the world to broker a peace that works for everyone, but rather to extract things that benefit only the U.S. This is simply a form of "us and them" thinking and helps to create suspicion, unreasonableness, conflict and violence. If our first loyalty is to our "tribe" rather than caring about everyone's interests, this will lead to trouble.

When the U.S. attempts to impose a highly materialistic and highly sexualized culture on deeply religious cultures of the Middle East, and then places a military presence nearby—all for the purpose of extracting oil to satisfy U.S interests—it should not be surprising that there would be anger and resentment and a desire to violently strike back.

A major cause of violence between individuals and between nations is unjust treatment. When people are exploited and treated unfairly, eventually they rise up against it—often in a violent manner. Doing the things that we can to stop exploitation of other countries and other people and promote social justice is a form of practicing reverence for life.

When other countries rise up against American ill treatment, they sometimes resort to terrorist attacks. Our standard way of responding to this is to attack the terrorists with violence. However, attacking terrorists just increases their anger and desire to strike back. An observation from Thich Nhat Hanh is very useful here: "Wrong perceptions are the [source of] ... anger, violence, and hate. You cannot remove wrong perceptions with a gun." (9) However if we *ask* terrorists why they want to attack us, and then really listen, we will discover underlying misperceptions: misperceptions they have about the U.S. wanting to harm them, and misperceptions that the U.S. has about its own actions as well as the actions of those who are attacking the U.S. When those misperceptions are recognized, we can begin to see how we all want not to suffer and that we are all part of one interconnected web of life on this planet. (10) Practicing deep listening, uncovering wrong perceptions in ourselves and others, and recognizing that *we are one* are things that each of us can do every day to create a world with less violence and harm.

Closely related to this is the realization that yes, we must restrain people who are harming and killing, but we must also address the underlying conditions that produce a person who is capable of placing such little value on human and other life. Areas of the U.S. and the world where people live under harsh conditions and are treated unjustly are the" factories" where violent people are created. If we do not address these conditions, the killer that we restrain today will just be replaced by another one from the same factory tomorrow. This is why looking for underlying causes and removing them—such as social injustice—is such an important part of what the Buddha taught about reverence for life. We must look for what we are doing that contributes to making these "criminal-producing factories" possible. We help to produce such factories by supporting corporations that plunder, and by voting for policies and candidates that cause harm.

Personal Food Choices

We like to think of ourselves as not killing or deliberately causing much harm, but we don't have to dig very deeply to discover that this is not true. Let's look in depth at a single example: our personal day-to-day food choices. Over a lifetime, the average American will eat 9 cows, 24 pigs, 208 turkeys, 1,750 chickens and 950 fish. (11) These are not creatures that we kill with our own hands, but we pay other people to do this for us by buying the animal flesh that we eat. In buying the products of killing, we help to keep the process of killing going.

Before these beings are killed, they are kept prisoner and fed an unnatural diet, filled with drugs and growth hormones, and kept in crowded and filthy conditions. Chickens, for example, are typically raised with each bird given only an amount of space slightly larger than a sheet of letter-size paper. (12) Pregnant pigs are kept in metal stalls measuring six feet by 2 feet for many months—so small an area that the pig can never turn around. (13) Since we could satisfy all our nutritional needs by eating fruit, vegetables, and grains, we are causing all this death, pain and suffering only to satisfy a habit and a *taste preference* on our part. And this is just the surface of this issue.

When we look a little deeper, we discover that the raising of animals for their flesh, milk, and eggs does enormous damage to the environment. When we eat animal flesh, eggs, or milk, we are actually eating food crops second hand. This is because we grow crops that humans could eat—corn, oats, soybeans—and feed these crops to cattle, pigs, turkeys, and chickens and then eat their flesh, milk, and eggs instead. In the U.S., about 90% of corn, oat, and soy bean crops are fed to livestock, not people. Additionally, in converting plant crops into animal-source foods, about 90% of the food value is lost. The animal foods industries call this a "conversion ratio." For beef, the conversion ratio is about sixteen to one. This means that it takes sixteen pounds of plant foods such as corn to make just one pound of edible beef. (14) To put this in perspective, buying a pound of beef and eating it is like going to the supermarket and buying 16 one-pound boxes of cornflakes, eating just one of the boxes and then flushing the other fifteen boxes down the toilet. In a world in which a child starves to death every ten seconds (15) this kind of behavior seems unconscionable.

Depletion of energy resources is also an issue here. John McDougall, M.D., provides some startling facts regarding energy:

> Crops like potatoes can produce 17 times the calories as animals on the same piece of land. [Changing to an all-plant food diet means that] Fossil fuels used in the production of food could be reduced fortyfold [4,000 percent]. Consider that about 2 calories of fossil-fuel energy are required to cultivate 1 calorie [of food energy from] starchy vegetables [potatoes, yams, corn, beans, grain]; with beef the ratio can be as high as 80 to 1. (16)

A plant-based diet requires only 5.5% of the land to produce one person's food compared to what is needed for a person eating the typical omnivore diet found in the U.S. Producing foods from animals requires eleven times the amount of diesel and gasoline that is required to produce an equivalent amount of plant foods. And all this is occurring in a world in which people are fighting and dying over shrinking oil resources. Additionally, burning eleven times more petroleum means producing eleven times more climate-changing greenhouse gases—a threat to all life on the planet. (17)

People have a long history of fighting over scarce water. The production of the typical U.S omnivore diet requires 4,000 gallons of water *per day, per person*. Eating plants, dairy, and eggs requires only 1,200 gallons per day. Making the change to a totally plant based diet would drop a person's water consumption for food to only 300 gallons per day. If we are practicing reverence life, we can begin to see such a change as an important step along the path. (18) Using so much land, water, and petroleum creates scarcity. When people don't have enough of critical resources, they often go to war. Recently, people have been fighting over access to petroleum. Historically, most wars have been fought over scarce resources.

Climate change is an unprecedented threat to the continuance of all human and other life. According to a United Nations report, livestock industries produce 18% of greenhouse gases worldwide. To put this in perspective, this amount is more than the *entire transportation industry*. All the cars, trucks, buses, ships, trains, and airplanes in the entire world produce only 13%. (19) Furthermore, the U.N. calculation leaves out the obvious fact that livestock breathe out CO_2, and this adds another easy-to-calculate 20% to the emissions total. So a minimum of 38% of greenhouse emissions are due to livestock.

Shockingly, Robert Goodland and Jeff Anhang from the World Food Bank determined in a meticulous set of calculations that livestock actually produce 51% of all human-caused green house gases. (20) As the Earth's climate continues to become less friendly to life, hundreds of millions of people will be displaced from their homes, and the number of deaths caused through lack of heat, floods, storms, and lack of food and shelter will be staggering.

Although rarely brought to conscious attention, something as seemingly simple as the choice of whether to have a hamburger or a bean burrito for lunch has an enormous impact on how much we contribute to harm and to killing. One serving of a quarter pound hamburger uses 425 more gallons of water to produce than a large bean burrito. Who would have thought that the implications of our food choices would take in such a wide spectrum of consequences? (21)

Another issue relating to personal food choices pertains to organic foods. Choosing organic foods enables us to avoid supporting the introduction of agricultural poisons into the soil, air, and water due to the use of toxic pesticides and other chemicals. Another piece of the food puzzle has to do with getting our food from sources closer to home. Food items on an American plate have travelled an average of 1,500 miles from farm to plate. (22) From the standpoint of depletion of scarce fossil fuels and the resultant introduction of greenhouse gases into the environment, there is a vast difference between a Montana resident buying an apple from Washington instead of a banana from Honduras.

These issues hit close to home and often provide us an opportunity to discover where we cling tenaciously to our deeply conditioned preferences. Our commitment to practicing reverence for life will receive a good test!   Western philosopher Peter Singer speaks eloquently to this issue.

> It is easy to take a stand on a remote issue, but [one] reveals his true nature when the issue comes nearer to home. To protest about bullfighting in Spain or the slaughter of baby seals in Canada while continuing to eat chickens that spent their lives crammed into cages, or veal calves that have been deprived of their mothers, their proper diet, and the freedom to lie down with their legs extended, is like denouncing apartheid in South Africa while asking your [white] neighbors not to sell their houses to blacks. (23)

Earning A Living

The kind of work we do to support ourselves profoundly affects us and affects the world around us as well. This is why the Buddha included teachings on Mindful Livelihood as an aspect of the basic Eight-Fold Program that he taught. A crucial aspect of Mindful Employment asks us to look deeply at the ways in which our occupation either protects or harms life. Am I involved in making a product which harms other people, living beings, or the environment? Some of the harm that our job supports will be close at hand and easy to see, while other types of harm might be difficult to see at first glance.

If we work for a restaurant that serves meat, unhealthy food, or alcoholic beverages, we are contributing to the harming of life. These products harm the people who consume them and also have large negative impacts on the environment. Harm is also often caused through eating establishments encouraging people to overeat, from waiters tempting people with unhealthy desserts to being offered all-you-can-eat buffets.

In holding a job, we may be participating in the production and sales of low quality products that break or don't work well, or products that people don't really need but buy because of dishonest advertising. Working in livestock or weapons-related industries obviously cause harm, as do jobs helping to make possible the showing of violent movies. Selling or promoting low gas mileage vehicles hugely damages the environment, depletes nonrenewable resources, and promotes climate change.

Sometimes the *product* manufactured is life enhancing, but the *process of creating it* produces highly toxic wastes, or pushes native peoples off their land, or destroys oxygen-making rain forest. Dry cleaning gets clothes clean but uses noxious chemicals which are then released into the environment.

Many businesses, such as fast food restaurants, produce mountains of trash and waste. Working in the profession of marketing typically helps to promote people being unhappy with what they have so they will buy something new just to increase company profits. It is not practicing reverence for life to work at a job that helps to cut down forests in a way that is not sustainable in order to create wood pulp for junk mail, newspapers, and magazines.

Some employers *externalize* the costs of running their business. As an example, think of soot from a factory that damages people's lungs, creates the need to repaint their houses, or clogs air filters. Clearing up these problems should be a cost of operating the business, but instead the health and financial burdens are pushed off onto individual citizens or government which are external to the operation of the business and do not share in its profits. Air pollution worldwide *shortens human life spans by an average of 2.6 years.* (24)

Perhaps the company I work for is spending vast sums of money to distort the democratic process and create laws that financially benefit the company but cause huge amounts of harm to people. Like it or not, my employment supports this harmful activity by helping the company to operate and generate a profit.

Additionally, our choices of which companies to support with our purchases will determine what kinds of jobs we help bring into existence for other people. Buying nuts from one company may mean supporting a business that uses virtual slaves in Central America as farm workers. Buying nuts from another company may mean that farmers can earn a livable wage and have their health protected. When we take the trouble to find out these things and then take action, we are practicing reverence for life.

These are just a few of the job related issues to begin to look at regarding reverence for life, and each person's situation will be different. No job is perfect, and every job will cause some amount of harm, but we can try to find jobs that minimize harm as a way of practicing reverence for life.

Moving From Excess Personal Consumption to Living More Simply

As we have seen, our personal food choices are quite likely the place where most of us can undergo the most improvement regarding changing consumption patterns in order to cause less harm to life. It is useful now to broaden our perspective and look at a more complete picture. As we learned in Chapter 2, the U.S., though only making up 5% of global population, uses 25% of all the resources used by humans everywhere each year, and also produces 25% of global pollution. Clearly, this excessive level of consumption contributes hugely to resource depletion and scarcity, and also to greenhouse gas production and climate change.

The Earth is literally a space ship and, like any space ship, there are three fundamental things that are true about it. First, the Earth is *finite*: there is only so much land, and so much water, air, petroleum, coal, natural gas, and forests. Second, the Earth is a *closed system*— with the exception of sunlight, nothing enters and nothing leaves and it is not possible to pick up more supplies along the way if we should run out of something critical. Third, *there is no such place as "away"* on spaceship Earth. This means that our belief that we can throw things away and get rid of them is false. If we produce some toxic substance as a result of a manufacturing process, it stays on the space ship—it could be moved to someone else's living space, but it cannot be thrown away. So when we look deeply, we see that these three principles accurately describe our situation in living on planet Earth. In many cases, once we see our situation more clearly, we will automatically see the ways in which we need to make different choices in order to cause less harm to life.

In 1900, our space ship had about one billion human passengers. Today, the number of human passengers has increased to about 7.7 billion. So while we have increased the number of passengers by almost 800%, our space ship has not gotten any bigger, and our supplies on board have actually dwindled considerably. We have less of almost everything except toxic waste. And sadly, we are adding 83 million *more* passengers to our space ship each year. (25) That's like adding the population of Germany each year, but without adding the German equivalent in new land, petroleum, coal, iron ore, timber, or fresh water and air.

To compound things, *humans have become larger* in the sense that the average person is using vastly more resources than one hundred years ago. Environmental author Bill McKibbon put this point quite powerfully. He notes that in the past, North America was populated by Native American hunter/gatherers. On average they used about 2,500 calories a day of energy, most of it in the form of food and a small amount in wood used for fires. However, today the average citizen of Earth uses 31,000 calories of energy, about 2,500 in the form of food, and the rest of it from burning fossil fuels. McKibbon points out that 31,000 calories is the same amount of energy required to keep a *pilot whale* going—a very large animal, twelve to fifteen feet long and weighing about 6,000 pounds. This is the sense in which humans have become much larger—each day each of us, as a global average, is using as much energy as it takes to keep a very large whale alive.

If we shift from looking at global population to the population of the U.S., McKibbon states that the average American uses a stupefying 186,000 calories of energy every day. Except for 2,500 calories for food, all of this energy goes to manufacture and power-up an unprecedented level of consumption. The energy used every day by one person is the same amount of energy required to keep a sperm whale alive—an animal that is 60 feet long and weighs over 100,000 pounds. And all of this on a space ship that has not grown any and that has become seriously depleted. (26)

Consequently, a huge part of practicing reverence for life is learning to live more simply and be content with fewer possessions. "Live simply that others may simply live," is a saying that fits well in this context. (27) If we choose to do this, we can do much less damage to life.

Worldwide, 15 billion trees are cut down each year, and the global tree count has fallen by 46% since the beginning of human civilization. (28) These trees support many human and other lives by providing food, shade, and erosion resistance. They literally serve as the oxygen-providing "lungs" of the earth and are part of the Earth's natural system for purifying toxic substances. Much of this tree loss goes for one-use products such as newspapers, magazines, advertisements, junk mail, and packaging—which we support with our purchases. 40% of the world's industrial logging goes into making paper products, and this is expected to reach 50% in the near future. The U.S. alone uses approximately 68 million trees each year for paper products. (29) If we buy fewer products and do most of our reading on-line or through libraries, we can save many of the Earth's forests.

We have been encouraged to recycle, but cutting consumption is a far better choice. A single example can show us why. To make glass soda pop bottles from raw materials requires heating those materials to 3,200 Fahrenheit. To make the same bottles from crushed recycled glass requires only 2,800 degrees—so there is an energy savings, but 2,800 degrees still represents a lot of energy, and even more energy is used to transport the glass. Drinking filtered water from the tap requires no energy for heat, manufacture, or transportation of bottles. It's also healthier and less expensive than soda. (30) Clearly, reducing our consumption of one way containers is much more effective than recycling.

Researcher Paul Hawken of The Natural Step organization, has calculated that for every 100 pounds of product sitting on a shelf in a retail store, 3,200 pounds of waste is produced that we never see before the product ever arrives at the store. (31) This waste is created all along the production chain that starts with resource extraction, resource processing, manufacture, packaging, and transportation. If we buy a hundred pounds worth of appliances, and then recycle the two pounds of cardboard packaging, that does help a little but it is tiny compared to the 3,200 pounds of waste we never see. The only way to seriously make a difference is to buy fewer products in the first place and live more simply. There are many places we can do this.

We might begin by thinking in terms of smaller houses. Over the years, house size in the U.S. has steadily increased from about 312 square feet per person in 1950 to 742 in the 1990's. (32) Why isn't a house that was adequate in the 1950's still adequate today? Is it simply that we are in the habit of always wanting more and more? Americans today are more than four and half times richer than their ancestors living in 1900: more electronics, more vehicles, more restaurant meals, more trips, more appliances, and so on. (33) We can begin to see that *our possessions come at the expense of the Earth and the welfare of all its inhabitants.* When we see this and begin consuming at a lower level, we are practicing reverence for life.

Anything we do to decrease greed and thereby decrease scarcity helps to create peace. There are thousands of ways we can reduce the harm we cause to life. We can use public transportation or walk instead of driving everywhere; stop using single-use containers; dry our laundry on a clothes line or indoor rack rather than a clothes dryer; discontinue our practice of recreational shopping ("mall therapy"); stop measuring our success by how much "stuff" we possess; avoid leather and other animal skins; buy secondhand products rather than call a new product into existence. We can also remember the statistics from Chapter 11 documenting the huge harmful consequences of our reliance on alcohol, cigarettes, marijuana, and other addictions: disease, death, resource depletion, impact on climate change, and loss of time and energy and money that could be used for better causes.

If we choose to live more simply, we can afford to work less and slow down in life and be less stressed because we no longer have to work so many hours to pay for all the stuff we have. When we do this, we have more time and energy and patience to be caring, take care of our health, do volunteer work and help others. These are all things that help to create a less violent world for everyone.

Some Frequently Asked Questions

1. *"I have heard that Buddhists believe that it is permissible to eat meat as long as it was not killed specifically for you. I would never ask someone to kill an animal for me to eat, but I do eat the flesh of animals that have already been slaughtered. How does this fit with what the Buddha taught about reverence for life?"*

This may have made some sense during the Buddha's time when monks made rounds with begging bowls to collect food and were perhaps collecting some piece of meat that would otherwise have been thrown out. However, our present day situation in this country is not like that. Very few of us beg for food. We purchase meat, milk, and eggs and in doing so we support and make profitable the ongoing exploitation and killing of other species when we could simply eat plant foods instead. The Dhammapada passage quoted earlier states very clearly that a wise person "neither kills nor helps others to kill." By making it profitable to kill, we are helping killing to happen.

2. *"I know I can carry out a spider in my house rather than kill it. But what about thousands of ants in my house? Do I have to be overrun with ants?"*

Buddhist teachings never instruct us that we "have to" do something. There are no rules to tell us what to do in Buddhism. We are given the guideline to cultivate mindfulness and minimize harm and killing. If we were on a ship that sunk and are now in a lifeboat and had only meat rations to eat or fish we could kill, we are not told that we cannot eat flesh. But this kind of situation is radically different from the vast majority of the situations we find ourselves in. The Buddha taught that we should do our best to minimize harm.

In the situation with the thousands of ants, it seems important to maintain a healthy environment in the home and the presence of great numbers of ants is not likely to be compatible with that goal. Thus the central question in this situation is: "How can I maintain a healthy home environment while causing the minimum amount of harm to the ant population and to life in general?" Progress toward answering the central question will likely be improved by asking other questions such as What is attracting the ants into the house in the first place? Where is their point of entry? Are there natural and harmless repellants or barriers available?

3. "It seems to me killing an animal and eating it or wearing its skin is still practicing reverence for life as long as I do it consciously, knowing that I am taking a life and expressing appreciation to the animal for giving up its life. What is the Buddhist response to this?"

Does the animal really "give up" its life or is it taken by violence rather than as a true gift? Can we really say that doing something and knowing we are doing it, and doing it with gratitude makes an act wise or compassionate? How would we feel if this same idea were applied to our treatment of members of our own species—or ourselves? What would we think of someone who stabbed someone in the park and took their money, but then defended their act by saying they did it knowing fully what they were doing and that they did it with appreciation for what the other person "gave" up?

4. "I often experience a great feeling of love for all of humans and for the natural world and all its creatures. Is this what the Buddha meant by reverence for life?"

This might be a good start, but what the Buddha taught goes deeper than experiencing a certain emotion. Practicing reverence for life is most centrally about manifesting caring in our behavior. Sharif Abdulla relates a personal story that expresses this quite eloquently.

> Even though we may profess to love others, what we do with others in real life is a different story. Years ago, at a psychology conference in San Diego, attendees at the plenary sessions were singing wonderful New Age songs, swaying back and forth, holding hands, openly expressing their love for each other. Many of them would then leave the conference room and treat the mainly Latino busboys and university staff like dirt. They would walk right by them, not make eye contact, not thank them or acknowledge them as human. The people wearing the conference tags were human; others were just furniture, to be used or ignored according to convenience. (34)

Notes for Chapter 14

1. Nhat Hanh, Thich, *The Heart of the Buddha's Teaching*, New York: Broadway Books, 1998, p. 94. Emphasis added.

2. *The Dhammapada*, translated by Eknath Easwaran, Tomales, California: Nilgiri Press, 1985, Chapter 19, line 270.

3. *The Dhammapada*, translated by Eknath Easwaran, Tomales, California: Nilgiri Press, 1985, Chapter 19, line 256.

4. *The Dhammapada*, translated by Eknath Easwaran, Tomales, California: Nilgiri Press, 1985, Chapter 26, line 405.

5. Citizens Climate Lobby website: https://citizensclimatelobby.org/basics-carbon-fee-dividend/.

6. *The Spirit of Peace*, a documentary video from https://www.peacepilgrim.org/free-offerings.

7. ABC News, https://abc7news.com/health/expert-celebrity-suicides-may-lead-to-uptick-in-suicide-rates/3578937/ .

8. Easwaran, Eknath, *Your Life Is Your Message*, Berkeley: Nilgiri Press, 1992 p. 9.

9. Nhat Hanh, Thich, "There Is No Path to Peace; The Path Is Peace," *Shambhala Sun*, Volume 12, No. 6, July 2004, pp. 43.

10. Nhat Hanh, Thich, "There Is No Path to Peace; The Path Is Peace," p. 68.

11. http://www.countinganimals.com/how-many-animals-does-a-vegetarian-save/. The number of cattle eaten by one person in his or her lifetime was calculated in the following way. The website states that the number of cattle slaughtered for meat in the U.S. in 2013 was 34 million. Dividing this number by U.S. human population of 315 million tells us that each person consumes .107 cattle per year. When this number is multiplied by the average human lifespan of 79 years this produces a total of 8.5 cattle consumed over the average person's lifetime in the U.S. The same method was used for chickens, pigs, and so on.

12. Farm Sanctuary, https://www.farmsanctuary.org/learn/factory-farming/chickens/.

13. Farm Sanctuary, https://www.farmsanctuary.org/learn/factory-farming/pigs-used-for-pork/.

14. Robbins, John, *The Food Revolution*, Boston: Canari Press, 2001, p. 293.

15. BBC News, https://www.bbc.com/news/magazine-22935692. Accessed Dec 4, 2018.

16. McDougall, John, M.D., *The Starch Solution*, New York: Rodale,2012, p. 8.

17. Andersen, Kip, and Keegan, Kuhn, *The Sustainability Secret*, San Rafael: Earth Aware, 2015, p. 161.

18. Tallman, Patricia, *The Restore-Our-Planet Diet*, Charleston: LOTONtech, 2015, p. 11.

19. "Livestock Impacts on the Environment," Food and Agriculture Organization of the United Nations. *Spotlight,* November 2006.

20. Goodland, Robert, and Anhang, Jeff, "Livestock and Climate Change," WorldWatch.org website, November/December 2009, https://www.worldwatch.org/files/pdf/Livestock%20and%20climate%20change.

21. Tallman, Patricia, *The Restore-Our-Planet Diet*, Charleston: LOTONtech, 2015, pp. 38-39. The particular figure used here was calculated by my me using Tallman's statistics.

22. Worldwatch Institute, "Globetrotting Food Will Travel Farther Than Ever This Thanksgiving," December 18, 2018, http://www.worldwatch.org/globetrotting-food-will-travel-farther-ever-thanksgiving .

23. Singer, Peter, *Animal Liberation*, New York: Avon, 1975, p. 167.

24. Berkowitz, Bonnie, John Muyskens, Manas Sharma, and Monica Ulmanu, "How Many Years Do We Lose To The Air We Breathe?, Washington Post, Nov. 19, 2018. https://www.washingtonpost.com/graphics/2018/national/health-science/lost-years/?utm_term=.fdaa66032b4b .

25. Calculated from taking the Earth's population growth of 1.11% for 2016 and multiplying that by the 2018 Earth population of 7.7 billion to yield a yearly growth of 83 million.

26. McKibbon, Bill, "A Special Moment In History," *The Atlantic Monthly*, May 1998, pp. 56-57.

27. This quotation has often been attributed to Gandhi, but there is no clear evidence that he ever said it. The same

saying has also been attributed, but also with no evidence, to <u>Elizabeth Ann Seton</u>. Whoever said it, it is excellent and succinct advice. In doing an internet search for the quote source, it is quite ironic that about half of the entries that showed up were advertisements for bumper stickers, refrigerator magnets, tote bags, T shirts and other consumer items with the quote emblazoned on them.

28. Worland, Justin, "Here's How Many Trees Humans Cut Down Each Year," September 2, 2015, *Time* website, <u>http://time.com/4019277/trees-humans-deforestation/</u>.

29. The Paperless Project, 2014. <u>https://www.greenamerica.org/sites/default/files/inline-files/Paper%20Facts%202017.pdf</u>.

30. *Lane County Master Recycler Training Manual*, Oregon State University, 2000, page II-9.

31. *Master Recycler Program 2019*, by Oregon State University,2019, p.131. Also available from <u>https://fa.oregonstate.edu/sites/fa.oregonstate.edu/files/recycling/resources/MR_Class/chapter_7_sustainability.pdf</u>.

32. Durning, Alan, "Saving the Forest: What Will It Take?" WorldWatch Paper #117, WorldWatch Institute, 1993, p. 33.

33. Durning, Alan, *How Much Is Enough?*, New York: W.W. Norton and Co., 1992, p.23.

34. Abdullah, Sharif, *Creating A World That Works For All*, San Francisco: Berrett-Koehler Publishers, p. 160.

CHAPTER 15

Ending Arguments and Power Struggles In Your Life

Eckart Tolle's *The Power of Now* contains the following passage.

> Once you have disidentified from your mind, whether you are right or wrong makes no difference to your sense of self at all, so the forcefully compulsive and deeply unconscious need to be right, which is a form of violence, will no longer be there... This is the end of all arguments and power games." (1)

When I first read this years ago I felt something shift powerfully inside of me. It was like a door opening onto a totally different landscape. I understood Tolle and knew that what he was saying was true—all arguments and power struggles can come to an end. All that is needed is to *disidentify from your mind*.

The idea of disidentifying with your mind is likely to sound strange to most people. However, it is a teaching that is as powerful as it is simple.

Understanding the Process of Identifying With the Mind

The best way to understand *dis*identifying with the mind is to start with the *opposite* process. What does it mean to *identify* with the mind? When we observe our minds, we find that there is a constant and ever-changing procession of thoughts, memories, desires, fantasies, and problem solving. Most people have a very strong tendency to invest this mental content with a quality of *ownership*. We say, for example, "This is *my* belief." We also talk about "*My* way of doing the dishes," and *my* preferences, perceptions, thoughts, and so on. We think that these things *belong* to us, and even that they *are* us—they are seen as a central part of what makes us *the person that we are*. This process, which is largely unconscious, is what is called *identifying with the mind*. Most people have been engaged in this process all of their lives, though they are typically not conscious of doing so.

We also have the habit of making the ideas produced by other people into part of their personal identities, so in addition to "my belief," we also have "my brother's belief," and "Senator Smith's belief," and so on.

Our habit of seeing beliefs and ways of doing things as part of who we are is so deeply ingrained and we have been doing this so long it does not occur to us to question it or even to become consciously aware of its existence. From early childhood, we have received countless messages that we need to stand up for "our" beliefs and develop a strong "personal" belief system. "Don't let people disrespect 'your' beliefs." "Your beliefs and ways of doing things are part of who you *are*."

People often make the same identification with external things as well, and speak of "my" car, shirt, house, team, political party, and so on. We say "I am a liberal" or "I am southerner," and think this is who we are as a person.

All of this seems quite natural to us. However, as we shall see, making the contents of our minds (and other entities as well) into a personal identity causes no end of conflict and suffering.

A central problem with all of this occurs when someone says something *questioning* about some piece of mental content that we have identified with. Since we think our ideas are part of who we are, when they are questioned or criticized it seems like we are being *attacked as a person*. This in turn leads to an impulse to *defend ourselves,* whether it is about our car, shirt, house, or belief. There is a sense of needing to "dig in" and "fight" to preserve our very *self*. We believe we need to "stick up for *our* beliefs" and "fight for *our* principles" as a matter of our own *personal honor*. When we feel attacked we fight back, and so does the other person who is typically equally identified with the contents of their mind. Thus, we become engaged in yet another combative argument or power struggle. And we suffer as a result.

Such arguments and power struggles are extremely damaging. As long as there is a "my" view and a "your" view, we will tend to see each other as adversaries or opponents. Our focus will remain on *winning* and being *personally right*.

When there is personal identification with views and an adversarial or *debate stance* is taken, the goal is to instruct or persuade the other party to adopt "my" point of view. Our focus is typically not on learning. We are *there to win*, not to *learn*. Not only is our *focus* not on learning but, as Thich Nhat Hanh points out, when we are entrenched in our personal views those views actually *block* our ability to learn.

> Usually when we hear or read something new, we just compare it to our own ideas. If it is the same, we accept it and say that it is correct. If it is not, we say it is incorrect. In either case, we learn nothing. (2)

Let's examine the debate stance more closely. When we have become identified with views and are in debate mode, there are likely to be *three key features in our thought process*. First, in debate, I *start from a belief*, a position I have staked out. I start from the assumption that I *already know* the truth, and then set out to convince others that I am right. For example, if I enter a debate on abortion, I start by taking some *position,* perhaps that "Abortion is always morally wrong." I have *identified* with this position, seeing it as *mine* and being part of who I *am*. Second, having already staked out a position (a territorial metaphor), I then set out to collect evidence. However, typically, I am only interested in evidence that supports my pre-existing belief. I collect only information that supports "my" view and undermines the views of my "opponent." Third, I then present the evidence on behalf of my belief and steadfastly *defend it* against all criticisms or "attacks" by others who do not agree, in the hope of persuading them that "my" view must be accepted.

218

When this kind of competitive debate occurs, frequently no one learns anything—and in truth, the participants are not *there* in order to learn. They are there to instruct, persuade, and defeat the other person. We tend to stop listening and use the time when the other person is speaking to formulate our rebuttal. It is interesting to note that in a debate we may not convince anyone else, but we almost always *convince ourselves.* As a result, we simply end up being *even more deeply entrenched* in our pre-existing view or prejudice than we were before the argument started.

Most of us have watched numerous debates between political candidates. As a little mental experiment, try to imagine one of the candidates saying "That's a really good point. I really learned something tonight. I was wrong in what I said earlier and will need to change my views on that issue." In the context of a debate, such a statement would be mind boggling, because to say such a thing would be admitting *defeat and be seen as a personal humiliation*.

Research in conflict mediation tends to bear this out. In their classic text *Getting to Yes*, Roger Fisher and William Ury found the following to be true.

> [It is important to] focus on [common] interests, not positions. At the Harvard Negotiation Project, researchers found that when people stated their goals in terms of positions that had to be defended they were less able to produce wise agreements [or wise thoughts]. The more you clarify your position and defend yourself, the more committed you become to the position. Arguing over positions endangers ongoing relationships, since the conflict often becomes a contest of wills... (3)

Disidentifying With the Mind

Identifying with the contents of mind is clearly problematic. But what exactly does the alternative of disidentifying with the contents of mind actually look like?   An analogy can be useful here to both help to *understand* nonidentification, and also to help us actually *accomplish it in our own lives.*

Imagine a collection of packages with name tags attached with strings—they could be presents sitting under a Christmas tree. Each package has a tag attached to it that has a person's name on it that the package belongs to. In this case, we can think of the packages as representing various beliefs or views, and the tags representing the people that those beliefs belong to. Over here is a package with a tag that says "John's view" and over there is another package with a tag that is labeled "Ann's view" and so on for each package. Now imagine snipping all the strings and throwing the name tags away. At this point we can *just examine the beliefs* and not concern ourselves with whether they "belong to" any particular person. Now there is no "your view" and "my view," there is only "the view that we are examining right now." When we have this metaphor in mind, it makes it much easier to let go of the idea that any belief is "ours," and to avoid feeling that we have to "dig in" and *defend* a personal position.

The following story can be helpful to build on what has been said thus far. Imagine that we are going for a hike in the Three Sisters Wilderness area in Oregon. It would be wise to take a map with us so we don't get lost, and so you have brought one with you to consult from time to time. The map shows trails, streams, mountain peaks, places where we can get drinking water, and so on, as well as distances between various geographical features. While we are consulting the map you brought, I notice and point out to you an error in the map—the map shows the spring where we can get drinking water as being three miles west of our present location, rather than its actual location which is three miles east. Because I have an aerial photo of the area, and hiked this trail last year, I have excellent reason to believe that the map is in error. When I help you to see the error in the map, do you get upset with me? Do you feel you must "defend your map" as being correct? Probably not, because you recognize that *the map is not you*—it is only a useful and important *tool* that helps us find our way around and make good decisions. If the map is inaccurate, we may make some bad decisions that will hurt us and/or others. Having someone help correct errors in the map we are using is something for which to be grateful.

In the same way, a belief can be viewed as a sort of verbal reality map. When someone points out an error in the map I am using, I can simply make the correction on the "reality map" and thank them for helping to produce a more accurate map. Beliefs do not have to be viewed as who we are, we can see them as only a map—an *impersonal tool*—which can and should be continually revised in the shared interest of making it more accurate.

Sometimes we have a hard time understanding the idea of not identifying with and attaching to beliefs because we live in a society in which virtually everything is *owned* by someone—so it is hard to think of something as not belonging to anyone. Again, an analogy can be very useful. Sometimes I would ask a student in class "Who does that backpack on the floor belong to?" and he would say "Me," or "It's mine." I would then ask the student about a statement he had made earlier in our class discussion: "Who does the belief that 'Only physical objects exist' belong to?" The student would again say "Me." On the surface at least, this all seems perfectly natural and accurate. But let's look at another situation.

Imagine now that we are at the beach and see a shell at our feet. Who does that shell belong to? Clearly, at this point, it belongs to no one. However, suppose you pick the shell up and look at it closely? Whose shell is it? At this point you have a choice. You could say it is "It's my shell," or you could say it is nobody's shell in particular, it is just a shell we are presently looking at. It might even be *useful* to us as a tool for scraping tar off our feet. But we don't *have to* see the shell as belonging to anyone. This is important. It is clear in this case that whether the shell is seen as belonging to anyone is *a choice.*

Suppose we now leave the beach, go across the street and I *buy* a shell in a gift shop. What if someone later says "That's an ugly shell?" Would I feel the need to *defend* it—and defend my *self*—and argue that it was really beautiful? This response is quite likely if I think of the shell as "mine," something that is attached to me and must be protected and defended. I am invested in it. But I could also *choose* to *not* see it as part of my personal identity, just as with the shell found at the beach.

In a similar manner, we can choose to do essentially the same thing in regard to beliefs and other mental content. They do not have to be viewed as *belonging* to anyone in particular. They are simply descriptions of reality. If they are accurate descriptions they can be useful to us. But they do not have to be viewed as "your description" or "my description."

This can be of enormous help in moving a discussion away from worrying about *"Who* is right?" to being concerned with *"What* is right?" This is a crucial distinction. Beliefs need not be seen as attached to specific people—once we have said or written something we can let it go; it is no longer "ours." It is simply a belief. What we have said is simply an attempt at drawing part of a map, if you will, that we can all look at and work with and try to make as accurate as possible. At this point our efforts can more easily become collaborative rather than competitive. We can look for where other people have something valuable to say, instead of being totally focused on finding where they are wrong and looking for faults. It can be a situation of "you and me working *together"* to find the truth—make a more accurate "map"— rather than an instance of "you *against* me" competing to determine who will "win" in some sort of personal contest.

The End of Arguments and Power Struggles

When we are able to let go of thinking that certain ideas are who we are, an important alternative to arguing and debate becomes available to us. This alternative is called *dialogue.* (4)

In *debate,* I start out with a belief ("my" belief) and the assumption that I already know the truth, followed by then looking only for facts that appear to support my pre-existing view so I can persuade others. In *dialogue,* the thought process used in debate is *reversed.* 1) I don't start with a belief, I *start from a question* and a *desire to find out.* Staying with the abortion example used earlier, one might start with the question, "Under what conditions, if any, is abortion morally wrong?" 2) I then set out to collect and evaluate facts and information on *all sides* of this issue, not just information that supports a pre-existing view I have come to view as "mine." And finally, 3) I decide (tentatively) which belief seems the most accurate, based on an analysis of the best evidence available so far. Choosing a belief is thus the *last* step in the process and is based on information provided from a number of perspectives. I accept a belief as true based on a thorough examination of all the available evidence, while also remaining open to the possibility that more information may well become available later and that, upon reflection, this belief may need to be altered in the future.

Choosing traditional debate rather than dialogue produces distinct negative consequences.

Being in debate mode and wanting to prove "our" particular thesis has a very real tendency to *blind us* to important pieces of information and avenues of thought. This is essentially the same thing that happens when we are driving on the freeway and intently trying to find the correct off-ramp. Because of our single-minded focus on the off-ramp, we may easily be oblivious to the important fact that traffic is suddenly stopping right in front of us. Our desires in general, and our desire to prove "our view" in particular, can likewise truly serve as filters that prevent us from seeing important parts of the situation right in front of us. Anything that doesn't support the cause of winning is either not noticed or is cast aside as irrelevant. This prevents learning and often keeps us stuck in arguments and fighting.

Being personally identified with views and entrenched in debate mode produces a number of additional undesirable consequences. In focusing on being right and winning, frequently the truth is lost in the quest to achieve a personal victory. After a while, we don't care what the truth is anymore, we just want to *win*. This is something we see quite clearly in our legal system, which is extremely adversarial and oriented toward winning. Frequently the side represented by the cleverest, most aggressive, and perhaps most unscrupulous lawyers "wins," but justice is not served in the process.

Additionally, in our tendency to identify with beliefs and act competitively, relationships between people are weakened rather than strengthened. Often at the end of a debate, people like each other less well and sometimes go away feeling angry and hurt. Collaborative discussions tend to produce the opposite result. If you and I have just spent an hour helping each other on some common project—whether it is talking through a problem to find a solution or helping each other build a boat—we are likely to feel closer and more connected than we did before we worked together.

What has been said thus far does not mean that there will not still be disagreements. There will always be differences of opinion. But we can eliminate disagreements in which there is a need to be personally victorious. Instead of competition, and winning and losing, there can be collaboration, shared purpose, and a focus on seeing reality clearly and uncovering the truth.

Not being personally identified with a belief does *not* mean you don't believe anything at all or that you cannot be strongly convinced of the truth of some particular belief—it's just that it's no longer *your* belief. You can still care passionately about a particular measure to mitigate climate change, but it is all about the *issue* of what is needed to reverse climate change, and not about whether you win or lose some sort of personal contest.

There need not even be any problem with presenting facts and reasons to persuade others—it is just no longer done on behalf of a belief that is *yours*. It is no longer in the service of achieving a personal victory, but rather in the service of truth and finding a solution that maximizes the well being of everyone. All of our attention can then be focused on determining *what* is right, rather than on *who* is right.

To some people, losing the need to be *personally right* may seem like something to be dismissed as hopelessly unrealistic and "possible only for a few saints." This attitude can surface when the teachings are understood *only as theories or words*. The practicality and power of these teachings is revealed in practice—in *doing*. We need to try them out in our own lives, and then see for ourselves how they change things. Otherwise, the teachings just become one more thing to argue about.

The Greek philosopher Epicurus once said "In a philosophical dispute, he gains most who is defeated, since he learns most." The "winner" has learned nothing new. Learning the truth of our present situation is absolutely crucial for making positive changes in ourselves and in the world. If we can take the step *of moving beyond the concepts of victory and defeat,* and "your" side and "my" side, our chances of finding the truth become much greater.

It is worth noting that everything that has been said about identifying with *beliefs* can be said about other forms of personal identity created by the mind. When I identify with "my" way of doing the dishes, I will think I need to defend it. If it's "my" truck, I likely will feel personally attacked if someone finds fault with it. If "my" occupation is attorney, I may easily fall into defending the honor of attorneys in general if someone says something negative about them. The same can happen in regard to "my" race, "my" ethnicity, "my" political affiliation, or "my" religion. If I think *who I am* is a parent, a smart person, a knowledgeable person, or a vegetarian, I am likely to be drawn into personalized competitive debates on topics related to these personal identities. However, if I have not made any of these mental categories into a "me," then my manner of engagement can be totally focused on the subject matter being discussed—what, in fact, is a good way of doing the dishes for example—without feeling personally attacked in any way.

Using Mindful Speech to Retrain Ourselves

An important strategy for freeing ourselves from competitive arguments is to become more sensitive to language. As we learned in Chapter 12, Buddhist teachings on mindful speech practice tell us that paying very close attention to our own speech can accomplish two things for us: 1) it can strongly *reveal* our present attitudes and beliefs, and 2) our language can also be used as a tool to *shape* those attitudes and beliefs. The language that we choose is both a symptom of the problem and a lever for change. Much of the language of our discussion of important issues uses territorial and even combative metaphors that help to create a certain *kind* of discussion. Talking about "attacking" an inference promotes a very different attitude than talking about "questioning" or "investigating" an inference. We can become aware of the language of identification and fighting that we use and begin to substitute the language of nonidentification and collaboration.

If we change the *words* we use it will help us to reframe what we are *doing*. Currently, our language is simply encouraging identification with views and adoption of a posture of attack and defense. The following list of expressions has been gleaned from newspaper and other articles and from panel discussions.

> We need to attack the assumption that..., a knockout argument , intellectual ammunition, deal a death blow to the theory that..., battle the assumption that..., the argument comes under fire when..., a crushing argument, defend the view that..., destroyed my argument, if you use that argument she will wipe you out, he shot down all my arguments...

I'm sure we could add many additional examples from our own experience. Clearly these are metaphors that encourage an adversarial, even warlike and highly personalized view of discussion. It need not be this way. With a little thought and effort we can re-train ourselves and get in the habit of using different expressions that create less hostile attitudes and conversations. Instead of "shooting down" arguments we can "look them over for possible problems." Instead of "running up the white flag," we can recognize that "the view we're considering is probably not true." Rather than talking about "defending a position," we could say we are "putting forth a view for consideration."

We can also drop entirely talk of "my view," "your view," and "Smith's view" in favor of constructions such as "the view that taxes are too high" and "this belief" or "that statement." There is no need to attach people's identities to various views. These are not difficult changes to make, but they will have a powerful effect on how we view what we are doing when we enter a discussion with someone.

If we are consistent with our efforts, consciously changing our speech will eventually change our perceptions, attitudes, and behavior patterns. We will begin to find ourselves in fewer and fewer useless arguments and power struggles.

Attachment, Detachment, and Nonattachment

Nonattachment is an important aspect of Buddhist teachings, and it relates closely to our tendency to fight about beliefs. A number of years ago I was present at a dharma talk given by the Buddhist monk Ajahn Amaro in Eugene, Oregon. He used the metaphor of holding a pencil in his hand to clarify an important aspect of what it means to have an appropriate relationship with beliefs and other mental content. He said that *attachment* to a belief, or an attachment to anything, was like holding the pencil fiercely clenched in one's hand. The person doing this almost has an attitude of "The only way you will get this pencil out of my hand is by prying it out of my dead fingers." In this state of attachment, I am gripping the pencil so tightly that I cannot write with it legibly, and break the pencil lead when I try to do so.

Another way of relating to pencils and beliefs could be called *detachment*. When I am detached, I simply *do not care* about the pencil at all and let it fall to the floor, or even throw it away. In this state of indifference, I cannot write anything—I have no pencil—and I am indifferent to all beliefs in regard to some particular issue. Neither attachment nor detachment are healthy states.

Nonattachment could be called *holding lightly*. When I hold the pencil lightly in my hand, I can make skillful use of it when it is needed and easily release it onto the desk when no longer needed. The same holds true for beliefs. When there is nonattachment to a belief, a belief is held lightly in mind, made use of when appropriate without getting tied up in knots about it, and easily released if it turns out to not be true or useful.

Our relationship with disagreement can be quite comfortable and unproblematic.

> [Thich Nhat Hanh states clearly that] No blame, no reasoning, no argument, just understanding. If you understand, and you show that you understand, you can love, and the situation will change. (5)

> [Jack Kornfield tells of a time he] ...asked a delightful old Sri Lankan meditation master to teach me the essence of Buddhism. He just laughed and said three times, "No self, no problem. (6)

Notes for Chapter 15

1. Tolle, Eckhart *The Power of Now*, Novato: New World Library, 1999, p.36.

2. Nhat Hanh, Thich, *The Heart of the Buddha's Teaching*, New York: Broadway Books, 1998, p. 12.

3. Hocker, Joyce, and William Wilmot, *Interpersonal Conflict,* 2nd Edition, Dubuque: William C. Brown. Publishers, 1985, pp. 102-3. Hocker and Wilmot are reporting on the work of Roger Fisher and William Ury (*Getting to Yes,* by Fisher and Ury, Boston: Houghton Mifflin, 1981).

4. Poliner, Rachel A., and Jeffrey Benson, *Dialogue: Turning Controversy Into Community,* Cambridge, MA: Educators for Social Responsibility, 1997. The explanation of dialogue presented in this chapter is an elaboration on the work of Poliner and Benson.

5. Nhat Hahn, Thich, *Peace is Every Step*, New York: Bantam, 1991, pp. 78-79

6. Jack Kornfield, *A Path With Heart*, New York: Bantam, 1993, p. 203

PART THREE

Going Deeper

CHAPTER 16

The Story of "Me"

Our False Idea of Who We Are

The Buddha taught that there is no self, and this has often been referred to as "the jewel of the Buddha's teaching." It is a teaching that is difficult to understand, and one that has frequently been misunderstood. To say that there is no self does not mean that we do not exist. It means that we have an incorrect understanding—a false idea—of who we are. This false idea of self is the cause of much suffering. However, as we shall see, the Buddha offered a radically different and very liberating understanding of the true nature of self.

Buddhist teachings on the nature of self are subtle, difficult, and quite alien to our normal way of seeing things. In order to come to terms with it, it will be necessary to unfold what the Buddha taught in stages. First, it is very useful to *uproot our existing false ideas* about who we are. Second, we need to understand the Buddha's teaching that *there is no permanent self*. And third, we need to achieve an understanding of the Buddha's teaching that *there is no separate self*. The first two of these ideas are moderately difficult to grasp for most people. The third idea is not at all easily understood, and typically requires a long period of study and meditation—often years—to fully grasp.

Seeing the Error in Our Prevalent Western View of Self

If we were to ask someone the question "Who are you?" there would typically be no difficulty in providing an answer—most of us believe we know who we are. Usually the first answer a person gives is their **name**. This seems natural enough. But, when we reflect on it, our name is only sounds in the air, or marks on a piece of paper or computer screen. It's just a marker tag that has been placed on us by our parents and society. People can and do change their names. Surely this cannot be who we are as a person.

One of the most central components of who we typically think we are is the **physical body.** There are several reasons that this is incorrect. When we talk about the body and make an identity out of it, what we are really doing is making an *idea* of the body into a personal identity or definition of self. We often say things like "I am short, fat, beautiful, bowlegged…. *That's who I am.*" However, we usually don't notice that when we do this we *pick* certain physical characteristics to identify with and completely ignore others. So someone might *choose* to identify with their "fat" legs, but *not* with their blue eyes or slender wrists. Consequently, what we call "our body" is very often simply a mentally constructed entity.

Additionally, the body is constantly changing: cells are dying and being replaced, aging is happening. My body now is not the body I had when I was ten years old. The body is constantly exchanging material with the outside world. I have molecules of oxygen in my blood and tissues that used to be part of the atmosphere and even part of trees and animals. The same is true of water. There is no clear boundary between "my body" and everything else. I have bacteria in my digestive tract that are absolutely *essential* for digesting food—are the bacteria part of me or are they separate beings?

People also have an extremely strong habit of taking their **mind** to be who they are. Let's begin with the thinking mind, "the little voice in the head." Could this really be who I am? When I'm not thinking does that mean I don't exist? The little voice is not always there—but I still exist during those periods when it is absent. This stream of words comes and goes and is constantly changing in its content and coherence. Isn't the little voice in my head now very different from the voice that was there when I was younger?

The *contents* of mind are also quite temporary and constantly changing: thoughts, beliefs, attitudes, and sense perceptions all come and go. Much of the time our thoughts are more like random statements from a radio—and someone seems to keep changing the station every few seconds. Thoughts just seem to arise on their own without our choosing them to be there.

We often think that the **experiences** we have had are a big part of who we are. But our experiences are gone. They exist now only as memories—thoughts and images in the mind that come and go—and perhaps in some fading photographs and souvenirs.

E**motions**—could that be part of who we are? As we saw in Chapter 7, emotions are constantly arising and leaving and being replaced with new feelings—essentially the same process that occurs with thoughts. These *temporary visitors* are important but the Buddha taught that they are not who we are, either.

Yet another common answer to "Who am I?" is our **occupation**. We often say "I'm a lawyer" or "I'm a teacher" or "I'm a truck driver" or "I'm a writer." But in truth, these are just *activities* that we engage in only for a certain numbers of hours each day. People have many jobs during their lifetimes. If I am writing a book, it seems more accurate to say that "I am writing something now" or "I spend a good deal of time writing" rather than making this into a definition of self and saying "I *am* a writer." I could just as easily—and just as mistakenly— define myself by saying "I am a thrower of tennis balls for dogs," since this is also an activity I engage in from time to time.

Is it possible that I am my **relationships?** This is another collection of activities and social roles that I take on. These roles come and go. We tend to say "I am a mother" instead of "I am doing some mothering now." My mother used to say to me "I will always be your mother." While it will always be true that she gave birth to me at some point in her life, whether she tends to relate to me in the role of mother is a choice on her part.

Could I be **my personality traits?** We tend to try to make a solid identity out of our behaviors or feelings. We say, "I'm shy, I'm an introvert, I'm not someone who gives public speeches." But the truth is these things also come and go. Sometimes "Shyness is visiting" and I don't want to speak in front of people. Other times it is gone and I speak publicly. If I fall down, I can create a personal identity by saying "I am clumsy." Alternatively, I can recognize that tripping and falling is only a single piece of behavior and say with more accuracy "Well, that was pretty clumsy." There is no need to make an identity out of it.

Talents and abilities? These also come and go. Some days I can play a particular piece of music on the guitar, other days I cannot. Some days I have a talent for writing or teaching, other days I don't do it very well at all. The abilities I have now are not what I had a few years ago and will be different a few years from now.

Am I **my accomplishments**—my *resume*? Are degrees hanging on a wall who I am? Accomplishments are *past events* that *do not exist anymore*. They exist only as thoughts, memories, marks on paper, or souvenirs—but that does not sound like a *person.* It is not who I am. The same can be said of people who make an identity out of what they see as their *failures.*

Some people have a strong tendency to make an identity out of nationality, race, or ethnicity. Let's consider **nationality** first. If I move to another country and gain citizenship, my nationality has changed, but it is only the result of having the right paperwork on file in the right places. Surely, changing my paperwork does not change who I am, though it does change my legal status. For most people, nationality is determined by birth place. Does the location of an event that happened one day years ago—my birth—realistically determine anything about who I am as a person?

And what of my race or ethnicity? According to philosophers and anthropologists, **race** is simply a way of dividing humans into subgroups—black, white, Asian, and so on—based on some physical characteristics that have some basis in heredity. If we look at a college classroom with thirty students in it, it is possible to divide them into five racial groups based on how light or dark their skin is. So we could say we have five races based on skin pigmentation. But we could also divide those thirty students into five subgroups based on height. This would result in a reshuffling of the groups. Someone who used to be part of my racial group based on having a skin color similar to mine is no longer a member of my racial subgroup when we categorize on the basis of height. The whole idea of race and races is really a set of categories or mental constructs that exist only in our minds.

The same analysis applies with equal force to **ethnicity**. "Italian," for example, is a concept used to form a mental category of people having some arbitrary characteristic in common—it could be having an Italian name, or it could be having ancestors who lived in Italy, or it could be participating in certain customs and traditions. The choice of what is necessary to be part of the Italian group is arbitrary and subject to disagreement. Some people with Italian names think of themselves as Italians—and some do not.

In summary, we can say that people often do, in fact, make personal identifies out of various combinations of the above elements. However, while this may be true, it is important to remember two crucial insights: 1) the identity that they have made is a *mental construct or story* and 2) whether they do this or not is a *choice*.

There Is No Permanent or Fixed Self

The Buddha taught that there is no fixed, permanent self. There is only a sequence of various and ever-changing "me patterns." Over the course of my lifetime, many Dale patterns have come into existence and passed away. We are afraid that when we die, the self will be obliterated. But what we mistakenly call the self is simply a temporary pattern of characteristics. Consequently, what you think of as your self has *already died* many times. The pattern that we called "Dale at five years old" does not exist anymore—it "died" a long time ago. The pattern that we called "Dale at age twenty" has also passed away. But there is no problem in any of this. These "deaths" are just the replacement of an earlier pattern with a later pattern.

The teaching that there is no permanent self can be seen as either frightening or freeing. It can be frightening because if I am not my job, not my beliefs, not my body... then who am I? I don't know who I am anymore! We've been taught in various ways that we *should* be able to say who we are. But why can't the answer be "I am nothing in particular?" Perhaps we can have a *flexible* identity. When I was first learning about no self, someone more knowledgeable than myself once asked me "Why do you *need* a personal identity or definition of self? What's it *for*?" These questions just totally stumped me when I heard them. I simply had no answer. However, after spending a good deal of time with the questions, I became comfortable with not being able to say who I was. I realized I didn't *need* a self image for *anything*. What I felt at this point was not fear, but an emerging sense of *lightness and freedom*.

If we begin to see our own mental process by which the impression of a fixed self is created, it will help loosen the grip that this false idea seems to have on us. In a 1988 dharma talk Joseph Goldstein touched briefly on a useful metaphor using The Big Dipper to explain how our false idea of self arises. (1) In my own teaching I have elaborated on this metaphor and combined it with a second metaphor about writing a fictional story.

If we go outside on a clear night and look up, we will see thousands and thousands of points of light in the sky which we call stars. Almost all westerners will also see a constellation of stars we call The Big Dipper. We have seen it many times and can spot it easily. But *does the Big Dipper really exist?* No, it does not. When people in China look at the same area of the sky, they see a different pattern which they call The Plow. With a little creativity, we could add a few more points of light to The Big Dipper so that it has a hook on the end of the handle so it can be hung on a wall peg! Are there five stars included in the object or seven or nine? Who decides whether it has a plain handle or one with a hook or whether it is really a dipper rather than a plow? *We do*, because the patterns we see are creations of our own minds. We *learn* to see the points of light in the sky in a certain way. The same is true of our idea of self or "me."

There is a *specific thought process* at work in the mind's creation of The Big Dipper. First, out of the millions of points of light we see, we *select a certain few of them* to see in separation from the rest. Second, we *mentally connect* these points of light to *create a pattern*— we "connect the dots" so to speak. And third, we *place a name on it* and call it The Big Dipper, and presto, the Big Dipper exists. However, the *only* place that it actually exists is *in our minds* .

If we observe closely, we will notice the exact same process in regard to the creation of a fixed self or "me." Out of all the literally billions of things that I have done, said, felt, accomplished, or experienced, I select a relatively small number of them to include in my concept of "Dale," the story of *me*. The mind then creates a sort of fixed pattern or image of who I am from these selected elements, and then the label "Dale" is attached to this picture and I say this is who I am. When we reflect on it, clearly this picture of who I am is literally a work of fiction—one, in fact, that is constantly being *revised*. In the same way that the author of a short story or a novel decides what characters, actions, and events to include in the story, I decide what elements of my experience to include in my fictional story of Dale. I may include graduation from college, but not getting fired from a job when I was twenty. I may include authoring articles, but not throwing sticks for dogs to chase. But all this, no matter how elaborate or dramatic, exists only in my mind. Yes, the events may have actually happened, but the Dale identity—the story of Dale, the definition of "me"—exists only in my mind as a work of fiction.

Other people, of course, will likely select other elements from my life and stick them together to form a *different* idea of who Dale is, and so yet another work of fiction is born. Various people create different ideas of who I am, and the very same person may see me differently at different times. In each case, someone is selecting a relatively small number of things I have done or said and sticking them together to form their own portrait of Dale.

Another useful metaphor for understanding Buddhist teachings on no self might be the moving image on a television screen. When looked at from close up, the image is essentially a "constellation" of dots, and the dots are changing from second to second. We organize a section of these dots into an image or a concept which we call "President Obama" or "President Bush." What we see has no solidity or permanence to it, the dots are constantly changing and forming new patterns.

It is also important to notice that the dots that make up "President Obama" are no different than the dots that make up "President Bush." "Bush" is simply a different temporary dot pattern than "Obama." In a similar manner, a person is made up of "dots" of thoughts, feelings, memories, actions, and body elements that come and go.

Clouds are another metaphor for understanding the idea of no permanent self. If we watch a cloud in the sky, we notice that it is continuously changing shape, color, pattern, texture. Sometimes the cloud looks like a flower, a little later it may look more like a face. What we call the self is also constantly changing, sometimes looking like one thing, sometimes looking like another. If we take a still photo of the cloud, we take an ongoing *process* and make it into something *fixed*. But in doing this, what we have created—the photo—is no longer anything like the real cloud; it is only how the cloud *appeared* for one very brief *instant* in time. Trying to make something permanent and fixed out of our ever-changing pattern of personal characteristics is exactly like this. Our fixed idea of self is nothing like the reality of who we are.

It is important to remember that the teachings on no self are a *practice* and not a theory. The *practice* of no self is the practice of *seeing* the absence of a permanent self in each moment of experience.

The Teachings on No Self Are Liberating

Rather than being frightening, recognizing the reality of the absence of a permanent self can be very liberating. This occurs in at least five ways.

First, because there is no permanent self, we don't have to defend or live up to some image of ourselves, or try to maintain a consistency of self over time. If I think I am "an intelligent person," then when I do something stupid, I will likely think I need to explain it away: "Well, what I did may have looked stupid but actually it was part of my intricate plan to..." Instead of defending my idea of myself as "an intelligent person," I can simply smile and say "That certainly was a dumb thing to do." Done, finished, no problem! Life just became so much easier and simpler. Endless justifying, defending, and explaining drops away. Rather than try to explain away my lack of consistency in my thoughts, I can say "Well, I did think that way before, but that is not what I think today."

Second, this way of understanding self opens up more *choices* for us. I don't have to be limited by some fixed picture of who I am: "I am an introvert, so I don't go to big parties or give public speeches." Rather than letting my mental definition of self make the decision, I can actually check in and *see how I feel in this moment*: "Being with other people and having fun sounds good right now; let's go to the party!" Our images of self frequently box us in: "I'm the kind of person who..." "Men do such and such," "Women do this or that," "I'm young, old, a mom, a dad, a student so of course I..."   If I recognize that I am not any "kind of a person" at all, the world has more choices in it for me.

Third, recognizing the absence of a permanent self helps us to understand that *we are not separate from other people*. The characteristics that flow through me are the same characteristics that flow through you— though perhaps part of a different overall pattern. The anger that was present in me yesterday is present in you today. We all experience the same kinds of feelings, thoughts, attitudes, concerns, impulses. The same "dots" flow through each of us at various times. When we grasp this, our sense of separation from other people can begin to drop away and be replaced by a sense of shared experience.

At the physical level, biologist David Suzuki has pointed out that if we have been in the same room for a half hour, my body has molecules in it that were once a part of you, and your body has molecules that were once part of me. We have molecules that were once a part of frogs, and trees, and Gandhi and Socrates. (2)

Fourth, understanding the nature of self from a Buddhist perspective can help us to relate to other people more fully. Instead of trying to present to others some image that we have of ourselves, we can share with others what is real for us in each moment—what we really think, what we really feel, what we really want. Oftentimes when two people are out on a first date having dinner in a restaurant, each is trying to present an image of who they think they are (or *want* to be or *should* be). At the end of the evening, they each know a lot about the other person's image of self, but virtually nothing about the real person sitting across from them. Their attachment to their self images prevents them from really getting to know each other and connecting on a deeper level.

This benefit of the no self view can play out in many ways. Suppose my friend Steve has promised to meet me at noon to help with a public event and doesn't show up. I might make this *single piece of behavior* into an identity: "Steve is an unreliable person." But there is much more to Steve than his failure to show up on one particular occasion. If I don't make a single act into who he is as a person, it is easier to choose to forgive him and start over fresh. The tendency to make one or a few acts into an identity is a strong one. An acquaintance in high school stole a car at age sixteen and was convicted of a felony. In the minds of many, *Dave is a felon.* Should we define Dave as *a felon* for the rest of his life because of a single act of a sixteen year old, or can we choose not to create such a limiting permanent identity and remain open and see Dave as more than just one action?

Fifth, coming from a place of no self, it is easier to change our beliefs, behavior, responses, and personality because we no longer think that these things are who we are; they are no longer part of a fixed definition of "me." If I think that my beliefs are who I am, I may feel the need to cling to them fiercely when they are challenged. If beliefs are just impersonal descriptions of some particular aspect of the world, I can let them go when I discover that they are inaccurate. If my behavior is who I am, the idea of changing may seem daunting. If my behavior is just what I did, I can more easily change how I behave in the new situation that is in front of me right now.

The following practice can help to make real for us how the teachings on no self can alter our experience of life. Each of us can ask ourselves: "What are some of the definitions or images of myself I carry around with me? What would it be like to *not* have the *concept* of myself as a failure, or an intelligent person, or a victim, or a funny person or any other self definition I might have?" In asking this last question we are *not* asking, for example, "What would it be like to not *have* intelligence." The question here is "What would it be like not to *think of myself or define myself* as an intelligent person?" If I think *am* an intelligent *person*, then perhaps I think I have to be, or appear to be, intelligent all of the time. This can be a burden, preventing me from asking questions that may seem ignorant or simple, or saying that I don't know and asking for help.

There Is No *Separate* Self

As stated previously, there are several levels of understanding in regard to the teachings on no self. So far we have been looking at the idea that there is no fixed or permanent self. For most people, this is moderately difficult to understand. Sometimes people mistakenly believe that this is the totality of what the Buddha taught about no self: "Everything about myself is constantly changing and impermanent, *but I still exist as a separate, individual, and distinct self.*" The last part of this is incorrect, because the *impermanence* of self is only the first level of the no-self teachings, though just understanding this first layer can be enormously liberating. The second level of understanding the no self teachings is that, in addition to the fact that there is no permanent self, there is also no *separate* self. As we shall also see, these teachings on no self apply not only to humans but to absolutely *everything that exists*: other living beings, pieces of paper, rivers, stars in the sky... *everything*.

The teaching that there is no separate self is very much more difficult to understand than what we have looked at thus far. In fact, when I first encountered the idea that there is not a separate self, it seemed to make no sense at all to me. Most people will need to commit themselves to working with these teachings over an extended period of time to really understand them. This work involves study of the teachings themselves, reflection, meditation, and the use of various practices. Though not an easy piece of learning to master, the results of doing so transform one's life at the very deepest level. What follows in the rest of this book is intended to serve as a good beginning toward a true understanding.

The Buddha taught that individual, separate things do not really exist: the only thing that is real at the most fundamental level is the seamless *oneness* which is reality. This is a difficult teaching. Let's begin by considering a simple example. If we were to go to a library we would be likely to find a globe—a sort of miniature model of the Earth showing continents, oceans, major rivers, and various nations. We would also find that there were lines of longitude and latitude on the globe: the lines of longitude running north and south and passing through the two poles, and lines of latitude running east and west and parallel to the equator. These two sets of lines divide up the surface of the globe into a number squares, and the lines are quite useful for the purposes of navigation.

According to maps, the 44th parallel of latitude runs right through Lane County, Oregon, which is where I live. But if we got in a vehicle and searched for it, we could not find it anywhere. The lines of latitude and longitude do not really exist anywhere except in the minds of people who have been taught about them. They are mental constructs, *ideas* we have created in our minds and they give the *appearance* that the Earth is composed of numerous squares.

In the same way that our mind-created lines of longitude and latitude *appear* to divide the oneness of our planet into individual separate squares of land or water, the human mind draws mental boundaries in the oneness of reality to create the appearance of separate individual things. The mind uses language *to segment* reality: the words we use segment what is a oneness into the appearance of many separate objects. But we forget that the boundary lines between separate things are merely the creations of our minds.

The Segmenting Function of Concepts and Words

In our Western way of thinking we believe that "separate things already exist, and then we give them names afterward so we can talk about them." Our Western thinking is exemplified in the following passage from the *Bible*.

> And out of the ground the Lord God formed
> [brought into existence] every beast of the field
> and every fowl of the air; and brought them
> unto Adam to see what he would call them:

and whatsoever Adam called every living
creature, that was the name thereof. (3)

However, in Buddhism (and Taoism as well), our Western way of seeing things is fundamentally *backwards*. The reality is that "Individual separate things do not appear *until we create them in our minds and then give them names*." As part of naming, we create mental boundary lines (like the lines of latitude and longitude) that define where a particular "thing" begins and ends in space, and often when it begins and ends in time as well. At first hearing, this is likely to seem incomprehensible to our Western minds. Let's investigate.

If there is a body of flowing water in front of us, it is a matter of *social convention* whether we call it "river" or "rio" (the Spanish word). It is a matter of social convention because if we live in an English speaking country we have *agreed* to call the things like what we have in front of us by the word "river." Social conventions are a matter of social *agreement*.

In Britain, people have agreed to drive on the left side of the road. In the United States, people have agreed to drive on the right side of the road. There is no objectively correct side of the road to drive on, though it is useful to have everyone agree to do it the same way. In cases such as this, it is easy to see the element of social convention. Though at first this is harder to see in regard to the mind's creation of separate things, the operation of convention works in exactly the same way.

But what we typically *do not see* here is that there are actually *two layers* of social convention present: 1) It is a matter of social convention whether we *call* a particular thing "rio" or "river," and 2) It is *also* a matter of social convention as to what *counts* as a particular *thing*. When we *decide* what counts as a particular *thing*, we *decide* where this particular thing begins and ends in space and in time. Does the "thing" we call "river" include only the water, or does it also include the bank containing the water? Is the valley surrounding both the water and the bank also included? And what about the trash on the bottom underneath the water, the mist in the air above the water, or the sounds the flowing water makes? Should the entire land area that makes up the watershed of the river be seen as part of this thing we call "river?" It is up to us to *decide* where this thing we label "river" begins and ends. Our human minds are what draw mental boundaries in what is in front of us, thereby *segmenting* reality into the *appearance* of separate things. But these boundaries, like the lines of longitude and latitude, exist only in our minds.

What counts as a "thing" is essentially a matter of social convention, and what label we stick on that thing is also a matter of social convention. The thing we label "river" is a mental construct because we decide where its boundaries are—where it begins and where it ends in *space*.

When the thing that we label "river" begins and ends in *time* is also a matter of social convention. Does the river begin when it has a certain amount of water flowing in it, or does it begin earlier: when it was a thin trickle of water, or when a crease first formed in the ground, or when the earth's crust first was uplifted to form a slope, or...? *What we see as a distinct thing such as the Colorado River, does not really exist except as a matter of social convention*.

It is the segmenting function of the mind, using words, that populates our world with the trillions of things that seem to reside in it. A person raised in a different culture would not see the same "things" we do when we look at a landscape because the mental boundaries they have learned are different from ours.

What is this *thing* we call a tree? Is the shadow on the ground part of the tree or part of the ground or a separate thing? Is the dirt that the roots are in part of the tree? What about the dust on the leaves? The sound of the wind in the tree? The rain drops rolling down the leaves or the moss growing on the bark?

244

What about the physical parts of a human being? That *thing* we call the neck—is it part of the head, part of the chest, or a separate thing? What we call the ankle—is it part of the foot, leg, or a separate body part? Cells in the human body never used to exist as separate things before the microscope and the decision to see them a certain way. Is blood *one* thing ("a pint of blood") or is it *many* things(a great many red and white blood cells floating in plasma)? We must also consider the fact that *ninety percent of all the cells in our bodies are not human cells—they are bacteria, viruses, and fungi.* And yet without these nonhuman cells, we literally cannot survive. Are these cells "me" or are they separate beings? Here is how Barbara Natterson-Horowitz, M.D., describes our situation.

> Deep inside every animal colon, ours included, thrives an entire cosmos of creatures... There are whip-tailed bacteria and tripod-legged viruses, frilled fungi and microscopic worms. Trillions of these invisible creatures make our intestines their home... Our skin, mouths, teeth (and even areas once thought to be sterile, like the lungs) so swarm with invisible creatures that *as few as one out of every ten cells in our bodies may actually be human.* The rest are much smaller microbes... Each of us is like a coral reef, an individual microhabitat harboring unique combinations of unseen wild inhabitants.
>
> In general, we should be grateful that these trillions of minuscule bugs and plants want to live in our guts [and elsewhere in our bodies]. Many of them break down our food and prepare nutrients for our cells to absorb— processes human cells cannot do on their own."
> (4)

We take it that things like individual and separate trees, rivers, clouds, rocks, and living beings really exist in the world. However, until the mind came along and used concepts and words to segment reality into the appearance of parts, they did not exist. Suppose I create a new word, "foop." A foop is a roundish rock somewhat larger than a basketball with a bird standing on top of it. When this word comes into common usage, all of a sudden we start seeing foops. When we are asked whether foops exist, we say "Of course—I've seen them; we all have." But before the word "foop" was invented, foops did not really exist. And they don't really exist in the world now. We have simply created the *appearance* of "foops" as a result of our minds having segmented out a piece of reality and labeled it "foop."

In the same way our minds can carve out an area of land and call it "Indiana" or the "Mojave Desert." For that matter, we are carving something out of reality when we call it "an area" or "land," or "water." These things no more exist as separate things than the squares of "land" marked off by the lines of longitude and latitude exist anywhere else other than as part of our mind-constructed maps. That portion of the oneness that is inside the mind-constructed boundary is real, but the *boundary* exists only in our minds.

Waves in the ocean provide a useful metaphor for understanding the illusion of separate existence. If the waves see themselves as separate entities, they may appear to be in conflict with each other, jostling with each other for dominance or space. But in reality, how can they struggle against each other when they are all just the one ocean of water? The construct of *separation* is an illusion and it is the source of all conflict. So an additional benefit of the no self teachings is that when we see the oneness which we truly are, there is no longer any point or desire to try to compete, dominate, or try to exploit others because what we call *others* is really *us*.

I once saw a spiritual teacher accept as a gift a picture of one of her students. She said, "Thank you for giving me another picture of myself." I found this puzzling at the time, but no longer find it so. If we showed a picture of wave A to wave B, wave B would recognize it as a picture of itself. This is because it is a picture of the *same water* of which all waves are composed. All pictures of waves are pictures of the ocean. It is only our conventional way of viewing things that causes us to see a multiplicity of separate waves instead of one ocean of water. We use our categories to carve out trillions of "things," from what is ultimately a whole, a oneness. We also create the concepts past and future as additional ways of segmenting reality—beginning, ending, before, after—when in fact there is only one "thing," *the oneness*, and only one "time," which is *now*.

Another useful approach is to reflect on how our left and right hands relate to each other. I like to build things and I am right handed. This means the left hand is the "holder" hand, the one that *holds* the nail, or holds the wood being belt sanded, or holds the piece being sawed, and so on. As a result, the left hand has been hammered, sanded, pinched, sliced, sawed, and burned many times over the years —and all as a result of actions on the part of the right hand. The left hand could feel abused and mistreated and seek revenge against the right hand saying to itself: "I'll get even and really hammer the right hand hard while it is asleep tonight!" But of course this doesn't happen because there is the realization that the left hand and the right hand are *one body*. In hurting the right hand, the left hand would only be hurting itself. So when the right hand accidentally hurts the left hand with the hammer, it naturally and spontaneously wants to care for the left hand. (5)

Alan Watts has put this idea of nonseparation quite beautifully.

> Especially as one grows older, it becomes ever
> more obvious that things are without
> substance, for time seems to go by more rapidly
> so that one becomes aware of the liquidity of
> solids; people and things become like lights and

ripples on the surface of water. We can make
fast-motion films of the growth of plants and
flowers in which they seem to come and go like
gestures of the earth. If we could film
civilizations and cities, mountains and stars, in
the same way, we would see them as frost
crystals forming and dissolving and as sparks on
the back of a fireplace. The faster the tempo,
the more it would appear that we were
watching, not so much a succession of
[individual and separate] things, [but] as the
movement and transformations of one thing—
as ...the apprehension of *one thing doing
everything.*" (6)

The totality of what exists—the oneness—can be appropriately
seen as *one life form.* Our temptation might then be to say "and we are
a *part of* that one life that exists." But strictly speaking, this would not
be accurate. We are not *part* of the oneness, because the oneness *has*
no parts. We *are* the oneness. This is true at the absolute or ultimate
level. At the relative level or the level of social convention, we are
separate individuals and parts of the universe. The individual wave
exists at the level of convention, but in the absolute sense it is simply
water.

Nirvana

[Nirvana is] ...the complete silencing of
concepts... the extinction of all notions. (7)

In Buddhism, nirvana does not refer to a place you can go to,
such as heaven. Nirvana means the extinction of all concepts, seeing
the world as it really is, which is devoid of all mind created boundaries.
So nirvana refers to two things. First, it refers to the *ultimate nature of
reality*, which is devoid of segmenting mental boundaries. Second,

nirvana refers to the *state of consciousness* in which reality is *seen* unsegmented by words and the mind-created boundaries that come with the words. No separation exists in reality, and no separation exists in the mind. What it is like to apprehend reality in this way cannot be described in words, since to do so would be an attempt to describe uncategorized reality using mental categories—an obvious impossibility. Words are useful here only as pointers. They can point and direct our attention to ultimate reality but they cannot describe it. The Buddha taught that the words used in connection with ultimate reality, are only like the finger that points at the moon—the finger is *not* the moon, and the finger is not a *description* of the moon, either. We can only know nonseparation through *direct experience*, not through verbal description. Verbal description, by its very segmenting nature, creates separation.

Sometimes our typical state of seeing things as separate is referred to as a dream in Buddhist teaching. This simply means that what we take to be the real world of Dale, Fido, tree, computer, this piece of paper, and so on is constructed by the mind, in the same way that everything we see in a dream is produced by the mind. At some point, we can awaken from this mind-created dream of separation and see things as they truly are.

Closely related to this is the Buddhist idea of emptiness. As a teaching device, Thich Nhat Hanh likes to hold up a sheet of paper and ask "Can you see the cloud in this sheet of paper?" The cloud is there.

> Without a cloud there will be no water; without
> water, the trees cannot grow; and without
> trees, you cannot make paper. ...Sunshine is
> very important because the forest cannot grow
> without sunshine... everything is here [in the
> paper]: the wheat that became the bread for
> the logger to eat, the logger's father—
> everything is in this sheet of paper. (8)

If we remove all the nonpaper elements from the paper there is nothing left. So the paper is said to be *empty*, which means that it is empty of a separate self. And of course, in another sense, the paper is full—full of the entire cosmos. So when viewed carefully, we see that every single thing is empty, including humans. The person we call "Dale" is composed entirely of nonDale elements.

It is not the fault of our words and concepts that we fail to see nonseparation. Concepts are, of course, very useful for finding our way around (navigation) and communication and figuring things out. We just need to remember that they are only mental constructs and social conventions. They are not reality. Maps and lines of longitude and latitude are useful, too, but we need to never forget they are only mind-creations and that they are not reality.

Some Practices for A Deepening Understanding of Emptiness

What could be called a Looking Inward Meditation on the self is a very useful practice. This consists of looking inward to actually *see* if there is a self, a "me." Begin the meditation the same way you would start a basic breathing meditation (see Chapter 4). Close your eyes, and just be aware of the physical sensations of breathing. After several minutes, expand your awareness to include anything that is arising in the present moment: thoughts, feelings, body sensations, sounds. Just observe what is there. What do you find? What is actually present in any given moment? When I do this I typically find things like itching sensations, pulsing, vibration, thoughts arising and passing away, sounds arising, patterns of moving colors. The intention here is to just be an *observer* of whatever is arising. Spend five or ten minutes just watching the "display." Ask yourself every thirty seconds to a minute: Is there anything in all these comings and goings that I am aware of that could be called "me?" Is there some kind of a "me" that *has* these experiences, or is there only the succession of one experience arising and falling away to be replaced by some other temporary content of consciousness?

We often say that a thought is "in here" but the sound of a bell is "out there." However, when we sit and pay attention, we see that both events are just things arising in the same field of awareness. It is very much like clouds moving through the sky. The open empty space of the sky is our awareness, and the clouds arising in the emptiness of the sky of awareness are sense perceptions, thoughts, bodily sensations, feelings, and all the other elements of our experience.

When we pay close attention to what is actually present in any moment, what we find is a succession of experiences arising and then passing away to be replaced by other experiences. There are *experiences*, but we are unable to find a *me* who is *having* these various experiences. At this radical level of investigating our experience, who we are simply seems to be a consciousness, that is to say an *empty space* in which various experiences arise.

For many people, the physical body is one of the most difficult things to understand as nonseparate and not who they are. However, when we pay close attention, our sense of the solidity of the body begins to disappear. Joseph Goldstein suggests an experiment which can be tried right now.

> ...press the palms of your hands together lightly,
> close your eyes, and notice what you are
> feeling. What sensations do you experience? In
> the sensations of pressure, warmth, tingling,
> and so on, what has happened to the notion of
> "hand?" (9).

There is no hand. When do we ever have an experience of anything that could be called *hand*? Hand is a mental construct. There is just a collection of sensations of pressure, warmth, and so on.

In just the same way, our notion of "body" is a *mental concept* that designates what is really just a collection of arising and vanishing perceptions. Seeing through the concept to the *direct experience* of what is happening helps free us from clinging to the body as who we are and as some kind of solid entity.

Also useful is Thich Nhat Hanh's suggestion to practice looking for interbeing. Interbeing refers to the teaching that nothing exists as a separate entity. Everything we see inter-exists with everything else and *depends* on everything else for its existence. When I tried the practice of looking for interbeing, I started with air. There is air all around, what we call the atmosphere, but that air is not separate from what I call me. I am constantly breathing it in and breathing it out, it dissolves in my blood and is carried to cells where it is used to burn glucose for energy. That air is totally part of, and inseparable from, "me." The air and "me" are *one*. And that same air is in all other living things. The same is true of water. There is water outside and inside "me" and it is constantly being circulated back and forth between "me" and "non-me." The water IS "me."

Notes for Chapter 16

1. Goldstein, Joseph, "Concepts and Reality," dharma talk recorded April 12, 1988 at Yucca Valley Retreat Center, video produced by InVision Productions, Corte Madera, California.

2. Suzuki, David, "An Environment In Crisis: What Our World Faces," video of a talk recorded May 13, 1989 in Los Angeles as part of Our Common Future: Healing the Planet Symposium. Video produced by The Healing of the Planet Symposium Committee, 1989.

3. *Bible, King James Version*, Genesis 2:19.

4. Natterson-Horowitz, Barbara, M.D., *Zoobiquity: What Animals Can Teach Us About Health and the Science of Healing*, New York: Alfred A. Knopf Publishing, 2012, pp. 148-149. Emphasis added.

5. This idea is adapted from Nhat Hanh, Thich, "There Is No Path to Peace; The Path Is Peace," *Shambhala Sun*, Vol. 12, Number 6, July 2004, pp. 43-68)

6. Watts, Alan, *Tao: The Watercourse Way*, New York: Pantheon Books, 1975, p. 94.

7. Nhat Hanh, Thich, *The Heart of the Buddha's Teaching*, New York: Broadway Books, 1999, pp. 136-137.

8. Nhat Hanh, Thich, *Being Peace*, Berkeley: Parallax Press, 1987, pp. 45-47.

9. Goldstein, Joseph, *One Dharma: The Emerging Western Buddhism*, San Francisco: HarperSanFrancisco, 2002, p. 140.

CHAPTER 17

A Different Understanding of Death

Before beginning an examination of Buddhist teachings on death, it is important to offer a cautionary note to readers. Sometimes people have a tendency to skip earlier chapters in a book and read a chapter from toward the end that they may have a particular interest in. In regard to understanding the Buddha's teachings on death, this is not a good idea. The earlier chapters provide an important foundation for understanding this subject. At the very least, the material in Chapters 2, 3, 4, 14, and 15 is needed as a good groundwork on which to build.

Like the previous chapter's discussion of the teachings on no separate self, most people find the Buddhist teachings on death quite difficult to understand, and it is best to be patient with ourselves and not to expect to understand everything right away. The process of achieving a real understanding can take many months or years.

The Buddha himself realized the difficulty of understanding the teachings in this area. After hearing the Buddha speak about no self and the nature of death, a wandering seeker named Vaccha said to the Buddha:

> " I am at a loss and bewildered." [The Buddha
> responded by saying] "You ought to be at a loss
> and bewildered, Vaccha. For this doctrine is
> profound, recondite, hard to comprehend, rare,
> excellent, beyond dialectic, subtle, only to be
> understood by the wise." (1)

The Buddha also said that the deepest truths cannot be captured in words. The words are like the finger that points at the moon. Words only point to something that we can and must see for ourselves through direct experience. The words themselves do not *contain* the truth, they only direct our attention so we can *experience* the truth directly. The various metaphors and verbal explanations that are used are like ladders that can be used to climb a tree or a wall; once we have a clear view of the landscape we are then able to see the real truth of our situation. There are many different metaphors and explanations in what follows because some metaphors will be helpful for some people but not for others. In offering several types of explanation, the hope is that one of them will snap the picture into focus for any given reader.

Once again, the words of Thich Nhat Hanh are useful.

> ...the concepts that we have do not reflect and cannot convey reality. ...According to Buddhism, we only reach reality through direct experience. Study and explanation are based on concepts. In conceptualizing we cut reality into small pieces that seem to be independent of one another. ...the faculty that directly experiences reality without passing through concepts is called nondiscriminative ...wisdom. This wisdom is the fruit of meditation. It is a direct and perfect knowledge of reality... It cannot be conceived by the intellect nor expressed by language." (2)

In what follows, the goal is to provide a good beginning toward reaching a sound understanding of these very deep teachings. Through study and restudy, reflection, meditation, and practice, understanding will eventually arrive.

A Third Possibility in Regard to Death

We can begin our inquiry by noting that the typical condition for many humans is to live in fear of death. We know intellectually that it will happen "some day," but we try not to think about it because we believe that doing so spoils our enjoyment of life. We often look for ways to distract ourselves from the inevitability of death. For most of us, what we fear is the annihilation of "me," which is understood as our individual consciousness or mind—our thought stream, our awareness of events and things, our unique emotions, memories, and personality. This is perhaps at the top of our list of fears, though for many there is also a strong fear of the destruction of the body as well. Our fears around death also extend to the final ending of loved ones who are special to us. How can the teachings of the Buddha relieve our fear and suffering in regard to death?

As far as death is concerned, we tend to see only two basic possibilities. The first idea is that death is the complete annihilation of the self—going from existence to total nonexistence. We often envision this as being like the light in a room being switched off and plunging the room into total darkness, or we may see it as being like a film reaching the end of the reel and the screen going blank. The idea of not existing at all is often very frightening.

A common second possibility is to see death as a transition into an eternal afterlife as essentially the same "me" that exists in our present life. In this understanding, the "me" that I am familiar with--my unique memories, knowledge, experiences, and personality—continues to live on. Sometimes this continued existence is seen as taking place in my resurrected old body, sometimes in a new body, and sometimes as an existence without any body at all.

The Buddha rejected all of these views. Death is not the annihilation of anything, nor is it followed by the continuation of the "me" that preceded death. The Buddha taught that both beginning and ending—birth and death—are *illusions created by the mind*. The key to comprehending these teachings on death is a clear understanding of what the Buddha taught about the nature of self.

The Ocean of the Unbounded Self: "You Are Everything"

At the deepest level, who or what are we? Many Buddhist teachers have used the metaphor of waves in the ocean. This metaphor was brought up briefly in the previous chapter and can be of great help to us here in regard to understanding death.

Imagine what we call "a wave" moving across the ocean. If it moves over a submerged reef, the wave gets taller and there is perhaps more foam, and then it flattens out again. Later, if there is some wind, the wave gets bigger. The wave is constantly changing. This is very much like the progression of the days and years of an individual person's life: we have experiences, we acquire things, have successes and failures, and many aspects of our life change.

As the wave approaches the shore, it gets taller and develops more foam and spray. When it finally crashes on the shore, what happens? We might ask: "Where does it go? Does it cease to exist? Does it die?" When we reflect on these questions, we realize that it doesn't "go" anywhere and it does not cease to exist, either. The water simply goes through another series of changes. Some of the water temporarily becomes spray in the air or bubbles, some of the water rebounds from the shore and flows river-like back out to sea, and so on. *The wave never was a separate entity*, it was just movement and pattern in the vastness of one vast ocean of water. The true nature of the wave is water, and the water is not destroyed. It does not cease to exist.

The vast ocean of water and its temporary forms is a metaphor for the vast ocean of *being*, which could also be called existence, reality, the universe, or the oneness. From this ocean of being our minds create the appearance of separate things by drawing mental boundary lines.

We saw how this worked in the example of the creation of "foops" discussed in the previous chapter. Once we have created the *idea* of a "foop," foops begin appearing everywhere. In the same way, we constantly mentally segment *everything* with imaginary boundaries to create the *appearance* of a separate individual objects that we then call by names such as The Big Dipper or the Colorado River.

As long as we see a person as a separate being, that person appears to have a beginning and an ending—a limited life span, at the end of which he or she disappears into nonbeing. When we recognize that there is no separation except what is created by the boundaries constructed in our minds, we see that who we actually are is the totality of reality. There are no boundaries in reality. We are the universe of being, and the universe of being is us. The totality, the Oneness of reality—which is who we are—does not cease to exist.

What we call a wave does not have a beginning or an end in space. We cannot really say where the wave ends on the west, east, north, or south sides of it. Nor can we say when in time it came into existence or when it no longer exists.

What we call "you" and "I" are essentially the same as the waves in the ocean. *Where* we say a person starts and stops in space is a matter of social convention. Does who we call Albert Einstein include the shadow he casts on the ground, the bacteria necessary for digestion in his intestines, the air inside his lungs, the books and articles he has written or the sounds he puts out into the air when he speaks? He is no different than the so-called "separate entity" called "river" that the previous chapter's analysis revealed to be a matter of our social conventions and mental ideas.

And *when* did Einstein come into existence in time? If he had been born in many of the native cultures of the Americas, his existence as a person would have been seen as beginning *when he was given a name*. This name would typically be given two to four months *after* his birth took place. Before that, he would only have been seen as a sort of

258

potential or possible person because of the high infant mortality rate in those cultures. (3)

In many other cultures, Einstein would be seen as coming into existence at birth. But without the gestation process in the uterus, there can be no person to be born. And without the contribution of a sperm and an egg from each parent at the moment of conception, there can be no fetus. Without the lives of the mother and father, and everything that made those lives possible, there can be no moment of conception. To say that a person begins at birth, or conception, or at any other point in time, is an arbitrarily chosen beginning point or boundary. In order for this particular birth to occur, everything else that has ever happened needs to have happened.

Similarly, when does Einstein pass into nonexistence? At the time the physical body entirely stops functioning? Or perhaps it is earlier, when Einstein loses the ability to *do* the things that we associate with the person we think of him to be? When the physical body stops functioning, does it not simply change form and go into the soil to be taken up by the roots of nearby trees and grasses? If Einstein has produced children, or students, or changes in the world, or ideas that continue to exist, don't those elements continue to exist after his body is buried? Our ideas about beginning and ending, and birth and death, are simply social conventions deriving from arbitrary decisions about where and when a person begins and ends.

The boundary between you and the atmosphere or a lake or a forest or a lizard is no more real than the lines of latitude and longitude that cut the Earth into the appearance of separate squares.

When a wave understands that its true nature is ocean, then it understands that there is no death, only oceanic continuation and change. When a human being understands that his or her true self or nature is the entire universe (the Oneness), then he or she understands that there is no death, only continuation and change.

So, though we have a strong tendency to fear death, in truth we have already "died" many times and have never seen it as a problem. The "me" patterns that existed at ages five, twenty, thirty, forty and so on no longer exist. Those earlier versions of "me" are gone. This happens to all of us, and yet no one sees this as some kind of a problem or something we need to fear. The wave changes, but the ocean does not cease to exist, and the ocean is ultimately what the wave is. In the same way, what we call the body of Einstein dies—changes form—but this is not who he really is. He is everything. He is the oneness. Einstein is the ocean of being, and the ocean of being was never born and will never die.

The Buddha taught that just as there was never a time in the past when you were nothing, so there will never be a time in the future when you will be nothing. You were and always will be everything there is. Put in the most simple terms, it is not possible for you to cease to exist because there is no "you" that exists as a separate entity. There is only the oneness which is the universe, and the universe does not cease to exist.

Relative and Ultimate Truth

Of course, there is a sense in which "you" as a separate individual do exist: there is a birth certificate with your name on it, a drivers license, a deed to your home, and the fact that you are held legally and morally accountable for your actions. This is all at the level of social convention, and it often serves a very useful purpose.

The Buddha taught that there are two levels of truth. The first level is called *relative truth*, or the truth of *social convention*. Separate individual entities—this tree, Einstein, the Mississippi River, that mountain over there—exist at this level of *relative truth*. These seemingly separate individual entities are like the waves in the ocean. We can *agree* to create mental boundaries in a certain way and we can *agree* to see the world and talk about it based on this agreement. This can often be useful. These mental concepts help us communicate with each other, build things, calculate and figure things out, and find our way around. This occurs in much the same way that the lines of longitude and latitude help us get around in the practical world.

So at the level of relative truth and social convention, you are a wave, a separate individual being. But at the level of ultimate truth, you are the vast ocean of water, the oneness of the universe.

Ultimately, our real nature is ocean. The wave that we call "me" is simply a pattern we carve out mentally in the ocean of Oneness. This thing I call a separate "me" is just an illusion. When I see that ultimately I am the ocean of water, what we conventionally call "death" is just the Oneness, which is also me, changing shape. All this is at the level of what Buddhism calls *ultimate truth*, which is also sometimes called *absolute truth*. The only thing that exists at this level is the Oneness of reality. Everything that happens is essentially the activity of *one living entity*, and it is constantly changing and creating. Seeing this oneness—which is seeing things unsegmented by our mental concepts —is called *nirvana*. Nirvana is reality as it truly is when not experienced through the lens of segmenting mental concepts. In Buddhism it is often called the world of no-birth and no-death.

Sogyal Rinpoche directs our attention to ultimate reality, and even links the teachings to western physics:

> To see through the eyes... of realization, is to
> look down on a landscape in which the
> boundaries that we imagined existed between
> life and death shade into each other and
> dissolve. The Physicist David Bohm has
> described reality as being "unbroken wholeness
> in flowing movement." What is seen [directly]
> by the masters... with total understanding, is
> that flowing movement and that unbroken
> wholeness. ...To see death, then, through

realized eyes, is to see ...death in the context of this wholeness, and [simply] as part... of this beginingless and endless movement." (4)

Thich Nhat Hanh puts it this way:

When we look at the ocean, we see that each...
wave can be compared with other waves, and
we can call it more or less beautiful, higher or
lower, longer lasting or less long lasting. [This is
at the level of relative truth.] But if we look
more deeply, we see that a wave is made of
water. While living the life of a wave [a
temporary form identity and a creation of social
convention], it also lives the life of water [the
oneness that is reality]. It would be sad if the
wave did not know that it is water. It would
think, some day, I will have to die. This period
of time is my life span, and when I arrive at the
shore, I will return to nonbeing. These *notions*
[mental constructs] will cause the wave fear
and anguish. We have to help it remove the
notions of self, person, living being, and life
span if we want the wave to be free and happy.
(5)

The Big Dipper metaphor, discussed in the previous chapter, can also help us to understand the two levels of truth. The Big Dipper constellation exists as a creation of social convention. People select various points of light and agree to draw and then see certain patterns among the points: The Big Dipper, Orion the Hunter, The Seven Sisters, The Plow, and so on. Some of these constellations can even be used to help us navigate at night, but nonetheless they exist only at the level of relative truth. At the level of ultimate truth, however, there is only the oneness of the nighttime sky with its millions of points of light. Who we truly are is the entire sky, which has no beginning or end and does not cease to exist.

Clearly, what the Buddha taught about death differs strongly from how Buddhism is often seen by the general population in Western society. According to the prevalent view, the Buddha taught reincarnation, and reincarnation has been taken to mean that after a person's death occurs, that person's *same individual consciousness* is transferred to a different physical body. So while death is the destruction of body, the same *individual consciousness* continues on in one lifetime after another. In this view, the body is seen as somewhat like a car, and individual consciousness or mind is seen as the driver of the car. At some point the car wears out and no longer works, but the *same driver* is given a new car to continue driving in. Essentially, the individual, separate, and unique personality, memories, and consciousness of a person are simply *transferred intact* from one physical body to another. As we have seen, what the Buddha actually taught about death is quite different.

When Buddhist teachings make *reference to past and future lives,* what this really refers to is past and future waves or patterns in the ocean of Oneness. It refers to all the previous shapes that the water has taken in the past, and all of the future shapes that it will take in the future. The references to rebirth really simply refer to the temporary shapes in the ocean being "reborn" as new shapes. The wave that crashes on the beach is "reborn" as a river-like stream of water running back out to sea to collide with new incoming waves to form yet more patterns. The unique characteristics or "personality" of "that wave over there" *do not continue,* but the ocean itself is not subject to birth and death. And it is the ocean that is who we truly are. In Buddhist teachings, *consciousness is not extinguished at the death of the body, but neither does it continue in the unique form that it had taken previously.*

In what the Buddha taught, what continues in us and cannot die is the empty field of awareness in which all phenomena arise: sense perceptions, thoughts, emotions. This awareness exists universally everywhere. The personality and unique attributes that we have—as a unique "wave," so to speak—are a sort of *lens through which* our true self, which is awareness, sees things. Adyashanti has put it this way.

> Once your world of conceptual knowledge gets put in its rightful place, it is transcended. You see that *you are eternal consciousness[or being] now appearing as* woman or man, this or that character. *But like every good actor, you know you are not what you are appearing as. [You are the water, not the wave.] Everything that exists is consciousness [or being] appearing as...* [*this or that.*] The Buddha called it no-self. When that's seen, you see unity. There is only God [unity or eternal universal being] appearing as a floor, as a human being, as a wall, as a chair. (6)

The Nature of Interbeing

Who we truly are exists in many places, and comes from many places. In Buddhism, the word *interbeing* refers to the fact that nothing exists separately and independently. Everything *inter-exists* with everything else. The existence of each thing is *dependent* on the existence of everything else.

Part of who I am today comes from my biological ancestors. Parts of my parents exist in me. I carry forward things they have said, parts of my manner of engaging life that I learned from them, their experiences that they have shared with me, and certain physical characteristics that I have inherited from them. They continue to live on in me and in the others that I touch in my own life.

Part of who I am today comes from my nonbiological, or spiritual ancestors. These are friends I have had, teachers, authors of books I have read, anyone who has interacted with me and added something to who I am today. Parts of these people now exist in me.

In exactly the same way, I also exist in many different places. If I have children, parts of me exist in them. I also exist in students that I have taught, people who have read things I have written, friends or acquaintances that I have touched and affected in some way. I also exist in the people that are touched and affected by the people that I have touched and affected—the children and friends of my students, for example. I exist in all of my biological and spiritual descendants extending without end into the future. These things are unaffected when this form I call "my body" stops functioning.

Thich Nhah Hanh uses a beautifully simple metaphor to help us see who we truly are in this regard.

> When I make a pot of oolong tea, I put tea
> leaves into the pot and pour boiling water on
> them... After I have poured out all the tea [so it
> can be drunk], what will be left in the pot is just
> the spent tea leaves. The leaves that remain
> are only a very small part of the tea. The tea
> that goes into me is a much bigger part of the
> tea. It is the richest part. ...We are the same;
> our essence has gone into our children, our
> friends and the entire universe. We have to
> find ourselves in those directions and not in the
> spent tea leaves. I invite you to see yourself...
> in forms that you say are not yourself. .. (7)

Rather than thinking in terms of birth and death, beginning and ending, we need to begin to see everything as continuation, evolution, and change. Let us draw on the wisdom of Thich Nhat Hanh one more time.

Imagine the birth of a cloud. *Has a cloud come from the realm of non-being?* Before expressing herself as a cloud, she has been the water in the ocean and the heat generated by the sun, and so on. So the birth of a cloud is really a continuation. It's not a moment of birth; it's a moment of *continuation*. The birth of a child is a continuation of the father and the mother. So our birthday can be considered a continuation day. Next time you celebrate your birthday, instead of singing, "Happy Birthday," sing, "Happy Continuation Day."

And can you imagine the cloud dying? Do you think that when the cloud dies, it passes from the realm of being into non-being? It's obvious that the cloud cannot die. A cloud can become rain or snow... There's no reason to cry. Because it is a moment of continuation, it can be a very happy moment. If you have the insight of no birth, no death, you can die happily without fear. You know that you are free from being and non-being, birth and death... Not only is the birthday a continuation day, but the death day is also a continuation day. (8)

We only suffer if we are attached to the idea of something staying in its present form forever. Seung Sahn makes this point very clearly.

"Steam, ice, water are all H20; but if you are attached to water, and water becomes ice, then you say the water disappeared. So it is dead! Raise the temperature; the water is born again!

266

Raise the temperature again; the water
disappears and becomes steam, and the water
is dead again!

...If you are attached to something and it
disappears, you suffer. If you are attached to
only doing what you like, you suffer. Don't be
attached to water [liquid form of H20], O.K.?
Being attached to [liquid] water is being
attached to form. Form and name are always
changing, changing, changing, nonstop..." (9)

Practices For Transforming Our Relationship With Death

The teachings on death are not doctrines or theories. The
words used can help us uproot false ideas from our minds, but the truth
does not lie in the words. All the metaphors and other verbal
explanations are intended as *pointers*—they point or *direct our
attention* so that we can deeply see the truth of the teachings on death
in our very *own experience*. The words are like the finger that points at
the moon. The Buddha taught that the teachings on death cannot be
truly grasped through thinking. They can only be known through *direct
personal experiencing*. This experiencing is achieved through the use of
practices. One type of Buddhist practice that is useful here is called
looking deeply.

The first Looking Deeply practice asks us look for ourselves in
other places. These other places might be friends, family members,
organizations we have been involved in, forests we have helped to
reclaim, people we have helped or been kind to, and so on. We call to
mind and reflect on all the various places and beings that now contain
parts of ourselves due to our previous interaction with them. This can
be done either as a sitting meditation or as a practice to be used
throughout the day. Most people who do this seriously are quite
surprised at how much of themselves has gone out into the world at

large, much as the essence of the tea leaves has gone out into the tea and then into the people who drink the tea.

When I did this practice again recently, I remembered another student I had known when I was in high school: Bob Green. I was a sophomore just starting high school and Bob was starting his senior year. We were both on the school gymnastics team. Bob was a very dedicated athlete with a huge work ethic. Very early on in the year Bob noticed my commitment and strong work ethic, reached out to me, and became my mentor and unofficial "coach" for the year. His impact on my development was huge. I had few friends, disliked high school, and felt lost in a sophomore class of a thousand students. Bob helped me excel in my sport and it gave me an anchor and a home in the sport that made high school bearable for me for the three years I was there. From his words and actions I learned self confidence, how to get the most out of my talents, how to become a student of a sport I cared about and to achieve a degree of mastery of it. I also experienced the good feelings that were generated by the act of reaching out to someone who needed and deserved help. Bob is part of the reason I eventually became a teacher and had a strong intuitive sense for finding students who were ripe to benefit from some special attention. I lost track of Bob after high school so he knows nothing of any of this. Nonetheless, some of who Bob Green was lives on in me and also in the many people I have interacted with during the course of my own lifetime.

Another form of Looking Deeply practice has the intention of helping us to see that "living" and "nonliving" are just mind-created boundaries and are not real. In the first half of this practice, we begin by turning our attention to noticing the many nonliving elements that exist in living beings, including ourselves. When we do this, we may notice that living beings contain nonliving elements such as molecules of various minerals like calcium that make up much of our bones and teeth. We also have molecules of oxygen and water in our blood and tissues that when they were previously not part of the body we considered "nonliving." We may reflect on the fact that we have an

268

outer-most layer of *dead* skin which is necessary for protection. Calluses are also dead, as well as protective, and so is the skin oil on our outer surface that prevents our skin from drying out and cracking. Sweat is another "dead" part of us and provides necessary cooling. All these things are important parts of us that we have categorized as "nonliving."

The second part of this practice reverses things and we turn our attention to noticing all of the elements of living beings that exist in so-called "nonliving things." When we look carefully, we see that a "nonliving thing" such as a rock, contains many living elements within it. One of the main characteristics we associate with living beings is the ability to respond to stimulus from the external environment: my hand gets too close to the fire and I pull it back; someone says something to me and my behavior changes. If we look closely, we see that so-called nonliving things also respond to events in their environment. A rock vibrates when it is struck by another rock. It contracts and gets smaller when the temperature around it gets colder, and expands and gets larger when the temperature increases. It absorbs moisture into its pores when the air is damp, and gives off moisture when struck by sunlight. The rock moves in response to the forces of wind and gravity and being struck by other objects. Planets and asteroids and meteors— so called inanimate objects—moving through the solar system respond to gravitational forces of other objects by altering their speed and direction of movement.

Practicing in this way help us to realize fully that there is no sharp or objective line between "living" and "nonliving." Living and nonliving are simply concepts that exist only at the level of social convention. This practice can be done either as a sitting meditation or as something done during normal daily activities.

A third form of Looking Deeply practice involves looking for the impermanence and change in each moment as we go though our day. We might choose to sit on the shore of the ocean or on the bank of a river and watch the continuous change of patterns in the water, rearrangements of sand on the shore, and the changes in how things look because of the constantly changing light. We can notice the clouds in the sky and the continuous change of one form into another. We can reflect on things that happened earlier in our day that have changed us —someone said something to us and we now see things differently; we had an experience changing a flat tire and now feel more confident than just a few hours ago.

Our thoughts and feelings are constantly changing from one moment to another and so are our sense perceptions and internal body sensations. The ancient Greek philosopher Heraclitus was right: it is not possible to step into the same river twice—the water is constantly changing, and *we* are constantly changing. We may say that we already know this, but this is knowing in terms of *concepts*. It is quite another thing to *actually see* the process of change in each moment. That is the true practice.

As part of this same Looking Deeply practice, we can also notice the commonness and pervasiveness of death—the change of one form into another— throughout our day: the sun dying at sunset, clouds coming into existence and changing and passing away, dead leaf litter on the ground, the no-longer-living plants we eat at dinner, the cotton threads in our clothing that used to be part of a cotton plant. Everything is always changing from one form into another, and death is simply another example of changing form. As Seung Sahn pointed out earlier in regard to the forms of water, as long as we can practice letting go of being attached to a specific form of water, or to anything else, there is no suffering.

A different kind of practice that is useful here involves combining mindful breathing with silent verbal acknowledgement of the reality of our life circumstances. The following are examples of useful phrases for this practice:

- Breathing in, I see that this body is not me, breathing out I smile to body is not me.

- Breathing in, I see that thoughts arising are not me, breathing out I smile to thoughts arising are not me.

- Breathing in, I see that I exist everywhere, breathing out I smile to existing everywhere.

- Breathing in, I see that my true nature is continuation and change, breathing out I smile to continuation and change.

After meditating for a while, the phrases used can be shortened to things such as "Thoughts are not me, smiling to thoughts are not me." A single phrase can be used for an entire meditation session, or it might work well to repeat one phrase six to eight times, and then move on to saying the next phrase six to eight times. With the second format, it might be useful to use a total of no more than about four phrases altogether so that things do not get too complicated and burdensome. Different phrases will work better for some people and less well for others. Each person can make up phrases that work for them, with the intention always being to help let go of our false ideas about who we are, and to see more clearly the real nature of what we call death.

Finally, we can make use of the Looking Inward Meditation on the self from Chapter 16. This can be a very useful practice when applied to death. This consists of looking inward to actually *see* if there is a self, a "me" in any given moment of experience. Is there really anything there in my experience that could be called "me" and which could "die" and pass into the realm of nonbeing? We begin the meditation and proceed in the same manner described in Chapter 16, observing what is arising in consciousness in each moment: sounds, body sensations, thoughts, emotions, and so on. What is actually present? We can ask ourselves at various points during the meditation, "Is there anything in all these comings and goings that actually *has* these experiences and which could be called "me," and that could pass into nonexistence?" We can spend five or ten or even twenty minutes just *watching* what flows into our awareness and *sitting with the questions* "Is there a self or a me anywhere?" and "Who or what is here that could die?"

Really *getting* the teachings on no self and death (so it becomes more than just *words*) typically takes time, often a *long* time. So adding some additional practices to work on *acceptance—dropping our mental resistance to the change that we call death*—is useful during this transition time. We can modify and make good use of several practices for dropping resistance examined in Chapter 10. This will enable us to achieve some peace through our acceptance of death while we are on the road to realizing the deep truth of the teaching that death is an illusion.

If we can begin to see our resistance to death well up in us, we can use the practice of simply acknowledging its presence. We can say silently "Hello resistance to death, I know you are there." We can acknowledge its presence without judging it or ourselves for it's being there. As an alternative, we might say silently "Noticing resistance to death... Smiling to resistance to death," or "Noticing resistance to death... letting go of resistance to death." Whatever our choice of words, it is useful to coordinate the words with the in-breath and out-breath. When we do these practices, our resistance loses much of its grip on us.

Chapter 10 also discussed making resistance our primary object of attention during a meditation session. We open ourselves to fully experience the resistance as it exists in us, paying attention to where we feel it in the body—what does it actually feel like, and what is the thought stream that is there along with it? This is a powerful practice that works with mental resistance of any kind, including resistance to the inevitable change in the body that we call death.

And lastly, the teachings from Tara Brach and Epictetus from Chapter 10 are relevant here. Tara Brach's teachings can inspire us to practice saying "Yes" to the things that we resist mentally. In this case, when resistance to the prospect of death arises, we can practice silently saying "I say yes to inevitability of the change we call death." Epictetus encourages us to use the practice of reminding ourselves that the body has the same essential nature as a clay vessel, and that the nature of all clay vessels to eventually break. The nature of the human body is the same—at some point, the human body ceases to function in the way that it used to. If we keep this reality as a permanent part of our awareness, we can have much more peace.

Notes for Chapter 17

1. Smith, Huston, *Religions of the World, Revised Edition*, New York: HarperCollins Publishers, 1991, page 117.

2. Nhat Hanh, Thich, *Zen Keys*, New York: Doubleday, 1995, pages 41-43.

3. This is information is from a July 17, 2018 e-mail correspondence from anthropologist Bruce Sanchez, Lane Community College, Eugene, Oregon.

4. Sogyal Rinpoche, *The Tibetan Book of Living and Dying*, San Francisco: HarperCollins, 2002, revised and updated edition, p. 345.

5. Nhat Hanh, Thich, *The Heart of the Buddha's Teaching*, New York: Broadway Books, 1998, p. 124.

6. Adyashanti, *Emptiness Dancing*, Boulder, CO: Sounds True, 2006, pp. 69-70. Emphasis added.

7. Nhat Hanh, Thich, *No Death, No Fear*, New York: Riverhead Books, 2002, pp. 125-126.

8. Nhat Hanh, Thich, "Our Cosmic Body," *Mindfulness Bell*, Winter/Spring, 2015, p. 7. A dharma talk transcribed for *Mindfulness Bell* from a talk given August 24, 2014 for the European Institute of Applied Buddhism. Emphasis added.

9. Sahn, Seung, *Only Don't Know: The Teaching Letters of Zen Master Seung Sahn*, San Francisco: Four Seasons Foundation, 1982, pp. 48-49.

Appendix: Staying On the Path of Self Transformation

A book can be interesting or mentally stimulating to read, but what happens when we have finished reading this or any book about personal transformation? Maybe we feel excited and motivated to actually use some of the new ideas to begin the process of fundamentally changing our lives. But often, very gradually, we fall away from our chosen path and find that we have slid back into our old patterns, habits, blindness—and suffering. If we want to make our chosen path of spiritual transformation—whether Buddhist, Christian, Hindu, or some combination of teachings— an on-going part of our lives, what can done to prevent us from sliding back into unconsciousness?

The teachings of the Buddha provide a path that has the potential to be life changing. But only if we actually make use of them consistently. Here are some things that can help us.

Setting Priorities. Unless we make a *commitment* to doing the practice *each day*, our lives will fill up with busyness and we will not stay with it. We must make our manner of being in the world—how we engage life moment-to-moment—our top priority every day. This means that we make *how we move through the world each day* more important than the *end results that we accomplish.* Getting dinner prepared is important, but even more important is the state of mind and heart we are in as we do it. We can make dinner in a hurried and resentful state of mind, or we can do it in a state of presence, gratitude, and enjoyment of the moment. Engaging life in this way does not mean that we do not accomplish things. In fact, most people find that they actually accomplish more of what is worth accomplishing when engaging life in a wiser and more present state of mind.

In regard to my own experience, and that of many others as well, the single most productive arena for producing personal change lies in changing my own behavior in my day-to-day experience of life. Many people miss this and think that the most important part of practice is sitting on a meditation cushion or listening to a dharma talk. These things have importance, but it is consistently *catching ourselves* at unskillful old behaviors more and more often throughout the day, and then *doing something different* that is perhaps the single most powerful tool we have for changing ourselves.

Reading and Dharma Talks. Continuing to read for inspiration and to deepen understanding of the teachings is important. There are a number of excellent books in the "Suggestions for Further Reading" section at the end of this book. I find that when I go back and re-read a quality dharma book, I always learn something that I missed on the previous reading. As for the things I didn't miss in the first reading, just being *reminded* of them again is very inspiring and motivating. It is a good idea to make doing some reading every day a habit. Even just reading one page a day chosen at random from a trusted book in your personal library can make a huge difference.

Listening to quality dharma talks on-line, and on DVDs and CDs on a regular basis helps keep us on track. This can be done alone or with other people who share our chosen path. Like a good book, a good dharma talk is worth experiencing again and again over the years.

Finding Others to Walk the Path With Us. Many practitioners find it very useful to meet with a group of like-minded people once a week or once a month in order to talk about their ongoing spiritual practice or to meditate together. It is very encouraging to find that other people face the same questions and challenges. Another advantage of group work resides in the fact that it is often much easier to see a personal issue or blind spot as it exists in someone else than it is to see it in ourselves. However, once we see the issue and how it operates in others, it then becomes easier to see the very same process in ourselves. Then we can work with it.

Corresponding with other practitioners by e-mail can serve a similar purpose if it is difficult to find suitable companions on the path in the area where we live. Looking in the phone book and on-line to see if there are practice centers nearby is worth doing. We can put up a notice about forming a group, check the phone book for local Buddhist centers, search on line, and use the on-line Mindfulness Bell sangha directory to find a group in our area. If it is not possible to find supportive people to practice with, it is important to know that people can and do make very good progress working on their own.

Keeping a personal journal can be a powerful tool, whether we are working on our own or in a group setting. Writing can be a good way of helping to sort out our experience of life. Just the act of putting things into words and then reading our own words on a page or a screen can help us see things about ourselves that we couldn't see before.

Many people find it very useful to do retreat work. There are Buddhist centers all over the country that offer retreats anywhere from a single day to ten days or more. During this time there are extended periods of sitting and walking meditation, regular instruction or dharma talks, and a chance to have extended periods of silence. Near-by retreat centers may be listed in the local phone directory and can also be searched for on-line. It is best to find a center that seems to emphasize the kind of approach and practices that support what we already know works well for us.

Meditation. We often begin a meditation practice with good intentions but find ourselves unable to stay with it. This happens for several reasons. Many times, we stop meditating because *we do not see any results*—we still get distracted all the time while meditating, our minds are all over the place, and we never seem to get any better at it. The problem here is that we are looking for results in the wrong place.

The place to look for progress is in our own lives, not in our meditation sessions. It is not wise to decide whether our practice is going well by looking at the quality of our meditations or other practices. Instead, we need to look at how things are going in our lives. Do we have more patience, or not get angry as much or stay angry as long? Do we have less of a tendency to take things personally (see events as something "done to me")? If so, then our meditation practice is working.

It helps to get out of the habit of judging our sittings as good or bad—we can just do it and have faith that it is benefitting us. We can remember that meditation is not about achieving some particular mental and emotional state, whether it be blissful or calm or relaxed. The basic intention is to learn to open to and experience each moment as it arises, training ourselves to be able to stay present with more and more of what life throws at us. Meditation is not some kind of a gimmick to "zap" unwanted emotional states and make them go away. We are learning how to be more at peace with whatever our experience might be.

Trying to "get good at meditation" misses the point. The real purpose of practicing meditation is not to get better at meditation, but to *get better at life*.

Another reason we stop meditating is that *we become impatient*—we want to see big results and we want to see them immediately. But meditation is not like that. If a lifetime of eating unhealthy food and sitting on a couch has left us unhealthy and unfit, this condition cannot be totally corrected in a week or a month. And if we do become healthy and fit, we won't stay that way if we give up the practices that got us there in the first place. Meditation works the same way: the change that happens is mostly gradual and it is a lifetime practice.

The following is one of the best strategies for establishing a consistent meditation practice: Make a commitment to put yourself in your regular meditation posture for at least thirty seconds every day. No one can truthfully say they are so busy that they do not have thirty seconds. We can always do at least this much. Once we are in our posture, frequently something more happens and thirty seconds becomes a five minute or a twenty minute sitting. Perhaps even more important, just doing even a thirty second sitting *keeps the habit going—it is yet another day in which we remembered to sit and did it*.

We can also remember the Zen saying from Chapter 4: "You should sit in meditation 20 minutes a day, unless you are too busy. Then you should sit for an hour." When we are scattered and distracted is when we really *need* to sit. We can learn to *connect* this scattered feeling with the need to sit. We can learn to consciously notice that internal feeling of stress or anxiety and view it as a *message* letting us know that we need to sit and become present.

We can, in addition, be prepared for negative thoughts to come up: "I feel like skipping meditation today" or "I don't want to read a page from a spiritual book today," or "I'm too tired." When this happens we can remember that they are just thoughts—they can be there and we can still do the things that assist our progress anyway. As we saw earlier, the thoughts that bubble up in us are much like highway billboards. We can simply notice they are there but then choose not to act on some mental billboard that says "I don't want to meditate." We see the billboard, and meditate anyway. Another creative option is to make our emotional resistance to doing meditation into the primary object of attention in our meditation—we get *interested* in that feeling and simply observe it!

Meditation can be viewed as a *gift* to ourselves, rather than a duty or a something we "should do" or "have to do." If we make meditation into a daily ritual—same time, same place, same routine—it helps to create a solid habit. At some point, meditating becomes the new "default setting" and we don't have to argue with ourselves about whether we are going to do it or not. If for some reason we miss a day, we simply start over again the next day. The practice becomes an established part of our lives at this point.

Suggestions for Further Reading

Beck, Charlotte, *Everyday Zen: Love and Work*, San Francisco: HarperSanFrancisco, 1989.

Beck, Charlotte, *Nothing Special: Living Zen*, San Francisco: HarperSanFrancisco, 1993.

Brach, Tara, *Radical Acceptance: Embracing Your Life With the Heart of a Buddha*, New York: Bantam Books, 2003.

Chodron, Pema, *The Places That Scare You: A Guide to Fearlessness in Difficult Times*, Boston: Shambhala, 2002.

Goldstein, Joseph, *One Dharma: The Emerging Western Buddhism*, San Francisco: HarperSanFrancisco, 2002.

Kornfield, Jack, *The Wise Heart: A Guide to the Universal Teachings of Buddhist Psychology*, New York: Bantam Books, 2008.

Ladner, Lorne, *The Lost Art of Compassion*, San Francisco: HarperSanFrancisco, 2004.

Nhat Hanh, Thich, *The Heart of the Buddha's Teaching*, New York: Broadway Books, 1999.

Nhat Hanh, Thich, *Interbeing: Fourteen Guidelines for Engaged Buddhism, Third Edition,* Berkeley: Parallax Press, 1998.

Nhat Hanh, Thich, *Old Path, White Clouds: Walking In the Footsteps of the Buddha*, Berkeley: Parallax Press, 1991.

Nhat Hanh, Thich, *Zen Keys*, New York: Doubleday, 1995.

Salzberg, Sharon, *Lovingkindness: The Revolutionary Art of Happiness*, Boston: Shambhala, 1995.

Salzberg, Sharon, *Real Happiness: The Power of Meditation*, New York: Workman Publishing, 2011.

Tolle, Eakhart, A *New Earth: Awakening to Your Life's Purpose*, New York: Dutton, 2005.

Tolle, Eakhart, *The Power of Now: A Guide to Spiritual Enlightenment*, Novato: New World Library, 1999.

Watts, Alan, *Tao: The Watercourse Way*, New York: Pantheon Books, 1975.

About the Author

Dale Lugenbehl has for 14 years been the Principle Teacher for Ahimsa Acres Sangha, an affiliate of the Thich Nhat Hanh Foundation. He has taught both Eastern and Western philosophy classes for 40 years in public colleges and universities, including 7 years of Buddhist Meditation Traditions at Lane Community College—the first college credit Buddhist meditation class ever offered in Oregon. He is also a member of Dharma Voices for Animals, Environmental Editor for American Vegan magazine, Director of Ahimsa Acres Educational Center, and the author of more than 50 published articles.

Made in the USA
San Bernardino, CA
11 January 2020